Agricultural research and technology in economic development

The impact of agricultural research and modern technology on food production, economic growth and income distribution in developing countries

PER PINSTRUP-ANDERSEN

International Food Policy Research Institute, Washington, D.C.

Longman
London and New York

Longman Group Limited,
Longman House,
Burnt Mill, Harlow, Essex, U.K.

*Published in the United States of America
by Longman Inc., New York*

© Longman Group Limited 1982

First published 1982

British Library Cataloguing in Publication Data

Pinstrup-Anderson, Per
    Agricultural research and technology in
    economic development.
    1. Technological innovations – Underdeveloped
    areas – Economic aspects
    2. Underdeveloped areas – Agricultural
    research – Economic aspects
    I. Title
    630'.7'201324   S540.A2

Library of Congress Cataloging in Publication Data

Pinstrup-Andersen, Per.
    Agricultural research and technology in economic
development.

    Bibliography: p.
    Includes index.
    1. Underdeveloped areas—Agricultural research.
2. Underdeveloped areas—Agriculture.
3. Agricultural research.   I. Title.
S540.A2P56   338.9'009172'4   81-14297
ISBN 0-582-46048-4   AACR2

Printed in Singapore by
Singapore National Printers Pte. Ltd.

Contents

iii

Introduction

The standard of living is low for the majority of people in developing countries. Absolute poverty results in severe human suffering among many of these people. Continuation of a situation in which a large proportion of the world population lives near the absolute subsistence minimum where at the same time the standard of living is very high for a small minority – whether it is found within the individual developing country or among different countries – is unacceptable from a humanitarian point of view. Such a situation also constrains economic growth and is politically untenable in the long run. Improvement of the living standards of the poor in developing countries is one of the most important tasks facing humanity.

Agriculture and food play a very important role in carrying out this task. This is because the agricultural sector provides or has provided, the basis for economic development in the majority of developing countries. However, most of the poverty in these countries is found in the agricultural sector itself, leading to insufficient food production. The consequent hunger and malnutrition largely account for the widespread suffering, both within and outside agriculture. Possibly as many as one-third of the people in Africa, Asia and Latin America suffer from hunger or malnutrition. Attempts to meet the basic needs of the poor in developing countries must focus heavily on food and agriculture. The future does not look bright. While favourable weather may assist in the creation of temporary food surpluses in some developing countries, current projections show that the next 10–15 years will bring increasing food shortages in many others. The projected shortages imply a deterioration in the already very delicate food and nutritional situation in many of these countries unless special efforts are made to counter it.

However, there is reason to believe that attempts to improve, or at least avoid, a worsening of the food and nutritional situation in the developing countries could be successful. Results from international and national research on wheat and rice have shown that modern science-based agricultural technology can assist in obtaining large increases in food production in developing countries. Similarly, evaluation of a series of research projects on other crops has demonstrated that public investment in agricultural research and diffusion of the results are capable of contributing to very large gains to society in terms of food production, economic growth and improved living standards.

While agricultural research offers great possibilities for expanded food production and improved productivity in developing countries, these possibilities have been utilized only to a very limited degree. Lack of a clear understanding of how agricultural research may best be used to promote economic growth and improve the standard of living among the poor has been – and to a large extent still is – the most important barrier to a better realization of these possibilities. A larger and more effective effort within the area of agricultural research and complementary public policy, investment and institutional change in the developing countries are needed.

This book discusses how agricultural research and the resulting technology may be applied effectively to meet the individual country's growth and equity goals. The role of international agricultural research is emphasized, and how the results of such research are effectively utilized by the individual developing country.

Agricultural research has traditionally played a very minor role in most developing countries. Until 10–15 years ago, such research was primarily focused on export commodities such as rubber, sugar-cane and bananas. The emphasis on export commodities was a logical consequence of the desires of the former colonial powers to expand the production of these commodities primarily for their own consumption and for export to developed countries. Research and the development of new technology for commodities which were primarily consumed by the population within the colonies were very limited. Expansion of production of these products came about primarily through an increase in the area under cultivation while attempts to increase yields and productivity in cases where they did occur were based primarily on technology imported from developed countries. Such technology was in many cases unsuited or poorly suited to the agricultural conditions in the developing countries and yield and productivity increases were small.

Foresight among agricultural researchers and research administrators, both in developing and developed countries, resulted in the initiation of cooperative research activities for food commodities in developing countries. These activities proved to be extremely effective in expanding food production and yields per unit of area. Among those who promoted such research activities were agricultural scientists and the management of the Rockefeller Foundation. Rockefeller Foundation support for research in a number of developing countries was a forerunner to the creation of a number of international agricultural research institutes for the developing countries. The results from two of these institutes were the foundation for the so-called green revolution, which has contributed to large increases in the production and yields of wheat and rice in many developing countries. Because of these increases and the research and technology that made them possible, malnutrition and hunger has been reduced in some countries while in others, predicted deteriorations in food production and nutritional conditions have been avoided or lessened.

Thus, results from rice and wheat research have illustrated that large and rapid increases in the food production of developing countries are possible without increases in the cultivated area. This does not mean that the food production problem of these countries has now been solved. However, the success of the green revolution does suggest that agricultural research and modern technology are extremely powerful tools for expanding food production in such countries.

In addition to its impact on food production and nutrition, technological change in agriculture may have strong influences on other factors which contribute to economic growth, patterns of income distribution and well-being of people. The critical issue then becomes one of best possible utilization of agricultural research and technology within the overall development strategy.

Interaction between research and technology on the one hand and public policy (existing, as well as potential) on the other, is an important element frequently overlooked in discussions and analyses of the socio-economic effects of the former. Assessment of agricultural research and technology in isolation ignores the potential benefits from optimal combinations of research technology and policy. Conclusions drawn from such isolated assessments are frequently misleading and, if used in research decision-making, would in many cases lead to wrong research priorities and the forgoing of large potential socio-economic benefits.

The relationships between agricultural research and modern technology on the one hand, and food production, economic growth, nutrition and income distribution on the other, are complicated. However, a thorough understanding of these relationships is essential for using research and technology as effectively as possible as tools for achieving the economic and social objectives of the developing countries. The primary purpose of this book is to explain some of the most important relationships among international and national agricultural research, related national activities, e.g. technology diffusion and public policy, modern technology and economic growth, income distribution and nutrition. Analysis of quantitative as well as qualitative relationships will be emphasized. Methodology for estimating the former is excluded for the purpose of making the book of interest to a wider readership. However, references are given to publications where the methodologies may be found.

The author hopes that the content may be useful for people interested in economic development in general and agricultural development and research in particular. Although focusing mainly on developing countries, a considerable portion of the content is relevant to agricultural research in general and might also be of interest to agricultural researchers whose research is not directly concerned with problems of developing countries. This would particularly be the case for the chapter dealing with the basic relationships between research and economic development and those chapters where the estimated benefits from research and the distribution of these benefits are discussed.

The book is divided into ten chapters. A brief discussion of the existing and expected future food and agricultural situation in developing countries is presented in Chapter 1. The most important factors determining food supply and demand are also discussed in this chapter. In Chapter 2, the basic relationships between agricultural research and technology and economic growth, income distribution and nutrition are discussed. Then follow two chapters describing agricultural research for developing countries: national research is examined in Chapter 3, and Chapter 4 describes the international agricultural research institutes and their activities. The estimated pay-off from agricultural research is discussed in Chapter 5 and the distribution of the associated economic benefits among groups in society is analysed in Chapter 6. The role of fertilizer in efforts to expand agricultural production and improve productivity in developing countries is discussed in Chapter 7. Particular emphasis is placed on an analysis of the contribution of fertilizer to food producing in these countries. The primary factors limiting fertilizer usage are identified and public policy measures to expand economically sound fertilizer usage are suggested. Chapter 8 deals with the environmental effects of technological change. National activities to expand research pay-offs are discussed in Chapter 9. Public policy measures aimed at the achievement of the desired distribution of research benefits are also discussed in that chapter. Chapter 10 deals with international assistance within the area of agricultural research and closely related areas, and the book terminates with some concluding remarks.

This book was written while the author was a senior research fellow and associate professor at the Economic Institute, Royal Veterinary and Agricultural University, Copenhagen. However, a large part of the material and experience underlying the content was acquired during previous work at the International Centre for Tropical Agriculture in Colombia and the International Fertilizer Development Centre in the United States. Final revisions of the manuscript were made after the author joined the International Food Policy Research Institute.

The author is grateful to a large number of colleagues in the agricultural and social sciences who provided inspiration and ideas for the manuscript, including Dana Dalrymple and Grant Scobie who reviewed all and parts of an earlier draft.

1 Food and agriculture in the developing countries

This chapter presents a brief description of the existing food and agricultural situation, recent trends and the prospects for the future. The primary purposes of the description are to show the need for expanded food production and productivity in the developing countries, and to place agricultural research and technology in the proper perspective within the overall set of factors influencing food production and productivity. It is important to emphasize at the outset that increased food production and improved productivity are but some of the necessary means to increase economic growth and improve living standards in developing countries. On the other hand, while recognizing that the direction and speed of economic development are determined by many factors, the role of food and agriculture in the development process is extremely important. This importance is derived from the relative size of the population found in the agricultural sector, the large proportion of total consumer spending on food and agricultural products and the importance of food in efforts to meet the basic needs of those with low incomes.

FOOD PRODUCTION AND ECONOMIC DEVELOPMENT

A presentation and discussion of the development process as such is beyond the scope of this book. It might be useful, however, to illustrate very briefly how increased food production and improved productivity may contribute to the process.

Successful economic development cannot be uniquely defined. Development is a dynamic process. Whether it is desirable and satisfactory for the individual, for groups within society or for a society as a whole depends partly on whether it moves in the direction necessary to meet the established goals and partly on the speed of the process. But the goals may vary considerably among individuals, groups and countries. Therefore, a given development process may be acceptable to some while unacceptable to others.

Development goals generally include three principal elements. These are efficiency, equity and security. The efficiency element focuses on growth and best possible utilization of scarce resources. If development goals were based exclusively on the efficiency element the distribution of the resulting economic goods would be determined by the distribution of ownership to resources, the efficiency of the individual resources and existing conditions regarding power and competition. In societies where such distributional mechanism does not lead to the desired result, elements of equity are introduced into the development goals. Finally, security aspects play an important role in development goals of many countries. These aspects may relate to national and territorial security, supply security for strategic goods, e.g. food, and a host of other security-related matters.

In cases where more than one of the three principal elements play a major role in a country's development goal – and such cases are the rule rather than the exception – conflicts may develop. Efforts to meet efficiency goals may lead to a worsening of income distribution while efforts to meet equity goals may be successful only at the expense of efficiency and growth. Such conflicts need not be present in all cases and are, of course, not limited to developing countries. The relative value given to each of the elements and the acceptable trade-off among them is determined by those possessing the political power in the particular country.

Development goals should be established by each individual country and not by outsiders. However, it is generally accepted that certain basic elements should be present in development goals irrespective of country, political structure and philosophy. The human element must be the key in any development goal. Freedom from hunger, malnutrition and other basic deprivations for as large a proportion of the population as possible, both in the short and the long run, should take priority. The existing distribution of personal incomes and resources is very skewed in many developing countries. The result is that a large proportion of the population in these countries may suffer from lack of even the most basic elements in life, while a minority may enjoy standards of living that exceed those found in the richest countries. For these reasons the distribution of the economic benefits from increased food production and improved productivity among groups in society should be given careful consideration when establishing development strategies for food and agriculture. This does not mean, of course, that redistribution of existing incomes and resources should be carried out irrespective of the impact on production and productivity. Such redistribution may have catastrophic consequences for economic growth and future living standards in general, unless due consideration is given to production and efficiency. Capital accumulation is essential for self-sustaining economic growth and the associated possibilities for improved standards of living irrespective of political structure and philosophy. The relevant question is how the growth is distributed. Redistribution without growth or with negative growth is not a viable solution to the problem of poverty in poor countries. What is needed is growth with a more even distribution of income, at least to the point of fulfilling basic needs.

In addition to their impact on growth, expansion of food production and improvements in productivity may contribute to a more even income distribution and improved security and stability.[1] Thus, all three main elements in the development goals – efficiency, equity and security – may be taken into consideration. A simplified example may illustrate this point. Increased food production contributes to capital accumulation within and/or outside the agricultural sector. Such capital accumulation provides the basis for further production expansion within the agricultural sector and promotes expansion of production in other sectors. This, in turn, tends to accelerate the demand for factors of production and provides opportunities for increasing employment and higher wages. Whether these opportunities are fully utilized depends on how the additional capital is invested. This issue is further discussed in the following chapters with particular reference to the employment effects of modern technology. Owing to increasing incomes among resource owners, the above-mentioned production expansion will result in increases in the demand for consumption goods. The foundation for self-sustaining economic growth is established.[2]

Expanded food production is expected to contribute to lower food prices than would have occurred in the absence of the production increase. Such price drops or reductions in price increases tend to benefit the consumers.[3] The benefit distribution among consumers would be determined by the quantities of food purchased and the reaction to price changes.[4] The distributional pattern among income strata would generally be such that lower-income consumers will obtain smaller absolute benefits than higher-income consumers. This is so because the quantity of food consumed generally is positively correlated with income level.[5] On the other hand, low-income consumers tend to spend a larger proportion of their incomes on food. Therefore, the benefits from decreases in food prices relative to incomes will be higher for those with low-incomes. In other words, decreases in food prices will generally result in smaller absolute but larger relative increases in real incomes among low-income consumers than among those with high incomes.

Results from an analysis of food consumption behavior in Cali, Colombia, support the above arguments (Pinstrup-Andersen, 1977). According to these results, increases in real incomes caused by decreasing food prices were positively correlated with income levels. However, the distribution of the income increases was less skewed than existing income distribution. Thus, a price decrease would contribute to a more even income distribution among consumers. Although these findings apply only to the city of Cali, it is likely that similar results would be found in many other cities in developing countries.

The distribution of economic benefits from measures to expand production and improve productivity among income groups within the agricultural sector would, of course, depend heavily on the distribution of resource ownership, e.g. the existing land tenure, and the adoption pattern. Early adopters of successful measures may obtain large economic gains while non-adopters may experience economic losses due to the downward pressures on prices. Early adopters are frequently found among the more affluent farmers. Thus, if a more even income distribution within the agricultural sector is an important element of the development goals, it may be advisable to focus agricultural research and the development and diffusion of modern technology towards the specific needs of poor farmers to the greatest extent possible. Introduction of policy measures aimed at adjustment of the benefit distribution or compensation for undesirable distributional effects might also be required. These issues will be discussed and analysed in considerable detail in the following chapters. However, before leaving the topic of benefit distribution, one additional argument should be made. The fact that some modern technology may not by itself meet equity goals should not necessarily imply its rejection. Modern agricultural technology should not be expected to contribute equally to all elements of development goals. Rejection of modern technology that is capable of making a major contribution to production and efficiency on the grounds that its contribution to equity is insufficient or undesirable may well be a mistake. Instead, it is likely to be better to accompany such technology by policy measures that ensure the desirable distributional effects while obtaining a positive impact on production and efficiency. This point has been misunderstood by many critics of the green revolution who have advocated, explicitly or implicitly, that technology which does not by itself satisfy equity goals should be rejected. The relationship between modern technology and public policy will be discussed in detail in other chapters. However, the need to view agricultural research and the introduction of modern technology as integrate parts of an overall development strategy and not as isolated activities is important and should be emphasized here.

The nutritional effects are implicit in the above-mentioned distribution of benefits from expanded food production and downward pressures on food prices. The nutritional situation is catastrophic in a number of developing countries. This situation is caused by a series of factors, and is closely associated with poverty among large segments of the population of many developing countries. These factors are related partly to limited food demand and partly to limited food production. Therefore, it may be useful to distinguish between the nutrition and demand problem and the production problem. The former is principally a result of rapid population growth, limited purchasing power – which in turn is due to low incomes and/or high prices – and a skewed income distribution. Population growth implies increasing food needs. These needs may, however, not be translated to market demand and consumption owing to limited purchasing power and a skewed distribution of personal incomes. The result is malnutrition among low-income people. This does not imply, of course, that lack of purchasing power is the only cause of malnutrition, only that it is a major one. Neither does it imply that expanded food production by itself will eliminate nutritional problems. It clearly will not. But it may be a very important part of a solution. This is further discussed later in the book.

The production problem consists of low yields and productivity, poor utilization of the production factors and a relatively small production with limited increase. The problem is caused by a series of factors including the existing structure of the agricultural sector, limited use of modern technology and problems related to the marketing and pricing of food. Marketing and price problems are to a large extent a result of lack of purchasing power among consumers. Therefore, on the one hand, severe limitations on purchasing power among consumers hold down demand and prices while, on the other hand, adverse structure in the agricultural sector and low production efficiency mean relatively high costs of production, low levels of production, relatively high prices and/or low incomes in the rural areas. The solution to the problem is a combination of increased purchasing power, improved production efficiency and expanded output. Improvements in efficiency will generate economic surpluses, which in turn may increase real incomes and standards of living within and/or outside the agricultural sector. These improvements in efficiency and output may be obtained through the expanded use of modern technology and improved production and management practices. Agricultural research plays an essential role in the development of modern technology and improved practices. It follows that agricultural research is one of the principal keys to the solution of the food and agricultural problem in developing countries. But before the relationships between research and agricultural production is pursued further, it may be useful to take a closer look at the magnitude and structure of the food and agricultural problem.

NUTRITION AND DEMAND ISSUES

The number of people suffering from starvation and malnutrition is unknown. There is no general agreement about the minimum calorie and protein requirements; a great deal of calorie–protein deficiency is seasonal and very difficult to estimate, and the statistical information on the extent of starvation and malnutrition is generally poor. Bearing these sources of uncertainties in mind it is estimated that as much as one-fourth of the world population or about 1 billion people may suffer from starvation and/or malnutrition (Mayer, 1976). About three-fourths of the world population is found in Asia, Africa and Latin America. Since these are the continents where almost all of the starvation and malnutrition occur, the implications are that about one-third of these people may be affected. It is estimated that about four hundred million people live very close to the minimum subsistence level, and between 4 and 5 million die from starvation and malnutrition every year. It is also estimated that about 2 million people died from starvation and malnutrition during the seventeenth century. This figure increased to about ten million in the eighteenth century and to twenty-five million in the nineteenth century (National Academy of Sciences, 1975). The figure for the twentieth century will be four hundred–five hundred million, if we accept the above figure of 4–5 million as an annual average for the century.

There is considerable evidence that starvation and malnutrition will increase between now and the end of the century unless current trends in the growth of population, production and incomes are changed. Accordingly, a Dutch study concludes that the number of starving or malnourished people will quadruple within the next 35 years under the assumption of a continuation of the above-mentioned trends (De Hoogh et al., 1978). Other analyses to be discussed at a later stage project large increases in food deficits in the developing countries. Such projections are, of course, based on a series of assumptions, the accuracy of which is difficult or impossible to determine. However, even though the projections are very uncertain, it appears that we may experience a deterioration in the existing nutrition and food situation in developing countries before the end of the century unless some very special endeavours are made to alter current trends in population, food production and income distribution (within and among countries).

Rapid population growth is one of the most important factors contributing to a worsening of the nutritional situation. The current global growth rate is around 2 per cent per year, while it is about 2.7 per cent in the developing market economies. It follows that food production in these countries must grow by at least 2.7 per cent annually, just to maintain the current food production per capita.

Malnutrition and starvation reduce the general well-being of the individual, lower resistance to diseases and diminish labour productivity. Malnutrition among small children may have irreversible effects on their intellectual development. Improved nutrition contributes to economic growth through increased labour productivity and intellectual capacity, at the same time as it contributes to the well-being of the individuals *per se*. Therefore the incorporation of improved nutrition into development goals is justifiable on the basis of its impact on current as well as future standards of living.

Malnutrition and starvation are caused partly by shortage of food and partly by an uneven distribution of available foods. Skewed income distribution and absolute poverty are the primary reasons for the existing uneven food distribution among population groups. In many developing countries skewed income distribution causes food consumption levels far above nutritional needs among high-income groups, while malnutrition and starvation are widespread among the poor. An analysis of consumption pattern in Cali, Colombia, illustrates this point (Pinstrup-Andersen *et al.*, 1976). Total food consumption was estimated to amount to 119 per cent of total energy requirements and 112 per cent of total protein requirements. Thus, the food consumed was sufficient to cover nutritional needs of the population as a whole. However, more than half the population received less than the minimum calorie and/or protein requirements. The amount of food consumed was closely associated with the income level. Food consumption by the group with the highest incomes (14% of the population) was approximately twice that needed to meet minimum calorie and protein requirements. At the other end of the income spectrum, food consumption by the group with lowest incomes (18% of the population) amounted to only 72 per cent of the protein requirements and 89 per cent of the calorie requirements. The high-income group spent 35 per cent of their incomes on food while the low-income group spent 87 per cent. Thus, even though they spent almost all their incomes on food, the low-income families did not meet nutritional requirements.

Although these findings are valid for Cali only, results from other studies support the argument that a similar situation may be found in many other cities in developing countries.

Average figures for food consumption at country or regional levels do not provide a true picture of the nutritional position because of the very uneven distribution of food consumption within an individual country or region. Thus, malnutrition and starvation are widespread in a number of developing countries and regions for which average nutritional intakes are above average requirements. Average figures show to what extent available food *could* meet nutritional requirements, not whether in fact it does.

Total energy availability in Africa amounts to 95 per cent of energy requirements according to available data (World Food Council, 1980). This implies that 95 per cent of the requirements would be met if the available food was evenly distributed. The corresponding figures for the Far East, Latin America and the Near East are 94, 108 and 109 per cent. Increases in food supply are essential to solve the nutrition problems in Africa and the Far East because there is absolute shortage in these regions. Theoretically, the nutritional problems in Latin America and the Near East could be solved with existing food supplies through redistribution of these supplies. But in reality, considerable increases would also be needed in these regions because a completely even distribution of available food according to needs is neither practically nor politically possible.

THE IMPORTANCE OF PURCHASING POWER

In market-oriented societies, family food consumption is determined by a number of factors including the needs of the family, incomes, preferences, food prices and the prices of other goods. The purchasing power possessed by the individual family, i.e. incomes in relation to prices, is the most important constraint on market demands for food in developing countries. If the purchasing power is very limited, nutritional needs may not be translated to market demand and consumption falls short of requirements. Consequently, while malnutrition may also be caused by other factors, e.g. lack of knowledge among consumers regarding nutrition and food, increasing purchasing power among poor people is the key to nutritional improvements in developing countries. The purchasing power among malnourished families may be increased in two ways. Firstly, incomes may be expanded either through economic growth or income redistribution. Secondly, food prices may be lowered through technological change which causes expanded food supplies and lower production costs. Reduction of the prices of other goods consumed by those with low incomes could, of course, also contribute to increased purchasing power.

Developing countries as a whole have experienced considerable economic growth during recent years. Thus, the gross domestic product (GDP) for these countries increased by 5.7 per cent annually during the period 1970–76 (World Bank, 1979). Among developing countries, those with low incomes, i.e. countries with per capita incomes of US$300 or below, experienced a growth rate of 3.4 per cent while the growth rate of developing countries with per capita incomes above $300 was 6.2 per cent. The population growth rates are high in many of the low-income developing countries and the growth in gross national product (GNP) per capita is very limited. Serious nutritional problems are found in these countries and the growth in GNP does not appear to have had any significant impact on these problems. In fact, the nutritional situation in many of these countries may have deteriorated during the 1970s. However, for developing countries as a whole, economic growth has been considerable. This, together with population growth, has contributed to expanded market demand for food. Unfortunately, however, as discussed in a preceding section of this chapter, food production did not increase sufficiently to meet the expansion in demand. This was a particular problem during 1972–74. The result was drastic increases in food prices in many developing countries, as shown later in this chapter. Thus, the nutritional impact of general increases in incomes without corresponding increases in food production is doubtful unless a change in the distribution of incomes in favour of low-income families occurs simultaneously. However, with the exception of a few countries, there are no indications of improvements in income distribution.

An annual growth rate in developing countries' GNP of about 5.6 per cent may be expected for the next 10 years (World Bank, 1979). This, together with the expected population growth, implies that food production must be expanded considerably in the future to avoid large increases in food prices. The following section focuses on the factors associated with such production expansions.

FOOD PRODUCTION ISSUES

The purpose of this section is to discuss briefly some of the food production issues judged to be of considerable significance for agricultural research and technology in developing countries. A complete treatment of the food and agricultural production problems in developing countries is not attempted.

The agricultural production problem in developing countries consists of low productivity levels for land and labour and a small agricultural production with limited increase. These elements are inter-related. The amount of food produced in relation to food needs was discussed earlier. The rate of increase in food production will be examined below. Then follows a discussion of existing low productivities and how they may be increased. The chapter finishes with a discussion of the perspectives regarding future food production and nutrition.

The food production of developing countries increased by 2.9–3.0 per cent annually during the period 1961–79 (Table 1.1). The population of these countries increased by 2.3–2.4 per cent during the same period. Thus food production per capita increased by 0.6–0.7 per cent per year. The annual rate of increase varied considerably during the period. A very poor performance was found during the period 1972–74 while production increases were high during 1975. Considerable differences in the rate of production increase were found among continents. The poorest performance was found in Africa where population increases exceeded the increase in food production. Small increases in food production per capita were found for developing market economies in Latin America and Asia, while the largest increase in food production per capita was found in the Asian centrally planned economies. This relatively large increase was primarily due to the relatively slow population increase in mainland China.

The smallest rates of increase in food production were found in the

Table 1.1 Average annual increase in food production in developing countries, by region and period (%).

	Increase in total food production		Increase in food production per capita	
	1961–70	*1970–79*	*1961–70*	*1970–79*
Developing market economies	3.0	2.9	0.4	0.3
Latin America	3.5	3.6	0.7	0.8
Far East	2.7	2.8	0.2	0.4
Near East	3.2	3.4	0.5	0.7
Africa	2.6	1.5	−0.1	−1.3
Asian centrally planned economies	2.9	3.2	1.1	1.6
Total developing countries	2.9	3.0	0.6	0.7
Total MSA countries	2.5	2.2	0.1	−0.3

Sources: World Food Council (1980a).

so-called 'Most Seriously Affected Countries' (MSA countries), i.e. the poorest countries. Production increases in these countries were barely sufficient to keep pace with population growth during the 1960s and fell short of this target during 1970–79. Since these countries are faced with severe nutritional and poverty problems and lack of foreign exchange for food imports, the slow increase in food production is of particular concern.

On the basis of the information given in Table 1.1 it may be concluded that the increases in food production in developing countries as a whole during the period 1961–79 have been insufficient to allow significant improvements in nutrition. Because of the slow increases in food production, increasing demands caused by higher incomes have, to a large extent, been translated to higher food prices. Hence, unless malnourished families have obtained at least their equal share of higher incomes, the food price increases may have re-distributed food away from these families and thus worsened the nutritional position.

Increased food production is a result of increasing the area under cultivation as well as increasing yields per unit of area. The relative importance of increases in area and yields vary among continents and time periods (Table 1.2). These increases each contributed about one-half of the production increase during 1948–1961/65 for developing countries as a whole. The relative importance of expanding agricultural areas fell to about one-third for the period 1961/65–73. An increasing reliance on yield increases and a corresponding relative decrease in the importance of extending the areas under cultivation is characteristic for all continents. This trend will continue as a larger proportion of potential agricultural areas is drawn into production and further

Table 1.2 The relative importance of area expansions and yield increases in the increase of food production in developing countries, 1948/52—1971/73.

| | (% contribution to production increases) | | | |
| | Area expansion | | Yield increase | |
	1948/52–1961/65	1961/52–1971/73	1948/52–1961/65	1961/65–1971/73
Africa	35	*	65	*
Latin America	62	53	38	47
Near East	78	40	22	60
Far East	42	1	58	99
Developing countries	49	37	51	63

* Not available.

Source: Pinstrup-Andersen (1976b).

expansion becomes more difficult and costly. FAO estimates that expansion of agricultural land will account for 28 per cent of output growth up to the year 2000 (FAO, 1979). It is further estimated that the area of potential arable land per capita will fall from 0.9 in the mid-1970s to 0.5 by the year 2000 (FAO, 1979). The possibilities for further expansion in agricultural areas are rather limited in the Far East, while Latin America and Africa still possess large unused or poorly used regions which may be drawn into agricultural production. However, utilization of these regions will, in many cases, require large capital outlays for infrastructure, water availability, improvement in soil quality, removal of tropical forest, etc. Furthermore, replacement of tropical forest and other natural vegetation may cause unacceptable ecological consequences (further discussed in Chapter 8).

LOW PRODUCTIVITY

Low productivity of land and labour is the basic production problem in the agricultural sectors of developing countries. Yields of agricultural products per unit of land in most of these countries are far below those found in industrialized countries. This point is illustrated in Table 1.3 for three crops of considerable importance in developing as well as certain developed countries. Yields of maize, rice and wheat in developing countries are estimated to be 29, 34 and 61 per cent respectively, of the yields of these crops in industrialized countries. Furthermore, the difference between average on-farm yields and yields on experimental stations in developing countries are much larger than the corresponding differences in Western Europe and North America. Two examples illustrate this large difference. The average on-farm yield of cassava in Colombia is estimated to be around 6 tons/ha while yields of more than

Table 1.3 Average yields of maize, rice and wheat in developing and developed countries 1977 (kg/ha).

	Developing countries		Developed countries	
	kg/ha	Index*	kg/ha	Index*
Maize	1.366	29	4.681	100
Rice	1.981	34	5.840	100
Wheat	1.348	61	2.196	100

* Yields in developed countries = 100.

Source: FAO, *Monthly Bulletin of Agricultural Economics and Statistics*, **26**, No. 9, Sept. 1977.

50 tons/ha have been obtained on Colombian experimental stations. Similarly, while rice yields of more than 10 tons/ha are not uncommon on experimental stations in developing countries, average on-farm yields are around 2 tons/ha.

The yield variation among individual farms in developing countries may also be very great. This point may be illustrated by data from a recently completed farm survey for cassava in Colombia. In this survey it was found that cassava yields varied from 300 to 34,000 kg/ha among the participating farmers, with the above-mentioned average yield of 6,000 kg/ha.

The large yield differences between: (1) developing and developed countries; (2) farms and experimental stations; (3) individual farms, together with the fact that current yields are far below biologically potential yields under many environmental conditions, seem to imply that large increases in production may be obtained within the current agricultural area.

Low productivity limits agricultural production and contributes to low incomes and limited capital accumulation in the agricultural sector. The immediate consequences are limited purchasing power and low standards of living for that part of the population which depends directly on agriculture. Limited capital accumulation in the agricultural sector implies that new investments necessary to facilitate improvements in productivity to a large extent depend on external capital. But shortage of operating capital is one of the most severe limitations to accelerated economic growth in developing countries. Thus, the agricultural sector must compete with other sectors in a capital market with strong capital demands and relatively limited supply. In such a market situation, capital owners will require relatively high interest rates and a considerable degree of security for loans. The individual farmer is in a weak bargaining position in such circumstances, partly because the necessary security for loans may be lacking, as might be the case for tenants, and partly because a farmer who owns a small plot of land may be unwilling to use this land as security for a loan. Uncertainty in agricultural production caused by climatic variations, diseases, pests, price variations and other factors beyond the control of the farmers, together with the fact that in most cases the farm provides the only opportunity for survival for the low-income farmer and his family, influences the farmer not to use his land as loan security even though the loan is expected to increase production and incomes. The prospect of being unable to repay the loan and thus losing the land is unacceptable to many low-income farmers. The risk associated with loans may be reduced or eliminated through various policy measures.

These measures will be discussed in Chapters 6 and 9. High interest rates are, of course, also limiting investment in the agricultural sector. Government subsidies aimed at reducing interest rates on agricultural loans are widespread among developing countries.

Therefore, as shown above, low productivity in the agricultural sector contributes to – and is affected by – lack of capital accumulation.

In addition to capital shortages, a number of other factors contribute to low agricultural productivity in developing countries. Some of these factors are closely associated with those mentioned above because they affect productivity through limitations in capital accumulation, while others affect productivity in some other way. The importance of each individual factor varies from one situation to another. However, six factors tend to be important for many developing countries. These are: (1) unfavourable structure of the agricultural sector; (2) limited infrastructure; (3) lack of effective technology suited to the local environments; (4) limited usage of modern factors of production and available technology; (5) unfavourable agricultural policy; (6) marketing and price problems. Each of these factors will be briefly discussed below.

THE STRUCTURE OF THE AGRICULTURAL SECTOR

The agricultural sector is of great importance within the total economy of most developing countries. Thus, it is not uncommon that more than 50 per cent of the population is found in the agricultural sector. Table 1.4 shows the proportions of the populations of Africa, Asia and Latin America that are found in the agricultural sector in 1965, 1970 and 1976. The agricultural sector accounts for 60–70 per cent of the total population of Africa and Asia and about 35 per cent of the Latin American population. A large proportion of the rural population of developing countries consists of low-income families. It follows that economic development strategies aimed at improving the standards of living of the poor must pay considerable attention to expanding rural incomes either through better incomes within agriculture or through increased earning opportunities for the rural population outside the agricultural sector. As shown in Table 1.4, the rural population accounts for a decreasing percentage of the total population in developing countries. This is caused by a considerable out-migration, partly because of poor earning opportunities in agriculture and partly because earning opportunities outside agriculture improve or are perceived to improve. However, the number of jobs outside agriculture does not expand sufficiently fast to absorb the additions to the labour force and

Table 1.4 The rural population as a percentage of total population 1965, 1970 and 1976.

	1965	1970	1976
Africa	72	69	66
South America	42	39	35
Asia	68	65	61
Europe	24	20	17
The world	54	51	48

Source: FAO, *Production Yearbook*, 1976.

high rates of urban unemployment are common in developing countries.

Farm size is another important structural aspect. This may vary greatly from one developing country to another. A large number of very small farms is a common characteristic of many of these countries. In Asia, 40 per cent of all farms larger than 1 ha are smaller than 2 ha and 92 per cent are smaller than 10 ha (Table 1.5). Farm sizes in Africa tend to be slightly larger, and about one-half of the South American farms are larger than 10 ha. It is not uncommon, particularly in South America and Africa, to find a large number of very small farms accounting for a relatively small proportion of the agricultural land, and a small number of very large farms accounting for the greater part, while middle-size farms are relatively unimportant with regard to both number and area.

The presence of a large number of very small farms tends to complicate attempts to increase productivity. The introduction of modern factors of production and technology aimed at increase of productivity on a large number of small farms is difficult, not only because of the capital and uncertainty issues mentioned earlier but also because a large number of individual decision-makers must be informed and convinced of the desirable characteristics of these factors of production and technology. The issues surrounding the introduction and adoption of modern technology will be traced in more detail in Chapters 6 and 9.

Table 1.5 The percentage distribution of farms on farm sizes in South America, Asia and Africa (% of farms above 1 ha).

	1—1.9 ha	2—9.9 ha	10 ha and larger
South America	13.3	38.3	48.4
Asia	40.1	52.3	7.6
Africa	35.4	51.5	13.1

Source: FAO (1965).

Many developing countries have traditionally emphasized the production of plantation crops such as bananas, rubber and sugar for export. Such a production emphasis was, of course, a result of the interests of the colonial powers. The export crops were usually grown on large holdings on the best soil. The remainder of the agricultural sector might be oriented to the production of food crops for local consumption. But most of these farms were very small and a large part of the production was used for on-farm consumption. While the technological level could be high on the large farms producing export crops, very little was done from outside the farm to improve the productivity on the small food-producing farm. As will be shown later in this chapter, this position has been changed somewhat in many developing countries. However, the general pattern of large numbers of small farms with low productivity and little or no access to modern technology alongside very large farms employing the most appropriate technology in the production of export crops may still be found in many regions of developing countries.

Existing land tenure is another factor of considerable importance for the adoption of modern technology. Separation of land ownership and land use is widespread in developing countries. Rental agreements for land are frequently of very short duration, e.g. one cropping period. Such agreements tend to have adverse effects on the investment in soil improvement because the current tenants have no certainty of obtaining the longer-term benefits of such investments. It is also more difficult for tenants to provide security for loans. Hence, lack of capital may hinder the adoption of modern technology and use of purchased production resources.

INFRASTRUCTURE

Lack of transport facilities or unreasonably high transport costs for agricultural products as well as production factors is a serious problem in many regions of developing countries. Insufficient infrastructure is a major cause of such a situation. The results are that production factors such as fertilizers are difficult or impossible to obtain at prices that make their use economically sound. It also implies that the local demand for food plays a very important role in the prices obtained by farmers. Since a relatively limited local market tends to have a stable demand for food commodities, production increases due to, say, favourable weather or introduction of modern technology may result in drastic price decreases unless it is economically feasible to export some of the additional production to markets outside the local area. However, lack of transport facilities and high transport costs may prohibit such export. In a situation such as that described above, food marketing is often dominated by one or a few middlemen. Operating between a relatively large number of farmers and consumers, these middlemen may possess a considerable degree of power over prices at the expense of farmers, consumers or both.

Introduction of modern technology with the aim of expanding production and improving productivity in regions such as those described above may not be economically sound unless simultaneous improvements are made in existing infrastructure, such as storage and transportation, to permit an economically sound outflow of agricultural products to other regions. This issue has often been overlooked by idealistic extension agents or other experts in developing countries, and for that matter by foreign experts and volunteers who have tried to promote large increases in food production within certain regions.

A number of other aspects of infrastructure could be mentioned. Institutions promoting relevant training and information at the local level are essential for the improvement of agriculture. Access to credit implies the need for local lending institutions, and investment in physical infrastructure of various kinds in the agricultural regions, possibly in connection with the development of agro-industrial complexes, may be of high priority.

LACK OF APPROPRIATE TECHNOLOGY

Available technology is often poorly suited to existing production environments including the physical, biological, socio-economical and institutional limitations found by the farmers. The result is low levels of technology adoption. It is generally agreed that farmers. irrespective of farm size, make production decisions on the basis of a rational assessment of economic and social consequences for the purpose of maximizing the well-being of the farm family. Low levels of technology adoption cannot be explained by irrational farmer behavior. Rather, it is a consequence of conflicts between the particular technology available and the limitation within which the farmer must – or does – operate. Such limitations may be caused by a series of factors including: (1) risk and uncertainty due to climatic or price variations; (2) lack of ability to cope with large variations in income; (3) lack of knowledge, resources and capital; (4) soil and climatic conditions unsuited to the particular technology or production system. The need to develop and adapt modern agricultural technology to fit the needs, resource endowments and desires of the farmers and the particular production environments cannot be overemphasized. This is a key issue in the discussion on the value of agricultural research and will be analysed in considerable detail in other chapters.

USE OF APPROPRIATE TECHNOLOGY

Fertilizer is the most widely used modern factor of production in developing countries. But even this is used only to a very limited degree. The issues surrounding the use of fertilizer and its influence on food production in developing countries are analysed in Chapter 7.

The use of other modern technology and factors of production, e.g. irrigation, high-yielding varieties and chemical disease, pest and weed control, is widespread in certain regions and for certain crops. However, considering the agriculture of developing countries as a whole, the use of these factors is very limited although growing – and large segments of the farmers of these countries use virtually no modern aids to production. Irrigation was used in ancient times and can hardly be called modern technology. However, application of modern know-how for construction of dams and development of irrigation equipment have contributed to a rapid expansion of the use of irrigation. Furthermore, the introduction of fertilizers and improved varieties have made irrigation more advantageous.

The use of modern technology developed through agricultural research will be discussed in considerable detail throughout the book.

AGRICULTURAL POLICY MEASURES

Government intervention may have positive or negative effects on food production and productivity, depending on the character of the intervention and the conditions under which intervention takes place. Since this section is focused on factors limiting production and productivity, only those policy measures which have negative effects are discussed here. Government intervention which, together with modern technology, contributes to improved productivity and expanded production will be discussed in Chapter 9.

Government intervention aimed at ensuring relatively low and stable prices for staple foods is common in many developing countries. Such intervention is popular because a large part of consumer income is spent on food. Consequently, food prices play an important role in the standard of living of the majority of the population outside agriculture, particularly the low-income groups. High food prices or food price increases may contribute to high rates of inflation, political instability and requests for large wage increases which in turn will have adverse effects on industrial growth. Thus, low food prices facilitate low urban wages and may contribute to improved welfare among the poor who do not depend on agriculture for their income. This may also accelerate short-run economic growth outside the agricultural sector. For these reasons, low and stable food prices are an important element in development strategies focused on rapid industrial growth. These development strategies were adopted by many developing countries during the 1950s and 1960s and are still used by some. The negative impact on food production and productivity, as well as incomes and capital accumulation in the agricultural sector, is obvious. The results are poor utilization of the resources in the agricultural sector, low standards of living among farmers, farm labour and the rural population in general, limited demand for goods and services, rapid out-migration of labour and adverse effects on long-run economic development.

Government policies that have adverse effects on food production and productivity are common in developing countries. Thus, export taxes on agricultural products and overvalued exchange rates are frequently enforced. Furthermore, import restrictions for agricultural inputs, e.g. import taxes and/or quotas for fertilizers, are common. Finally, it should be mentioned that many developing countries maintain policies aimed at promotion of the production of export crops while neglecting the necessary expansion of the production of food for the domestic market.

MARKETING AND PRICE ISSUES

Limited food demand and resulting low prices may be a serious obstacle to increase in food production and improved productivity in some developing countries. Local demand and price problems in areas with deficient infrastructure, particularly with respect to transport facilities and local competitive structure, were discussed previously. Similar demand and price problems may occur in larger markets and even at national levels. Even though nutritional needs may remain unsatisfied, the market demand for food is constrained by low consumer incomes. Under severe income constraints expanded food production may lead to drastic price falls which, in turn, would have a negative impact on the desire of the farmers to expand production. In this connection it is important to distinguish between food needs and food demands. Needs are determined by biological and physical factors and are translated to market demand only to the extent permitted by existing purchasing power and consumer preferences as to how the purchasing power is to be utilized. Thus, it is not uncommon to find situations where limited food demand makes otherwise feasible production expansion uneconomical, at the same time as starvation and malnutrition are widespread. Increasing purchasing power among the needy is the only viable solution to the problem. This may come about either through higher incomes or price reductions. But low food prices are a barrier to expanded food production. Therefore, reduction of food prices in isolation would make matters worse.

However, there is one way by which food prices may be lowered while food production is increased: through improved productivity which may lower the costs of production per unit of output. These cost savings may be passed on – partially or in total – to consumers through decreases in food prices. Modern technology contributes to such improved productivity by increasing yields per unit of land or other resources. But if total benefits, i.e. cost savings, associated with the use of modern technology are passed on to the consumer, why would the farmers be economically motivated to introduce such technology? In general terms the answer is that those farmers who introduce modern production-expanding technology may be able to acquire economic benefit through greater sales and reduced unit costs. The increase in production would tend to lower prices for all farmers producing the particular product, irrespective of whether or not they introduced modern technology. Therefore, farmers who do not introduce modern technology will experience a net loss due to price falls while those introducing the technology may obtain a net gain because unit cost savings exceed the price falls. This implies that farmers would be interested in the introduction of unit-cost-saving technology even though the producing sector as a whole may obtain little or no economic benefit. The question of who gains and who loses from the introduction of modern agricultural technology is crucial to the subject of this book and will be treated in considerable detail in Chapters 2 and 6.

Although demand and price problems in many cases hamper efforts to expand food production, it should be pointed out that high food demand and rapid demand increases, together with very limited expansion of food production, tend to be much more common. This may result in drastic increases in food prices and, consequently, economic growth and standards of living outside the agricultural sector will be adversely affected. During the period 1972–74 increases in food production were small in many developing countries while incomes rose considerably. The result was drastic price increases. Higher rates of increase in food production during 1974–75 slowed this increase. Table 1.6 illustrates this development for 65 developing countries. Food prices increased by more than 30 per cent annually during the period 1973–75 in about one-fourth of these countries. In comparison, only 8–9 per cent of the countries experienced increases in food prices of this magnitude during the years immediately before and after that period. Similarly, only 8 per cent had food price increases of less than 10 per cent annually during the period 1973–75, while about two-thirds were below that level during 1975–76.

The impact of increasing food prices on inflation, economic growth and standards of living is much more significant in developing than in developed countries because expenditure on food occupies a larger share of total consumer incomes. Drastic food price increases are, therefore, unacceptable to many developing countries, and while artificially low food prices are harmful to the agricultural sector the use of price increases beyond free market levels to expand food production is viable only within somewhat narrow price levels. The best solution to the food production problem lies in productivity improvements and unit cost savings while maintaining reasonable food prices.

PERSPECTIVES FOR THE FUTURE

As mentioned above, the future food and nutritional situation may be influenced by a large number of factors. Some of these factors may be manipulated by man, others may not. The extent to which such manipulation will occur is a matter of technical and economic feasibility as

Table 1.6 Increases in food prices in 65 developing countries, 1972–76.

Increase (%)	(% of the countries)			
	1972/73	1973/74	1974/75	1975/76
Less than 5%	16	2	8	30
5.1–10	30	6	20	28
10.1–15	23	11	14	11
15.1–30	23	54	36	22
More than 30%	8	27	22	9

Source: FAO, *Monthly Bulletin of Agricultural Economics and Statistics* 25 (July/August) 1976 and 26 (July/August) 1977.

well as political will. But what will the food and nutritional situation look like in 10–15 years if past trends for the key factors continue? Most available projections conclude that the situation will not improve significantly, and results from a number of these projections point in the direction of increasing food shortages in developing countries unless food imports are increased considerably.

The future food and nutritional situation may be viewed as a race among population and income growth, reduction of absolute poverty and growth in food production. The average population growth in developing countries is around 2.4 per cent annually. There is reason to believe that this growth rate will be reduced significantly within 15–20 years, but for some time to come, food production must be increased by more than 2 per cent annually to maintain current food production per capita. Nevertheless, population growth will only influence market demands for food if purchasing power is available. Thus, future food demands depend on a combination of population growth, changes in incomes and prices and the distribution of incomes. It is estimated that the GDP of developing countries will increase by about 3.3 per cent per capita annually (World Bank, 1979). It is further estimated that growth in population and incomes together will cause an increase in food demand in food-deficit developing countries of 4.1–4.4 per cent annually between now and 1990 (IFPRI, 1977). An unchanged income distribution is assumed in these estimates. If incomes are distributed more evenly, food demands will increase further. However, there are no indications that a more even distribution of incomes will occur in the near future.

As mentioned earlier, food production in developing countries increased by about 3 per cent annually during the last 20 years. Accordingly, unless the rate of growth in food production is accelerated, increasing food shortages will occur in many developing countries. Worst affected are the MSA countries where current increases in food production are below the population growth rates and where the existing food and nutritional situation is very unsatisfactory.

The International Food Policy Research Institute (IFPRI) has estimated that grain-importing developing countries will face a grain deficit of about one hundred million tons by 1985, increasing to 120–145 million tons by 1990 if the recent rate of increase in these countries' food production continues. In comparison, the grain deficit of these countries was 28 million tons during the period 1969–71 and 45 million tons in the year of the food crisis, 1974–75. Africa and the Near East account for 45 per cent of the estimated grain deficit, Asia for 40 per cent and Latin America for 10 per cent. Regarding individual countries, India is expected to have the largest deficit by 1990 (17–22 million tons), followed by Nigeria (17–21 million tons), Bangladesh (6–8 million tons) and Indonesia (6–8 million tons).

These estimates indicate very clearly that a mere continuation of past rates of increase in food production in developing countries will lead to increased requirements for food imports. If foreign exchange earnings or availability of food aid do not permit deficit countries to meet these requirements, the results will probably be increasing domestic food prices, reduced economic growth and increased starvation and malnutrition. But if the food-deficit countries manage to come up with the necessary foreign exchange, world market food prices will tend to be pushed upwards. Furthermore, given the scarcity of foreign exchange in most food-deficit, oil-importing developing countries, large increases in the use of such scarce foreign exchange for food imports is likely to hamper growth and development through reduced imports of investment goods. Thus, while expanded rates of increase in food production in developing countries is not a sufficient condition for solving the food and nutritional problems it is certainly a necessary and essential condition. Such accelerated food production must be based primarily on increasing yields per unit of land.[6]

NOTES

1. Including national and regional political security as well as internal social and economic stability.
2. This, of course, is a very naïve and incomplete description of the economic growth process. The interested reader is referred to the list of references for a more complete treatment.
3. This implies that price decreases at the producer level are passed on to the consumer and that food demand is inelastic. While the latter is usually the case, the former may not be permitted to happen if the middlemen possess considerable power over price and quantity manipulations. If such power exists and is utilized, a large part of the economic benefits associated with price decreases at the producer level may be appropriated by the middlemen.
4. The relationship between price changes and the resulting change in quantities demanded of a given product is called the price elasticity of demand.
5. For basic staple foods this may not be true above certain income levels.
6. Replacement of non-food crops offers another possibility for expanding food production. However, the economic consequences of such replacement for the agricultural sector may be unacceptable.

2 Agricultural research, economic growth and improving living standards: The relationships

The primary purpose of this chapter is to show how agricultural research and technology may contribute to economic growth and improved living standards. Emphasis is placed on a description of the process which converts research resources to improved living standards, and how the elements of this process interact with other elements of overall development. An explanation of the relationships between these factors is also given. The actual impact on economic growth and income distribution is dealt with in Chapters 5 and 6.

Research results and technology differ from other economic goods in many ways. Knowledge of the most important differences is essential to obtain the largest possible benefits from research. Such knowledge is also important to better understand why, when and to what extent it is necessary and useful to invest public funds in agricultural research and under what circumstances international research is useful.

In most developing countries the enormous potential of agricultural research to increase food production and improve resource productivity has been utilized only to a very limited extent. There are many reasons for this, including historical developments and a lack of priority for food production in some countries. Insufficient understanding of the nature of research results and how agricultural research and technology may be most effectively utilized to promote economic growth and increase living standards is undoubtedly an important reason. A better understanding of these issues, both in developing countries and in the donor countries, is likely to contribute to more effective resource utilization within the area of agricultural research and technology.

The first section of this chapter deals with the general research and technology diffusion and adoption process. Then R&D supply and demand factors are discussed. The third section deals with the adoption of technology. The relationship between agricultural research and technology and economic development is discussed in the fourth section and the chapter terminates with a discussion of the nature of agricultural research results and technology. Externalities in research and their influence on the demand for public research funds at national and international levels are also discussed in this last section.

GENERAL FRAMEWORK

A general and grossly simplified framework is illustrated in Fig. 2.1. Decision-making on R&D priorities and activities are influenced by a series of R&D demand and supply factors. The results of R&D expected to be useful for, and of interest to, the potential user (the farmer in the case of agricultural production technology) are fed into a diffusion

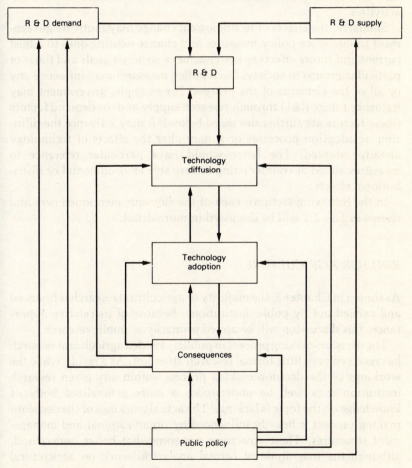

Fig. 2.1.   Overview of process framework.

mechanism which, if successful, will lead to technology adoption by farmers or other appropriate users.

Adoption or non-adoption will have consequences for: (1) decision-makers on adoption/non-adoption (farmers); (2) other groups in society, e.g. consumers and farm labour; (3) society at large, e.g. some types of environmental impact. These consequences will, in turn, influence researchers and their future research work. Farmers will be motivated to make further adjustments in the production process, including possible changes in technology adoption. Furthermore, in cases where the diffusion mechanism is – or can be – controlled by farmers or farm groups, the consequences may lead to changes in this mechanism. Finally, farmers may attempt to influence future R&D activities.

Similarly, the effects of technological change may motivate government to introduce policy measures and change existing ones to adjust current and future effects to better achieve society's goals and those of particular groups in society. Such policy measures may influence any or all of the elements of the process. For example, government may influence future R&D through research supply and/or demand factors (these factors are further discussed below), it may influence the diffusion or adoption processes or it may alter the effects of technology already adopted. The latter would have particular reference to measures aimed at counteracting undesirable environmental or distributional effects.

In the following sections, each of the elements mentioned here and shown in Fig. 2.1 will be discussed in more detail.

R&D FOR AGRICULTURE

As shown in Chapter 3, the majority of agricultural research is financed and carried out by public institutions. Because of its relative importance, this discussion will be aimed primarily at public research.

The decision-making process in publicly funded agricultural research has received very little formal research attention. As a result, while the workings of the decision-making process within any given research institution may well be understood, a more generalized body of knowledge on the topic is lacking.[1] The actual workings of the decision-making process is heavily influenced by organizational and management structures. These structures are somewhat better understood, although the magnitude of formal analytical work on agricultural research organization and management is also rather limited.[2]

This section discusses the factors influencing the content of the research and thus the type of technology sought. While the decision-making process as well as research organization and management are important in that respect, no attempt will be made to analyse these matters in detail.

Factors influencing the content of the R&D undertaking may be divided into two closely related groups: research supply and research demand factors. The interaction of these factors and the decision-making, organizational and management structures leads to the establishment of a research strategy including a set of intermediate and final goals, although neither the strategy nor the goals are necessarily explicitly stated in the individual case.

Research supply factors
Among research supply factors, five seem to be of particular importance (Fig. 2.2). First, the professional interests of the researchers and research managers are likely to exercise great influence on the R&D content. Secondly, the research capacity, i.e. available financial, physical and human resources, provides the framework within which R&D must be carried out. Thirdly, the existing body of knowledge, the 'state of the art' and recent trends in R&D will influence the type of R&D to be carried out. A fourth factor influencing R&D is inertia in the planning and execution of research.

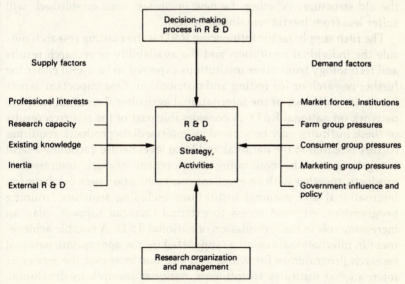

Fig. 2.2. Factors influencing goals, strategy and activities in agricultural R&D.

Continuation of current R&D activities, tasks and programmes with very little or no change or adjustment taking place is very typical for a number of public agricultural research institutions. Immediate research goals are vaguely specified and effective mechanisms for terminating or drastically changing individual research tasks and programmes, including periodic reviews of progress, are frequently absent. Changes in overall resource availability, e.g. budget cuts or increases, are frequently distributed across existing activities more or less in proportion to current resource use.

Where such inertia is strong it may effectively prohibit other supply and demand factors from having their proper influence. The inertia problem is most pronounced in well-established institutions with a small staff turnover and only marginal resource changes over time. New research programmes and tasks and major changes in existing ones can come about primarily through the granting of additional, earmarked resources to existing institutions or the creation of new ones.

Replacement of existing research institutions (frequently a department of the Ministry of Agriculture) with new semi-autonomous institutes has been carried out in a number of developing countries recently. While the overall purpose of such organizational change has been to obtain a more flexible and effective research environment, it has provided the opportunity for major revisions in research goals, strategies and activities which might have been prevented by inertia in the old structure. Whether the new institutes, once established, will suffer less from inertia remains to be seen.

The fifth supply factor influencing R&D is the existing research outside the individual institution and the availability of research results and technology from other institutions expected to be useful either for further research or for testing and distribution. One important aspect here is the influence of the international agricultural research institute network on national R&D. A considerable part of the research results of these institutes may be viewed as 'intermediate products' requiring further research at the national and local level before becoming useful to agriculture. The continuing development of such intermediate products, together with an excellent communication network between international and national institutions including seminars, training programmes, etc. and access to external financial support, play an increasing role in the formulation of national R&D. A notable achievement in international research, supported by the appropriate national research programmes for wheat and rice has increased the power of international institutes to influence national research in developing countries. The rapid expansion of international agricultural research may also have replaced some national research. This will be further discussed in Chapter 4.

Research demand factors

Relative prices of agricultural resources and output may have considerable impact on the direction of technological change through their influence on R&D. The theory of induced innovation advances the hypothesis that the trend of technological change and the supporting R&D tend to be heavily influenced by relative resource endowment and factor prices (Binswanger and Ruttan, 1978; Hayami and Ruttan, 1971.) Thus, in societies with a relatively ample supply of labour but severe land scarcity, R&D will focus on the development of labour-using, land-saving technologly. Similarly, changes in relative resource prices, e.g. increasing energy prices relative to the price of other resources, would tend to adjust R&D accordingly. The proponents of the induced innovation theory do not claim that relative resource and output prices are the sole determining factor in the prevailing direction of agricultural R&D, only that they play a major role. The extent to which market forces can be expected to ensure a socially desirable pattern of R&D will be discussed in a subsequent section. What is of interest here is that market forces may be expected to influence R&D priorities.

The majority of agricultural research is financed by public funds. The primary reason why the private sector does not enter into these research activities to a greater extent is that a private firm may be unable to acquire a sufficient proportion of the economic gains associated with the research results to make a research undertaking profitable. This, of course, is a familiar problem in cases where the use of research results cannot be protected or controlled by the research agency. However, such research may be highly profitable for society as a whole. Therefore, public investment may be justified.

The distribution of economic benefits from publicly funded agricultural research among groups in society will depend on the particular R&D goals, strategies and activities. It follows that various groups in society will attempt to influence the R&D projects in order to obtain as large a share as possible of these benefits. Such influence may come about in different ways, depending on the organizational structure of the R&D decision-making body and the various pressure or interest groups. Interest groups from the producer, consumer and marketing sectors are likely to be actively trying to influence agricultural R&D (Fig. 2.2).[3] Considerable conflict of interest may exist among the three sectors and even among pressure groups within a given sector, e.g.

small and large farmers, farmers in one region versus another, and among organizations representing producers of different commodities.

The relative influence of each of the interest groups may vary sharply among countries. In some countries, notably the United States, it appears that the food-processing firms have had a very great impact on agricultural R&D. In other countries, particularly some market-oriented developing countries, larger farmers seem to have had considerable access to the decision-making on R&D, while farmers with smaller landholdings have not. In some countries agricultural R&D is heavily influenced by the desires of farmers, while in others, communication between the farm sector and the agricultural research institutions is virtually non-existent. In general, consumers seem to have had very little direct impact on agricultural R&D, although in most cases they have been the major beneficiaries. Of course, consumers exercise a considerable influence through their demand behaviour. Finally, it should be mentioned that, while suppliers of capital inputs, e.g. fertilizers, pesticides, etc. exercise some influence on publicly funded R&D, the rural labour force seems to have had absolutely no direct impact, in spite of the fact that alternative technological change may have very different effects on employment and wages.

The above-mentioned group pressures may be brought to bear on R&D, either directly or through some government policy measures. A series of other policy measures may influence agricultural R&D. Some of these may be directly focused on R&D, while others may concentrate on different matters but indirectly affecting R&D to a great extent. The means available to government to influence agricultural R&D directly or indirectly are many and varied and cannot be discussed in detail here. It should be pointed out, however, that failure to take into account the relevant policy measures – whether existing, potential or likely future measures – in analyses of technological change in agriculture may greatly reduce the validity of the results.

TECHNOLOGY ADOPTION

The term 'adoption', as used here, refers to the act of incorporating something into the production process. Adoption of a new technology or a technology not previously used in the production process implies 'technological change'. The technological state of any given production process is a description of the composition and combination of inputs and technologies that exist at a given time. Thus, technological change describes a movement from one technological state to another. Adoption of technology must be preceded by technology diffusion where the latter terms refers to the act of making technology available to potential adopters. Diffusion, then, is the link between R&D and adoption. Thus, effective diffusion is an essential but not sufficient condition for adoption. Decision-makers on technology adoption must be made aware of available technology and they must believe that adoption will be in their best interest. On the basis of the consequences of adopting a certain technology, the expected benefits from continuing, modifying or discontinuing its use will be assessed. Furthermore, the consequences of adopting a certain technology among some farmers may create awareness of its existence and potential benefits among others. This somewhat simplistic overview of the adoption process is illustrated in Fig. 2.3.

Figure 2.4 presents a more detailed schematic illustration of the farm level decision process related to adoption and use of new technology. Each of the elements in Fig. 2.4 is briefly discussed below.

The point of departure is an externally induced diffusion of information and materials which together form technology T_1. This diffu-

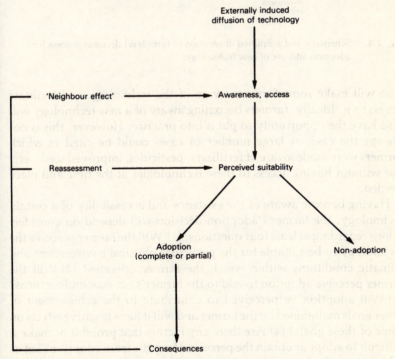

Fig. 2.3. Schematic overview of adoption process in agriculture.

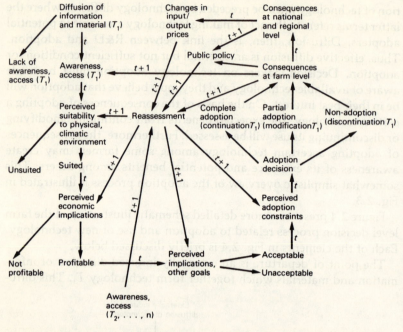

Fig. 2.4. Schematic and simplified illustration of farm level decision process for adoption and use of new technology.

sion will make some farmers aware of the technology and facilitate access to it. Ideally, farmers becoming aware of a new technology will also have the opportunity to put it into practice. However, this is not always the case. A large number of cases could be cited in which farmers were made aware of fertilizers, pesticides, improved seeds, etc. but without having access to these technologies at the time and place needed.

Having become aware of the existence and accessibility of a certain technology, the farmer's adoption decision will depend on considerations regarding at least four questions: (1) Will the farmer perceive the technology to be suitable for the particular physical environment and climatic conditions within which the farmer operates? (2) Will the farmer perceive adoption to add to the farmer's net economic returns? (3) Will adoption be perceived to contribute to the achievement of other goals maintained by the farmer and will it have negative effects on some of these goals? (4) Are there any factors that prohibit or make it difficult to adopt or obtain the perceived benefits from adoption? Let us take a closer look at each of these four questions.

A considerable proportion of agricultural technology is commodity specific, such as improved crop varieties and animal breeding stock. Such technology would, of course, only be relevant for producers of the particular commodity. Furthermore, the potential benefits from agricultural technology may be obtained only within certain physical environments and/or under certain climatic conditions. There has been a tendency to develop agricultural technology primarily for regions with the most favourable physical and climatic conditions. Such technology may be poorly suited or completely unsuited for farmers in regions where such conditions do not apply. Many of the world's agricultural research and experimental stations are located on very good soil. If climatic conditions are not optimal at these sites, considerable efforts are made to approach optimality, particularly with regard to water availability. Soil fertility is maintained at close to optimal levels (unless, of course, soil fertility factors are being studied) and adverse crop or animal conditions such as diseases, pests, weeds, etc. are being eliminated or controlled by means of chemical and other measures. These are the places where a considerable proportion of new or modified agricultural technology is being developed and tested.

In all fairness, it should be noted that there are exceptions to the above. Some agricultural research is now being carried out under more realistic farming conditions and local testing under actual farming conditions is becoming more common. Furthermore, research aimed at obtaining maximum yields may provide useful guidelines for further research. The principal point to be made here is that a large part of available agricultural technology is suited only for limited and usually most favourable ecological environments.

If a farmer perceives that a given technology is suitable for his farm, his next question is whether and to what extent its adoption would be profitable. In estimating the profitability, the farmer will probably take into account not only the change in costs and returns regarding the particular technology to be considered but also the effect on costs and returns from corresponding adjustments in other farm activities. The thoroughness of the economic analysis would vary among types and sizes of farms and, at least among smaller farmers, experience-based guesses are probably more common (and they may give more realistic results!) than more structured estimates. Profitability is closely linked to the above suitability of technology for the particular environment. Because agricultural technology may not have been tested under conditions relevant for a given farmer, any indications of profitability implied in the recommendations from the diffusion agency may be grossly invalid for the individual farmer. Reliance on such recommendations has resulted in great losses to adopters. One single set of fertilizer recommendations for a region with great variation in soil type and fertility is but one example of this problem. Recommendations which fail to account for farm level prices of fertilizers and other inputs are also common.

While a perceived increase in net returns may be necessary for the adoption of new technology, it may not be sufficient.[4] The anticipated impact (positive or negative) on the achievement of other goals may be of great importance. Among low-income farmers in particular, objectives such as income stability (reduced risk and uncertainty), assurance of a desired crop mix, adequate supplies for home consumption and reasonable family work loads are common and may greatly affect adoption decisions. Thus, failure to consider farm level goals other than profitability in *ex ante* analyses of technology adoption may result in erroneous estimates of the expected adoption rates. The interaction between technology characteristics and farm level goals should be considered in any such analyses.

The influence of risk and uncertainty on technology adoption has been widely studied and various models have been developed for farmers' risk behavior (e.g. Binswanger, 1980). Much less research has been carried out on the other objectives.

The issues treated here are integral parts of the total farm-household decision process regarding production, consumption, time allocation and other farm-family matters. While traditional economic analysis tends to look at production, consumption and time allocation as separate sets of activities, recent methodological and empirical work on so-called 'household economics' has been successful in providing additional insights into the interrelationships among these and other sets of activities and objectives. Ignoring this approach in analyses of the adoption decisions, particularly among low-income farmers, would be to forgo an excellent opportunity of gaining a better understanding of the decision process and a related improvement in the power of the analyses to project adoption rates of various technology alternatives. On the other hand, household economics models may become very complex. Hence, care must be taken to select only those relationships of greatest importance for the technology adoption and use decisions, to avoid excessive complexity of the overall models.

A number of factors may make adoption difficult or impossible or they may prevent the farmer from obtaining the benefits associated with adoption, and thus make adoption undesirable. Such constraints would tend to be location specific and may only be identified through a thorough knowledge and understanding of the production environment (including physical, climatic, cultural, social and economic factors) in which the farmer operates. Some constraints may be internal to the actual farm household activities, e.g. lack of sufficient family labour during peak labour demand periods and unwillingness to use hired labour, while others would be external, e.g. lack of access to the necessary inputs. It would be inappropriate to attempt a clear distinction between internal and external constraints because they are highly interdependent. Labour constraints may be considered an internal constraint if we ignore the possibility of hiring labour, but an external constraint if we look only at the supply of hired labour, ignoring the possibility of increased family labour. Similar examples could be given for capital constraints. Social and cultural constraints may be imposed from the community in which the farmer lives or they may be deeply rooted within the individual farm family. In any case, some of these constraints may play a very important role in the adoption decision. Some may be removed, while others must be allowed for in the design and choice of technology. Those that are not expected to be removed either: (1) because it is too difficult or impossible or would have unacceptable side effects; or (2) because the appropriate policy measures or institutional changes are not likely to come about, must be explicitly incorporated into analyses of the adoption process if they are expected to have serious effects on the adoption behavior.

But what are these constraints? As mentioned above, the presence and importance of any given constraint tend to be specific to the particular case, e.g. region, farm size, even in some cases to the individual farm. This is why any effective *ex ante* analysis aimed at the estimation of expected adoption rates and efficiency of a given technology must be based on a thorough knowledge and understanding of the production environment within which the farmers involved are operating. Such understanding can only be obtained by interaction with the farmers and not through statistical tables. Thus, the specific constraints to be incorporated into the analysis will vary from one case (region, farm size group or some other disaggregation) to another.

A large number of studies have been carried out on constraints to technology adoption in agriculture.[5] These studies clearly illustrate the great diversity of constraints and the interdependence between the farm group studied and the factors of importance in the adoption decision. Thus, attempts to generalize the relative importance of individual constraints across farm groups, regions and countries are unlikely to be very useful. However, a few constraints frequently found to be important among low-income farmers may be mentioned. Lack of access to purchased input such as fertilizers and pesticides at the time and place needed, seems to play a major role. Uncertainty about the performance of a given technology under actual farming conditions is another constraint frequently encountered. Such uncertainty stems primarily from lack of technology testing under the relevant conditions which results in highly unreliable recommendations provided by the diffusion agencies. This situation tends to induce the farmer initially to adopt a new technology only on a small plot of land, in essence to do his own testing, before proceeding to rejection or full adoption. It also causes low-income farmers, who are unwilling to risk crop failure and its unacceptable consequences for the family's well-being, to postpone adoption until they have observed the results of technology on neighbouring farms. This is one reason why small farmers lag behind larger ones in adopting new technology.

A number of other constraints have been identified under specific circumstances. These include: adverse institutional arrangements and public policies, shortage of credit, certain cultural and sociological factors, limited output markets, complexity of the technology and land tenure. Each of these constraints and possible ways to eliminate them are discussed in Chapter 9. The important point to be made here is that adoption constraints must be identified on the basis of existing production environments, including physical, climatic, cultural, social and economic factors.

The adoption decision
Taking into account the above-mentioned issues and probably a few more, the farmer makes his decision whether or not to adopt a given technology. Adoption may be complete, i.e. for the total relevant production activity, where the farmer opts for a new variety of rice which he thinks appropriate for his total rice area,[6] or it may be partial, i.e. on a small plot of land for the purpose of observing the results. In addition, the farmer decides whether to make any other adjustments in farming practice, i.e. reducing or increasing the area sown with the various crops, purchasing more or less of certain complementary inputs, etc.

Adoption of new technology will have certain consequences for the adopting farmers, e.g. changing net incomes. These effects will, in turn, motivate the farmer to reassess his decisions on adoption and related adjustments within the farm. The additional experience obtained will influence his perception of the suitability, profitability and other aspects of the technology which, in turn, will influence his decision-making in the subsequent time period ($t + 1$). He may decide to continue 'complete use', he may discontinue or he may make certain modifications in the use of technology and other production activities (see Fig. 2.4). Awareness of other technology ($T_2, \ldots, n$) may also enter the reassessment. The farm level consequences among adopters may create awareness and desires to adopt among other farmers. In fact, in a number of cases, this demonstration effect has been found to be extremely important in accelerating technology adoption.

Widespread adoption will imply significant effects outside the individual adopting farm. Changes in input and output prices might result. Such changes would enter into the reassessment. Furthermore, policy changes on a number of issues such as prices, institutional structures, credit, extension service, crop insurance, etc. may be brought about. The perceived effects of such policy changes would also enter into the farmer's reassessment. It should be emphasized that the individual farmer will include in his reassessment only those issues which he perceives will affect him directly. Broader socio-economic effects such as environmental, employment, resource and foreign exchange effects will only enter into his decision-making to the extent that they are reflected in input/output prices, costs, resource availability or in some other way affecting him directly. If the relative resource endowment at the national or regional level is not reflected in relative input prices or absolute availability it will be discounted in his decisions. Scarcity of energy is of little concern unless it is reflected in the prices he pays (or expects to pay) or the access he has (or expects to have) to energy. Extensive unemployment will not affect his production decisions on labour use if minimum-wage laws or labour unions maintain relatively high wages. Effects on the local community, such as pollution of local streams, may be exceptions to this general rule because of community pressures. Such pressures may be strong, particularly in small, relatively closed, traditional communities.

AGRICULTURAL RESEARCH AND ECONOMIC DEVELOPMENT

RESEARCH RESULTS AND TECHNOLOGY

Figure 2.5 illustrates how agricultural research may contribute to economic growth and improved standards of living. As shown in step 1 of Fig. 2.5, agricultural research may result in new knowledge and new materials. The knowledge and materials may be used either as a basis for further research or directly by the agricultural sector. Research which is used only as a basis for further research is sometimes called 'basic research', while research producing results of direct utility for the

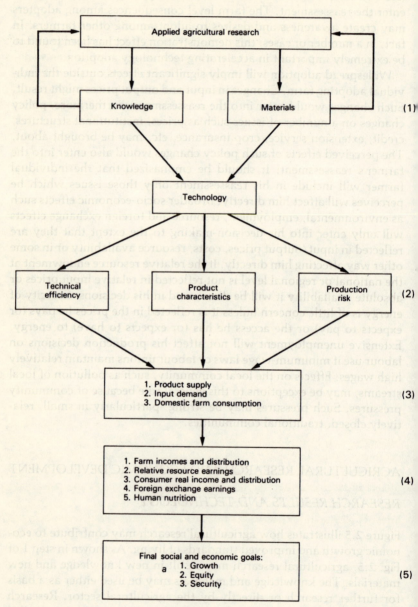

Fig. 2.5. Illustration of the potential outcome and implications of agricultural research.

agricultural sector is called 'applied research'. However, such classification of agricultural research is unsuitable and at times directly misleading.

Effective agricultural research should, to the fullest extent possible, be based on a desire to solve a defined research or agricultural problem. Such a problem orientation usually requires research programmes of a cumulative nature, i.e. new research must be based on the results of previous research. Thus, the research programme may be viewed as a chain, where the individual links consists of research projects, the results of one project providing the basis for the next. The majority of agricultural research projects are used only for further research. However, successful research will eventually lead to results which, alone or together with results from other studies, provides the basis for new agricultural technology (step 2 in Fig. 2.5). In addition, knowledge and materials used for the development of new technology are also normally used as a foundation for further research for the purpose of developing better technology.

Thus, narrow research objectives are relative, not absolute. As soon as an objective is achieved, another one, expected to meet better the overall development targets, is established. A certain technology may become available to the agricultural sector at the same time as efforts are made to develop an even better one. Such a stepwise process is characteristic of effective agricultural research. For some types of technology, continuation of the research along with the release of technology is essential to maintain effectiveness. This is true for some of the disease and pest resistance factors incorporated into crop varieties.

Stepwise improvement of agricultural technology does not imply that every step results in only a small improvement. In some countries, such as Denmark, where the use of modern technology is widespread, farmers may shift to new technology even though the associated economic gains are relatively small. In developing countries, where the use of modern technology is much less common and the perceived uncertainty of introducing new technology is greater, farmers may not adopt modern technology or change from one modern technology to another unless the expected economic gains are large, e.g. a doubling of yields. The new wheat and rice varieties developed during the 1960s were in fact capable of doubling yields in many cases. However, few technological improvements are likely to result in gains of such magnitude. Therefore, it may be necessary to accumulate a series of smaller technological improvements before releasing these, as a package, to the agricultural sector.

New materials developed through agricultural research may be biological, chemical or mechanical. A large proportion of the new knowledge obtained by means of agricultural research is associated with or embodied in these materials in the process of formulating new technology. Another part of the knowledge obtained may be used without the direct involvement of new materials. The use of this kind of knowledge is usually associated with improvements in the decision-making process and organization on individual farms. Thus, modern technology may be divided into four principal types: biological, chemical, mechanical and management technology. Biological technology includes new crop varieties, and other technology which incorporates materials of a biological nature. Chemical technology includes chemical fertilizers, chemical means for pest or weed control and similar materials, while mechanical technology includes farm machinery, equipment, etc. Management technology includes the knowledge concerned with decision-making and management of farming activities without directly involving the use of new materials. Clearly the distinction among the various technological developments are not as clear cut as may be implied above. However, even though there is considerable overlapping among the four principal technology types, it seems useful to adhere to such a classification in technology evaluation.

TECHNOLOGY AND EFFICIENCY, PRODUCT CHARACTERISTICS AND RISK

Modern agricultural technology may influence agricultural production in three ways (step 3 Fig. 2.5). First, modern technology may help in increasing efficiency, i.e. greater production for a given quantity of one or more resources, or unchanged production with a reduction in resource use. The classical example of such a case is the ability of much modern technology to facilitate increasing yields per unit of land. In addition, the application of modern technology may result in the more efficient use of other resources used in agricultural production, e.g. labour, water, plant nutrients – whether they are added to the soil through fertilizers or are already present in the soil – invested capital, e.g. buildings and machines. The choice of resource(s) for which efficiency increases are sought depends on a series of factors including goals and relative scarcity and prices of the individual resources. This choice may greatly influence the magnitude of economic benefits from agricultural research and technology, as well as the distribution of these benefits among groups in society. Thus, it is important that the choice is an explicit element of decisions on research priorities and specifications of the desired technology.

Technological change may greatly affect the resource-use pattern. Recent rapid changes in the price of some resources, e.g. energy and fertilizers, and prospects of absolute resource scarcity and negative environmental impacts have raised some serious questions regarding the current and predicted future path of technological change in agriculture. While some argue that relative resource and output prices accompanied by minor policy-adjusting measures will ensure that the optimal path for society will be followed, others would argue that the market mechanism is grossly inefficient as a guide to the future direction of technological change. Still others argue that relying exclusively on market forces to guide future technological development would lead to disaster, both from the environmental viewpoint and in the depletion of finite resources.

The time horizon required for the guidance of R&D and the resulting technological change in agriculture is long relative to the time horizon implied in the reaction of market forces. Thus, market signals pointing to a change in the technological direction may not come about sufficiently early to ensure that the required change is made at the most appropriate time. The time lag between changes in R&D strategies and the resulting impact in technological change at the farm level may be considerable, while relative market prices would tend to react immediately to changes in demand and supply factors, including changes in relative resource scarcity. Thus, rapid and abrupt changes in resource prices requiring immediate substitutions among inputs or outputs are unlikely to be immediately reflected in the direction of technological change. Considerable uncertainty regarding future resource prices calls for a somewhat broader focus of research in order to reduce the time necessary to adjust the path of technological change.

Input price distortions which create differences between social and private costs of inputs are another factor which makes market forces less effective in guiding technological change. Existing market conditions may not reflect the true social value of the various inputs. Furthermore, external factors peculiar to the individual firm, such as adverse environmental effects, may imply that certain social costs are not reflected by the market forces.

Agricultural technology may also contribute to a change in product characteristics, e.g. shelf life, nutritional content, length of required growing season and capacity for mechanical harvesting. Finally, modern agricultural technology may reduce production risks. Agricultural production is associated with considerable risks. Such risks may be related to the production process as well as to markets and prices. Production risk is caused by climatic factors, e.g. variations in rainfall and its distribution throughout the growing season, variations in temperature and solar intensity, etc., diseases, pests and other factors. The risk factors contribute to variations in yields and production and, as a result, may cause considerable variation in the incomes of individual farmers. For low-income farmers such income variations may be unacceptable. Therefore, the impact of modern technology on production risk is of considerable importance, particularly for these farmers and should be carefully considered in the specification of the desired technology.

Some modern agricultural technology is capable of greatly reducing the production risk. Irrigation reduces the risk associated with variations in rainfall. The development and use of crop varieties more tolerant to variations in water availability is another method of reducing the effect of this type of risk. The development of crop varieties with tolerance or resistance to diseases and pests plays, in fact, a dominant role in agricultural research, irrespective of whether the research is focused on developing or industrialized countries. The development of such crop varieties accomplishes the dual purpose of increasing production and reducing risks. The point to be made here is that the risk issue is more important in developing countries, particularly among small farmers for whom a crop failure may imply severe consequences.

While some types of technology may reduce production risks, others may increase these risks. The latter may be the case for new high-yielding crop varieties with little or no resistance to crop diseases. Replacement of traditional varieties with at least some resistance to existing diseases or pests by such new varieties may greatly increase risks. A trade-off between yield capacity and resistance to certain adverse factors need not be present, but it is not uncommon. The selection of improved plant material is frequently made on the basis of relative yield capacity under optimal growing conditions with respect to water, soil and nutrients and with the best possible disease and pest control. Thus, the selection of varieties may take place with little or no consideration given to the yield capacity under existing farming conditions. Varieties selected under such conditions may add significantly to the production risk faced by the individual farmer. The above-mentioned close connection between agricultural research and existing farming conditions, including on-farm testing of new varieties before release to farmers, is essential to avoid such increasing risk. An increasing emphasis is currently placed on maintaining this connection, particularly in international agricultural research. Such emphasis includes research to improve yield stability and reduce risks.

Another reason why new technology may increase production risk, or rather make it more difficult for the farmer to accept the consequences of such risk, is that the use of some new technology requires additional capital. If such capital is borrowed, possibly with the farm as the security for the loan, the effects of a bad harvest are likely to be worse than where traditional technology is used. Unless special arrangements are made, loans must be repaid irrespective of the amount harvested. Because of the limited capacity of the low-income farmer to absorb risk and the severe consequences of crop failure it is easy to understand that he is unwilling to adopt modern technology with high expected yield capacity if it implies higher risk. Accordingly, the effect of modern technology on production risk is an important issue to be considered in decision-making regarding the specification of the technology to be developed for low-income farmers.

IMPACT ON AGRICULTURAL PRODUCTION

Hitherto it has been shown that modern technology may influence agricultural production through changes in efficiency, product characteristics or production risk. It is further argued here that any contribution made by agricultural research to economic development must eventually involve changes in one of these three elements. But what are the results of these changes? What is the next step on the way to translate research resources, to economic development? What may occur is a change in either the quantity of agricultural commodities produced or the quantity of one or more resources demanded, or both (step 4 in Fig. 2.5). Changes in the quantities produced may result in changes in the market supply – i.e. the agricultural sector wants to sell a larger or a smaller quantity at existing prices – and/or changes in home consumption. Changes in home consumption may be important for nutrition and standards of living among low-income farm families in developing countries because a very large part of family's total food consumption may come from its own production. Furthermore, a large part of the total production may be used for home consumption.

The impact of new technology on the quantity of each commodity produced depends on the type of technology. New technology may be product specific, e.g. new high-yielding crop varieties, or it may be resource specific as in the case of improved fertilizer materials and chemical weed control. A combination of the two is not uncommon, such as new crop varieties with high-yielding capacity under application of large quantities of fertilizers. New technology may also be of more general types such as improved production systems for mixed cropping and improved crop-rotation methods.

New technology may have a direct or an indirect impact on the quantity of a given commodity produced. The direct impact refers to the impact on the crop(s) for which the technology is used, while the indirect impact refers to the impact on the production of other crops. It is important to be aware of the existence of both direct and indirect effects. While the direct effect is usually the one of immediate interest, indirect effects may greatly enhance or reduce the total benefits from research and technology. Introduction of product-specific, high-yielding technology for one crop may make the production of this crop more profitable to the farmer. This, in turn, may cause large increases in the area growing a particular crop while that with competing crops may be reduced. Such a substitution among crops is a natural result of changing relative profitability.

What is argued here is that attempts should be made to estimate these indirect effects and to take the necessary precautions. It has been argued that the introduction of high-yielding wheat varieties in India during the last half of the 1960s caused a reduction in the area growing grain legumes, and consequently a reduction in protein production. If such a development did in fact occur,[7] or is expected to occur, and if it is considered undesirable by the government responsible, it may be advisable to introduce policies to improve the profitability of legume production in the short run, while promoting research to improve its production efficiency in the longer run. Measures to slow down or stop the introduction of high-yielding wheat varieties would be an unacceptable solution because it would forgo large potential productivity gains.

This example illustrates the need to integrate research and technology priorities with public policy in related areas to ensure that both efficiency and equity goals are achieved to the fullest extent possible. Considering the effects of modern technology in isolation may lead to wrong decisions regarding research and technology. A great deal of the early criticism of the green revolution was prone to this error. Rather than suggesting facilitating, corrective or compensatory policy measures to ensure the best possible utilization of the opportunities offered by research and technology, it was implied and sometimes explicitly stated that technology that could not by itself contribute to the achievement of both growth and equity goals was unacceptable.

IMPACT ON RESOURCE DEMAND

Technological change may greatly affect the resource-use pattern in agriculture. Different technologies may have different impacts on the quantities of resources used and the optimal resource composition for a particular production process. A given technology may reduce the need for a given resource per unit of output (it is resource-saving) while increasing the need for another (resource-using). Introduction of a technology which needs less of a certain resource per unit of output does not necessarily imply that less of that resource will be used in total. It merely implies that current output quantities can be maintained with a smaller quantity of the resource, provided, of course, that the necessary resource substitution takes place. But since more is produced per unit of the particular resource, i.e. technical efficiency increases, it will be profitable to expand production and thus expand the use of the resource unless product demand or resource supply makes such expansion unattractive.

Thus, it is important that decisions on research priorities and the specification of the desired technology be based on clearly stated objectives regarding future demand and earnings of each of the resources, In societies with high rates of current and expected future unemployment and severe capital scarcity, labour-using technology would be preferable to capital-intensive, labour-saving technology. But while this seems fairly obvious, it is not uncommon to find cases where research priorities appear to conflict with relative resource endowment, e.g. emphasis on the development of labour-saving technology in societies with high unemployment. Failure to conform to existing relative resource endowments and prices is an important reason why new technology may not be adopted by farmers. In some cases, relative resource prices do not reflect relative resource endowments because of price or wage-distorting policies such as minimum wages or because powerful labour unions are capable of raising wages. In such cases, the technology should reflect existing relative prices and not relative endowments because the degree of adoption depends on the farmer who, in turn, is guided by relative prices.

IMPACT ON GROWTH AND DISTRIBUTION

Increasing efficiency of some resources, i.e. a larger production per unit of resource, expanded demand for resources and increasing profit to the residual factor, e.g. family labour or capital, lead to a larger total income for resource owners and/or consumers of agricultural products. The additional incomes are transformed into investment and consumption within and outside the agricultural sector. This implies further increases in earnings, consumption, production and investment in other sectors or, in other words, economic growth (steps 4 and 5 in Fig. 2.5). Therefore, although the growth linkages of agricultural technology are grossly simplified here, the conceptual relationships are straightforward.[8] The key is a combination of increasing resource efficiency and resource substitution which together facilitate increasing real incomes. But how are the additional real incomes distributed in society? Only the general concepts are discussed here. The specifics relating to the various types of technology and empirical findings regarding the distribution of the benefits of research and technology are analysed in Chapter 6.

Introduction of new agricultural technology affects functional as well as personal income distribution. Functional distribution refers to the distribution of incomes among owners of resources, e.g. landowners and workers. It is affected by changes in the quantities of each resource used and the prices paid. Changes in resource use and prices, in turn, are determined by the characteristics of the particular technology, the demand and supply structure of each resource, the demand structure for agricultural products and the institutional setting.

The personal income distribution may be influenced not only through changes in the functional distribution but also directly by changes in product prices. Expansion in the supply of agricultural products and substitution among the various products caused by the introduction of new technology may affect product prices. Such price changes may influence the distribution of incomes between producer and consumer sectors and among groups within each of these sectors. If increased supply caused by the introduction of new technology does not result in lower prices, the producer sector may obtain large gains. This may occur if prices are fixed by government or the increases in supply are offset by opposite adjustments in foreign trade of the same magnitude, i.e. more exports or less imports of the particular commodity. If, on the other hand, the additional output is added to the existing supply on the domestic market and prices are left to adjust to the new market situation, the consumer sector is likely to obtain large economic gains. The relationship between changes in the quantity demanded of most agricultural products and price changes is such that to sell more, prices must be reduced to the point that the consumer sector pays less for the total quantity, i.e. obtains a larger quantity at a lower total cost. Therefore, the introduction of new technology under these conditions will result in the increase of real incomes among consumers and the freeing of purchasing power for commodities other than those for which technology was introduced. On the other hand, total incomes of the producers will fall. More is produced at a lower total market value. The effect on the net incomes of producers depends on the ability of the producer sector to reduce total cost of production. While some types of new technology may be very inexpensive, for example improved crop varieties, others, such as fertilizers, may not. In any case, although new technology is likely to reduce costs per unit of output it can only reduce total costs if a sufficient amount of traditional resources are replaced or sector supply control is enforced. The traditional resources are land and labour.

Land may be shifted from one commodity to another, but it is unlikely that it will be taken out of agricultural production by the individual farmer unless such action is made profitable or forced by land deterioration, government policies or urban developments. Thus, labour is normally the resource to be replaced. Out-migration of labour from agriculture may be required to meet labour needs in other sectors. However, in societies with large urban unemployment, labour migration from agricultural to urban areas may not be in society's best interests. While such migration is undoubtedly necessary to promote economic growth in the longer run, the speed by which it occurs is important.

If only a relatively small group of farmers introduce production-expanding technology, these farmers may obtain large economic gains even though the agricultural sector as a whole loses. This is so, because unit cost savings exceed price falls. Farmers who do not introduce such technology will lose because prices fall while unit costs do not. These may well be those farmers which leave agriculture to join the urban unemployed.

If, contrary to the above, the additional output does not cause any price decrease or a smaller decrease than that mentioned-above because of adjustments in foreign trade or price policies, the producer sector may obtain large gains. If no price change occurs, consumers are not expected to gain or lose. To the extent that the additional output is exported or used for import substitution, new technology may increase foreign exchange earnings. These would also be affected if technology or other inputs are imported.

IMPACT ON NUTRITION

The distribution of economic benefits from agricultural research and technology may affect the standards of living in a number of ways. One of these – improved standards of nutrition – requires further mention. The nutritional situation is extremely bad for certain population groups in many developing countries. Agricultural research and technology may be powerful tools for its improvement. But the improvement obtained per dollar invested in agricultural research and technology diffusion depends to a very large extent on research priorities and facilitating, corrective and compensatory policy measures. Malnutrition is closely linked with poverty and is found among poor agricultural producers and poor consumers alike. Accordingly, the most effective technology from the viewpoint of improving standards of nutrition, is that which results in expanded real incomes among poor farmers and consumers. An example may be technology for food commodities primarily produced by low-income farmers and which occupy a large share of the budget of low-income consumers. Technology for commodities primarily produced on large farms and primarily consumed by high-income consumers may have little nutritional impact. In some cases, new technology may in fact have a negative impact on nutrition through commodity substitution and a reduction in incomes of the poor. These cases are exceptions. Nevertheless, the nutritional effects may differ greatly among alternative technology choices and research priorities, and the incorporation of definite nutritional targets into decision-making on research and technology may greatly improve the nutritional effect without unacceptable adverse effects on the achievement of other objectives (Pinstrup-Andersen, 1980).

THE NATURE AND CHARACTERISTICS OF RESEARCH RESULTS

As mentioned earlier, agricultural research produces knowledge and materials which may be used as technology in agricultural production to contribute to economic growth and improved standards of living. Therefore, research results and the derived technology may be viewed as being a productive resource like land, labour and capital. However, it is more useful to perceive modern technology as a factor that facilitates improved utilization of these resources. Research results and modern technology differ significantly from traditional production resources in a number of aspects. Five of these aspects will be discussed here; they are: (1) the uncertainty associated with agricultural research and technology diffusion; (2) time requirements; (3) interaction with other factors of production; (4) the importance of the production environment for the effectiveness of modern technology; (5) external benefits associated with research results and technology.

UNCERTAINTY ASSOCIATED WITH RESEARCH AND TECHNOLOGY

Research is a search for new knowledge and materials useful for society as a whole, groups within society or possibly the individual scientist. It is an exploration into the unknown. Therefore, when research is initiated, the results are normally not known and it is difficult or impossible to estimate time and resource requirements to obtain a particular research result and, for that matter, whether such a result can in fact be obtained. In some cases it may be possible to predict the results with a reasonable probability, but that is usually as far as one can go. In this manner, research differs considerably from more routine production processes where output can be readily predicted on the basis of inputs. Agricultural production is also subject to uncertainty, but to a much lesser degree than research. Because of the great uncertainty regarding research results, it may be very difficult to predict whether a particular research activity will be economically advantageous. On the other hand, the results of a single line of research may provide sufficient economic benefits to cover the total cost of all research projects in a certain institution or country for a number of years.

The difficulty of predicting the outcome of research activities and the potentially high return from successful research places a heavy burden on the individual researcher because the results of research depend to a large extent on his or her training, experience, intelligence, abilities and motivation. Likewise, the requirements for research organization and administration are somewhat special. The individual researcher or group of researchers must possess considerably more flexibility and freedom to carry out their work than is the case in more routine-type activities. At the same time the organizational and administrative structure must ensure that research activities focus upon the established goals and overall strategies.

Another factor of uncertainty has to do with the value to society of the research results obtained. As mentioned above, research results may be introduced into the agricultural production process as technology. But the value of such technology is influenced by a series of factors which, in turn, may change over time. The implications are that the value of a given technology may change considerably from the time of its initiation to when it is ready for use. On the basis of research objectives, a given research programme may be successful because the desired technology is developed. However, by the time this occurs the value associated with its use may be greater or less than anticipated at the time of initiation. In addition, benefits of new technology may vary because of the degree to which it meets, or does not meet, the requirements, of the farmers, not because these requirements have changed but because they were not taken sufficiently into account when designing the desired technology. It is not unusual for the value to society of research results to be less than that which the researchers anticipated. This is so because research priorities and technology specifications are frequently decided on the basis of insufficient information on existing farming conditions. A thorough knowledge and understanding of the factors influencing the use and pay-off from alternative technologies may reduce – but not eliminate – the uncertainty associated with the value of new technology. Various approaches to obtain the required information are discussed in Chapter 9.

TIME REQUIREMENTS

Agricultural research and diffusion of the resulting technology is frequently very time consuming. Total time requirements may be divided into three phases: (1) from the initiation to the completion of the actual research activities; (2) from the time research results are available until they are tested, combined and transformed to usable technology; (3) from the time the technology is available until it is adopted by farmers and introduced into the production process.

The time required to obtain research results which may be applied in new technology may be long, and depends to some extent on the amount of research resources available. More resources may reduce the time required, but only within limits. The need for a stepwise approach in which one research activity or project is carried out on the basis of those previously implemented, limits such reduction. Furthermore, the time required for research on plant and animal growth and development obviously imposes certain limits on the possibilities for reduction.

Testing of research results and technology may also require a considerable time. Because of variations in climatic and other factors at the test sites, it may be necessary to carry out the testing over more than one growing season. Finally, the time required to persuade farmers to adopt new technology may be long. The length of this period and the extent to which new technology is adopted at any given point in time depends heavily on the ability of the technology to meet the needs and wishes of the individual farmer and his resources. Technology that is well adapted to these needs and wishes may be adopted very quickly. Again, the need to focus agricultural research and technology development on what the farmer wants and needs and not on what the research community thinks he should want is extremely important.

The efficiency of the extension service is another important factor. Even though a certain new technology is well suited to the farmer's needs and desires, he must be informed of its existence and characteristics in order to adopt it. Time requirements associated with the diffusion of technology and the magnitude of adoption depend on a number of other factors including the structure of the agriculture sector, resource endowments and the farmers' attitudes. Experience from prior adoption of successful technology is likely to facilitate rapid adoption of future technological innovations, while lack of prior experience and experience with poorly suited technology are likely to have the reverse effect. In countries where farmers are accustomed to technological change and where close communication with extension and research facilities exists, as is the case in the UK, the United States, Denmark and certain other high-income countries, the time required for the distribution of new crop varieties and other technology may be very limited indeed. Farmers in many developing countries – particularly low-income farmers – have little or no experience of successful modern technology and communication with extension and research is poor or non-existent. In such circumstances, diffusion and adoption of modern agricultural technology may be a very slow process.

INTERACTION WITH OTHER FACTORS OF PRODUCTION

As mentioned earlier, new technology is frequently capable of increasing the efficiency of the traditional resources: land, labour and capital. However, the ability of a particular technology to facilitate increases in efficiency may be greatly influenced by the use of other types of new technology. This interaction among different types of technology and between technology and the traditional resources is of great importance for the impact of new technology on agricultural production. Two examples may illustrate this point. Use of fertilizers on traditional crop varieties may result in very little yield increase. Similarly, introduction of improved crop varieties without fertilizer application may result in little or no yield increase. However, if both improved varieties and fertilizers are introduced, the resulting yield increases may be large. This point is illustrated in Fig. 2.6 for two rice varieties in the Philippines. In this example the traditional and the improved varieties yield roughly the same without application of nitrogen. However, while the nitrogen response of the traditional variety is very limited and becomes negative even at relatively small amounts of nitrogen, the response of the improved variety is considerable. Thus, neither the improved variety nor nitrogen would greatly add to rice yields when applied in isolation. Applied together, however, large yield increases could be obtained. Similar interaction may be found between fertilizers and irrigation, varieties and irrigation, varieties and pest control, varieties and land preparation, etc. Such interaction means that the yield increase obtained from introducing a certain technology in isolation is frequently much less than that expected on the basis of results from research and testing.

The solution to the problem is to introduce a package of technology to ensure a proper balance among the various technology components to exploit the potential yield-increasing capacity of the individual components. Such a package may consist of improved varieties, fertilizers,

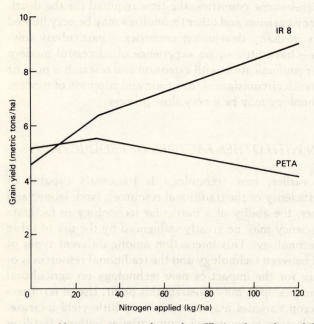

Fig. 2.6. Nitrogen response of a modern (IR 8) and a traditional (Peta) rice variety (Jennings, 1976).

pesticides and the relevant advice on how best to utilize the package. However, it may be difficult to get such a package accepted among low-income farmers in developing countries because the required changes in the production system and the decision-making may be more than such farmers are willing to accept at a given time.

Introduction of the package may also require more capital than the low-income farmer has at his disposal or is willing to borrow. For many low-income farmers with very little or no past experience with modern technology, the introduction of a complete technology package may be a bigger step than they are willing to take. Of course, such a package need not be applied on the total area. Instead it is common for farmers to try the package on a small plot of land to observe the results before deciding on full-scale introduction. Such 'on-farm testing' makes extremely good sense.

The effects of the above-mentioned interactions are to a large extent determined by the characteristics of the technology. Plant breeding and selection, for example, are carried out on the basis of certain assumptions regarding the use of alternative technology and factors of production. The objective of plant breeding and selection determines the effects of interaction to a considerable extent. Suppose the requirement is to obtain varieties with large yield potential under favourable water supply or high rates of fertilizer application. It should not be surprising that the varieties developed by successful research in terms of the above requirement would have little or no yield advantages under adverse water supply or without the application of fertilizers. As mentioned earlier, a large part of agricultural research, including plant breeding and selection, is carried out under optimal production environments. But such optimal environments may not be present on a particular farm. Thus, the yield advantages obtained on the farm may be considerably lower than those found under experimental conditions. This is further discussed in Chapter 9.

Planning and execution of the appropriate parts of agricultural research on the basis of more realistic production conditions would greatly enhance the value of such research in developing countries. Furthermore, it is of great economic importance to farmers that all possible attempts be made to incorporate tolerance or resistance to diseases and pests into new plant materials. Such tolerance and resistance reduce the need for other means to obtain the yield potential of improved plant materials. Resistance to a certain pest might, for example, make chemical pest control unnecessary for obtaining high yields. In general, it is important that the desired technology be specified on the basis of the framework within which the farmer operates and over which he has little control. This framework is called here the 'production environment'.

PRODUCTION ENVIRONMENT

The efficiency of agricultural technology greatly depends on the production environment in which it is applied. As defined here, this consists of geographic location, climatic and ecological conditions, soil type and structure, input and output markets, the structure of the farming sector (farm size, ownership conditions, etc.), production systems and other factors which together form the frame or limits within which the day-to-day activities of the individual farm and farmer take place. A particular agricultural technology may be advantageous only if applied within a particular production environment. The technology is said to be 'location or environment specific'. Such specificity is frequently found in biological technology.

The impact of the production environment on the efficiency of agricultural technology reduces the possibilities of the successful transfer of technology from one country to another. Even transfers from one region to another within a given country are frequently unsuccessful because of differences in the production environment and location or environmental specificity of the technology. Transfer of the results of agricultural research and technology from industrialized to developing countries is a particularly interesting case in point. Most industrialized countries are located in temperate zones, while most developing countries are found in tropical and subtropical areas. Thus, research and technology aimed at the agricultural sector of industrialized countries and heavily dependent on climatic and geographic conditions may have little to offer in developing countries. Furthermore, technology developed for the industrialized countries may be focused on economic, social and institutional settings quite different from those found in developing countries. This issue is, of course, of concern for technology transfer in general and not only for agricultural technology. Without going further into this topic, reference might be made to the present concern regarding the transfer of labour-saving technology in industry and commerce from industrialized to developing countries.

However, not all agricultural research and technology developed in industrialized countries suffers from lack of transferability. A considerable amount of more basic research may be equally applicable for the two groups of countries. Furthermore, broad types of technology, for example fertilizers and modern varieties, are obviously important to all countries irrespective of geographic location and income level. However, the specific technology needed, for example the type of fertilizer and the particular characteristics of a new variety, depends on the production environment in which it is to be utilized.

Likewise, while the majority of the agricultural research needed by developing countries must be carried out in these countries, some research results may be transferred from other countries. Similarly, some research is most effectively carried out by international research institutions. The reasons why international research may be advantageous are discussed in the next section.

EXTERNALITIES IN RESEARCH

The concept 'external economic benefits' or 'externalities' is used here to describe a situation in which a considerable portion of the economic benefits of a given activity is acquired by groups which neither carried out the activity nor paid for it (directly or indirectly). This concept is important to determine when and why private firms or certain groups in society may be motivated to promote, initiate and/or carry out agricultural research. It is also useful to assist in the division of labour between national and international research institutions.

It is intuitively obvious that it would not be economically advantageous for a small farmer to carry out agricultural research at his own expense for the purpose of improving his own production. Research costs would exceed the economic benefits he could obtain.[9] But if the research costs were distributed among a number of farmers for whom the research results were relevant, the economic benefits obtained by the group might exceed costs. Economic benefits similar to those obtained by the farmer who did the research could become available to the other farmers. Therefore, if more farmers had access to the research results, total benefits would increase while costs remain unchanged. If total costs were to be borne by the farmer who might want to initiate research, he would only do so if the benefits obtained exceeded the costs, irrespective of the magnitude of the benefits obtained by others. Since it is unlikely that benefits to the individual farmer would exceed costs, the research would not be initiated – even though total benefits exceeded costs – unless costs were distributed among beneficiaries. But when and to what extent would it be in the economic interest of a group of farmers or other groups in society to invest in agricultural research? And under what conditions would it be in the interest of private firms outside agriculture? Finally, under what circumstances would it be economically advantageous to society as a whole to invest public funds in agricultural research?

As will be shown in Chapter 5, society as a whole may obtain large economic gains from agricultural research. However, owing to the nature and characteristics of research results, it may be difficult or impossible for the agency controlling the research to acquire a sufficiently large portion of the economic benefits to make investment in research economically attractive. It follows that relying exclusively on private firms for agricultural research without government intervention or funding would undoubtedly result in suboptimal research investment and the forgoing of activities with a high pay-off to society. On the other hand, some agricultural research and technology is well suited for execution and development by private firms.

The circumstances under which private firms may obtain sufficient economic benefits from agricultural research activities to warrant such activities are further examined below. Then follows a continuation of the analyses regarding the conditions under which farmer groups or the agricultural sector as a whole might initiate or promote research. The third section analyses the conditions for which investment of public funds in agricultural research would be in the interest of society as a whole. The last section discusses the factors determining when and to what extent international agricultural research is advantageous.

AGRICULTURAL RESEARCH BY PRIVATE FIRMS

Private firms may obtain acceptable economic returns from agricultural research if they are able either (1) to sell the research results directly or as an element of a product or service, or (2) to increase earnings through complementary effects, e.g. if research results contribute to expanded demand for the products or services offered by the firm.

In many developing countries the access to patents and other exclusive rights protected by legal institutions offer certain possibilities to research agencies for acquiring at least some of the economic benefits associated with research and technology. However, in many cases effective protection of such rights is extremely difficult. While research and development related to new agricultural technology may be very expensive, difficult and time consuming, the copying and multiplication of such technology – once available – may be easy and inexpensive. Development of crop varieties with high yield capacity, disease and/or insect resistance or some other desirable characteristics may be difficult and costly. But once such a variety is made available to farmers, seed multiplication may be an easy task for the individual farmer. Thus, the ability of the research agency to benefit from the economic gains associated with the varietal development may be limited to initial sales, or alternatively, sales to a few farmers who in turn make seed available for themselves and possibly others for future growing periods.

Of course, there may be important reasons why farmers would prefer to continue to purchase seed from the research agency rather than producing it themselves or purchasing from neighbours. Production of seed under special conditions, e.g. with better pest control, the use of brand names and the provision of certain guarantees regarding seed quality are some such reasons. However, the farmer is paying for superior seed multiplication and not for the research behind the varietal development, and the possibilities for maintaining a large price differential between such seed and unimproved seed are rather limited. The price differential may be much less than the gain to farmers from changing to the new variety.

The price the farmer will pay for the new seed will be determined by the cost of producing it on the farm or obtaining it from neighbours or elsewhere, and the perceived quality difference between seed purchased at the research agency or some seed-multiplication institutions licensed by the agency and the seed he produces or obtains elsewhere. Therefore, the portion of the economic benefits associated with the new variety which the agency is able to capture may be insufficient to cover research costs.

The development of hybrids offers much better opportunities for obtaining a sufficient portion of the associated economic benefits because the hybrid seed is developed through crossing and must be purchased each year. Simple on-farm seed multiplication based on purchased hybrid seed would result in the loss of the high yield capacity associated with hybrid seed.

Other types of agricultural technology, such as certain chemical technology, agricultural machinery and equipment are better suited for protection by means of patents and other legal means. In general, it is probably fair to say that private firms have an easier time obtaining and exploiting exclusive rights on chemical and mechanical technology than on biological and management technology. This, of course, is a major reason why the former is primarily developed by the private sector while the latter depends to a large extent on public investment. It should be pointed out that ability to maintain certain rights over research results and technology does not ensure an acceptable return from investment in the development of such results and technology – it is a necessary but not a sufficient condition.

Another issue influencing the ability of private firms to obtain the value of research benefits is that the knowledge produced by research is not 'used up' or depreciated in value because it is applied. Sale of research knowledge to one farmer does not prohibit its simultaneous or subsequent use by other farmers free of charge. The farmer who initially buys the knowledge does not use it up as he would fertilizers or pesticides. Therefore, unless he keeps the knowledge confidential – something that rarely occurs among farmers – this neighbours would not have to pay for the knowledge.

Introduction of new technology may have a considerable impact on the demand for certain agricultural inputs. Thus, private input supply firms may acquire large economic gains from investment in agricultural research through the effect on the demand for their products (agricultural inputs). This was referred to above as the complementary effect. Research leading to a combined biological and chemical technology package is a case in point. Producers of pesticides may obtain large benefits from investment in research aimed at the development of improved varieties if the high yield capacity is dependent on the application of pesticides, even though the research benefits associated with the varieties as such cannot be obtained. Investment by the fertilizer industry in plant breeding aimed at the development of varieties with high fertilizer response is a similar example which has not been greatly exploited.

RESEARCH FINANCING BY THE AGRICULTURAL SECTOR OR GROUPS WITHIN THE SECTOR

It is reasonable to expect that the agricultural sector is willing to invest in agricultural research only if such investment is expected to provide an acceptable economic return to the sector. The factors influencing the distribution of research benefits between agriculture and consumers of agricultural products were discussed earlier. It was concluded that the agricultural sector as a whole may obtain large economic benefits from productivity increasing research and technology if some or all of the additional production resulting from such technology is either exported or used to replace imports. If, on the other hand, the additional production is added to the existing domestic supply, and prices are permitted to adjust, total incomes of the agricultural sector are likely to fall. In this latter case, the introduction of productivity-increasing technology will result in increasing net incomes to the sector only if the fall in the total costs of production is in excess of the fall in total incomes.

The total cost of production may be reduced through resource substitution, e.g. labour-saving mechanization. However, while productivity-increasing technology is likely to reduce cost per unit, it is unlikely that the resource substitution will be sufficiently powerful to cause a decrease in total costs that would exceed research costs and the fall in total sector incomes. Thus, it may be expected that an agricultural sector producing solely for the domestic market with no opportunity for export or import substitution would be unwilling to invest in research aimed at increasing productivity unless some market intervention measures such as supply control or price subsidies were introduced to limit the price decreases. On the other hand, an agricultural sector producing for export or for a domestic market with fixed prices, might obtain large gains from research investment. It is not uncommon that research on export crops is financed partly or totally by the producers.

In cases where investment in research is not of economic advantage to the agricultural sector as a whole, it may still be advantageous to certain groups within the sector. For this to be the case, the group must be capable of limiting the use of the resulting technology by farmers outside the group. Development and application of productivity-increasing technology by the group may reduce unit costs and expand production among the members of the group. If a relatively small proportion of the total production of the commodity to which the technology is applied comes from the group, the increase in production will depress prices only marginally, and total as well as net returns to the group are likely to increase. This situation is similar to the case where early adopters of new technology may acquire large economic gains while the producer sector as a whole experiences a loss.

Research aimed at changing product characteristics or developing new products has been carried out by producer groups with great economic success. Such research may result in product diversification, increased demand for the products resulting from the research measures and increased net returns. Extensive research is carried out in this area by agricultural processing firms, particularly in the industrialized countries.

PUBLIC RESEARCH INVESTMENT

As mentioned earlier, the consumers of agricultural products are the principal beneficiaries of agricultural research aimed at increasing production. For this reason, it is no surprise that consumers are willing – or at least not strongly opposed – to finance such research. Rather than contributing directly, the consumer finances agricultural research through public funds. These funds may be obtained through taxes on incomes, property, imports or exports or in some other way. Therefore, consumers as well as producers share in the financing of research, and this distribution of costs among individual consumers is not necessarily proportional to the distribution of research benefits. This issue is of interest in the impact of agricultural research on income distribution and will be further examined in Chapter 6.

INTERNATIONAL FINANCING

As mentioned above, certain research with large expected benefits to society will not be carried out by private firms because most of such benefits are external. In a similar manner, a number of research activities may not be carried out by an individual country because the proportion of total benefits that can be obtained by that country is insufficient. These research activities are most advantageously carried out at the international level. Research producing results and/or technology useful for a number of countries and research with extensive or very specific resource requirements are examples of activities suited for international research institutions.

Interaction between the production environment and the effectiveness of agricultural technology, together with large variations in the production environment among countries severely limit the extent to which international research is advantageous to national or local projects. In fact, international research should be viewed as a complement to and not a substitute for national and local research. The relevant question is to identify the areas within the overall research effort where international research may strengthen the research overall, and not replace national or local investigations. This will be examined in great detail in Chapter 4. The point to be made here is that, because of the nature of agricultural research and technology, there is a need for international research.

NOTES

1. Illustrations of some aspects of the decision-making process in selected agricultural research institutions in Latin America are presented in Pinstrup-Andersen and Byrnes, 1975. Recent innovations and suggestions for improvements in the decision-making process are discussed in Shumway (1977) and Pinstrup-Andersen and Franklin (1977).

2. Agricultural research organization is treated in Arnon (1968). See also Bredahl, Bryant and Ruttan (1980).

3. To the extent that research is supported by external sources, e.g. foreign assistance agencies, these sources could exercise strong influence on the type and focus of R&D. One view of the demand for agricultural R&D expressed by international donors is discussed by Scobie (1979), and questioned by Dalrymple (1980). Further discussion of research demand may be found in Guttman (1978).

4. Perceived increase in net returns is not always necessary for technology adoption. Some farmers may adopt technology which is perceived to contribute to other goals, e.g., income stability, even though net incomes are not expected to increase.

5. An excellent review of such studies related to economic constraints in developing countries is presented in Schutjer and Van der Veen (1977).

6. The farmer may perceive (rightly or wrongly) that a given commodity-specific technology is only advantageous on some of the area grown with the particular crop. Such a case is considered complete adoption as opposed to partial adoption explained above.

7. While the grain legume area was reduced, total protein production increased considerably (Ryan, 1977).

8. For additional discussion of the growth linkages associated with technological change in agriculture see Mellor (1975, 1976) and Bell and Hazell (1980).

9. The testing of new technology on a small plot of land mentioned earlier, is not considered as research here.

3 *Agricultural research in developing countries*

The agricultural research system for the developing countries is composed of five components (National Research Council, 1977a). These are: (1) national or regional (intracountry) research organizations; (2) regional (intercountry) research programmes; (3) international agricultural research institutes; (4) research carried out in industrialized countries but focused on or relevant to problems in developing countries; (5) inter-country research networks.

This chapter discusses national and regional (intracountry) agricultural research. It begins with a brief discussion of some of the historical and contemporary aspects of agricultural research in developing countries. Then follows an analysis of current magnitudes of research expenditure by continent and income level and trends in these expenditures during the last 20–30 years. The relative emphasis on research versus extension in developing and industrialized countries is analysed and the role of the private sector in agricultural research is discussed.

BRIEF HISTORICAL VIEW

According to Arnon (1968) 'the earliest measure taken to improve the agriculture of the colonies was the establishment of botanical gardens'. During the eighteenth and nineteenth centuries, such botanical gardens were established both in the countries of the colonial powers and in the colonies such as the West Indies, India, Jamaica and many others (Arnon, 1968). Through these gardens, new crops and crop varieties were introduced and tested in the various countries.

During the latter part of the nineteenth and the beginning of the twentieth century a number of agricultural experimental stations were established in the developing countries. These experimental stations were limited almost exclusively to exporting crops of economic interest to the colonial powers. Thus, experimental stations for coffee, cocoa, peanuts, rubber, cotton and possibly other export crops were established in West Africa during the period 1880–1915 (Anthony *et al.*,

1979). Similarly, in India, early emphasis was placed on research for export crops. Beginning in 1921, Central Commodity Committees were established for cotton, sugar-cane, tobacco, oilseeds, jute, coconut and other export crops (Menon, 1971). The purpose of these committees was to promote research, developments, extension and marketing for the particular crops.

In Indonesia, the first privately funded experimental station was established by the sugar-cane industry in 1885. Later, experimental stations were established for coffee, tea, cocoa, tobacco and other crops (Mangundojo, 1971).

As agricultural research expanded during the period up through the Second World War, the emphasis on export crops was maintained in most developing countries. Research stations for single commodities such as rubber and sugar-cane were common. In many cases the research was initiated, managed and funded by the private sector. Examples of such privately funded research stations include three in Sri Lanka for tea, rubber and coconut respectively; the Rubber Research Institute of Malaya; the Sugar Experimental Station of Mauritius; coffee research stations in Kenya; the Sisal Research Station in Tanzania; and the Tea Research Institute of East Africa (Masefield, 1972). At the same time, publicly funded agricultural research was being undertaken on export crops in a number of developing countries. The West Indian Central Sugar-Cane Breeding Station in Barbados, the Cocoa Research Station at Tajo in Ghana and the Tung Experimental Station in Malawi were examples of such publicly funded research institutions.

The research scientists in these stations were mostly recruited in the home countries, and only limited efforts were made to develop research expertise among the citizens of the various developing countries. Furthermore, because the primary objective of agricultural research in the colonies was to improve cash crops and increase earnings from the sale of these crops outside the colonies, very little attention was paid to research on food crops primarily consumed in the colonies themselves. Public and private support to agriculture – other than research – was also primarily aimed at export crops. The result was a dualistic structure of the agricultural sector consisting of a relatively progressive subsector of usually, but not necessarily, large production units for export crops and a stagnant subsector of peasants producing food commodities primarily for their own consumption.

There are, of course, exceptions to this general pattern. Thus, research on food crops for domestic consumption was carried out in some colonies because of pressures from large commercial producers or as components of famine prevention programmes (Anthony *et al.*, 1979).

The emphasis on export crops was maintained by many developing countries after independence. This, together with a shortage of research expertise and the priority on industrial development, resulted in very limited or no research on food crops in many developing countries between independence and the middle of the 1960s.

Since then, an increasing awareness of the need to focus development efforts on food and agriculture and the documented success of agricultural research and technology have contributed to expansion in agricultural research for the purpose of increasing food production for domestic use and improving living standards in rural areas. However, as will be further discussed here and in subsequent chapters, current research in food and agriculture in developing countries is still only very limited. Furthermore, the research of many developing countries still concentrates on export crops. Accordingly, more than two-thirds of the total expenditure on agricultural research in Sri Lanka went to export crops in 1975 (Bengtsson, 1977). In Ghana, about 40 per cent of agricultural research funds for 1977/78 went to cocoa and oil palm (Agble, 1980) and more than half of the agricultural research funds in Guyana went to sugar-cane in 1977 (Chesney, 1980).

However, a number of developing countries are now making relatively large investments in research on food commodities, whether for export or domestic use, for example India, Brazil and the Philippines.

The organization of agricultural research varies among countries. In general, a large part of the research on export commodities is carried out and funded by the private sector. Research on agricultural commodities for domestic consumption is primarily carried out under the auspices of the Ministries of Agriculture with a relatively minor amount of research by the universities. In some countries, publicly supported agricultural research institutions with varying degrees of autonomy have been created.

Post-Second World War developments in the content and organization of agricultural research in developing countries have been significantly influenced by external assistance. Although the total extent of external technical and financial support for agricultural research has been very limited, it has been considerable when compared to that of the individual developing country. Expatriates have played a significant role in the development of agricultural research institutions as well as university education in agriculture. Furthermore, a very large proportion of the leading agricultural scientists and research administrators in developing countries have received training in industrialized countries. While some countries now possess sufficient institutional and professional capacity to take care of their own research needs, the lack of such capacity is still a major bottleneck in effective agricultural research of sufficient magnitude in many countries and the need for external assistance is great. This will be further elaborated in Chapter 10.

MAGNITUDE OF RESEARCH EXPENDITURE

Global agricultural research expenditure for 1979 was estimated to be more than $7 billion (Schultz, 1979). The latest data for the breakdown of agricultural research expenditures on continents or groups of countries are for 1974. For that year it was estimated that about one-fourth of the total expenditure occurred in Africa, Asia and Latin America (Table 3.1). If agricultural research expenditure for Japan and Israel are subtracted, this figure falls to approximately 15 per cent. It thus, appears that around 15 per cent of global agricultural research expenditure for 1974 occurred in developing countries. If this proportion remained constant through the period 1974–79, developing countries spent about $1 billion on agricultural research in 1979.

Global expenditure on agricultural extension amounted to about one-third of the expenditure on agricultural research in 1974. Close to one-half of the extension expenditure occurred in Africa, Asia and Latin America (Table 3:1). Therefore, the ratio of research to extension expenditure differs greatly between these continents and the rest of the

Table 3.1 Agricultural research/extension expenditures by continent 1974 (1971 US$ m.)

Continent	Research		Extension		Research/ extension
	($ ml.)	(%)	($ ml.)	(%)	
Africa	141	3.7	225	16.9	0.6
Asia*	646	16.9	259	19.5	2.5
Latin America	170	4.4	122	9.2	1.4
North America and					
Oceania	1,289	33.5	288	21.7	4.5
Eastern Europe and USSR	861	22.4	250	18.9	3.4
Western Europe	733	19.1	183	13.8	4.0
Total	3,841	100.0	1,326	100.0	2.9
Developing countries	557	14.5	—	—	—

* Japan accounts for about 55% and Israel for 2% of the research expenditure.

Source: Boyce and Evenson (1975).

world. Western Europe spends about $4 on agricultural research for each $1 spent on extension, while Africa spends only $0.60 and Latin America $1.40 (Table 3.1).

Agricultural research and extension expenditure as a percentage of the value of agricultural production is shown in Table 3.2. Expenditure both on research and extension and the value of agricultural production are expressed in 1971 dollars rather than in current 1974 dollars. Agricultural output prices increased drastically from 1971 to 1974 while the price of research resources only increased moderately. Thus, if expressed in current 1974 dollars, the figures shown in Table 3.2 would be considerably smaller. In fact, the price of many of the major agricultural commodities doubled or tripled during the period 1971–74 while the price of research resources, which primarily consists of wages, increased much less. Use of a single price level makes comparisons of research expenditure and value of agricultural production over time less dependent on short-term changes in relative prices such as those occurring between 1971 and 1974. The choice of 1971, rather than 1974, prices was based on the assumption that the former was more representative of longer-term price trends.

Table 3.2 Agricultural research/extension expenditure as a percentage of the value of agricultural production, 1974.

	Research	Extension
Africa	1.40	2.20
Asia	1.85	0.90
Latin America	1.21	0.87
North America and Oceania	2.70	0.61
Western Europe	2.19	0.55
Eastern Europe and USSR	1.83	0.50

Source: Boyce and Evenson (1975).

Latin America and Africa spent 1.2–1.4 per cent of the value of agricultural production on agricultural research, while North America and Western Europe spent more than 2 per cent. On the other hand, Africa, Asia and Latin America spent a larger percentage of the value of agricultural production of extension than did the rest of the world.

If research and extension expenditure is disaggregated on the basis of national income levels, a clear relationship emerges (Table 3.3). Low-income countries spend less on research and more on extension than do high-income countries. Very poor countries spend less than one-third of the amount spent by high-income countries on research when measured as a percentage of the value of agricultural production. On the

Table 3.3 Agricultural research/extension expenditure as a percentage of the value of total agricultural production by income level, 1974.

Income level (GNP/capita, US$)	Research	Extension	Research/extension
Less than 150	0.67	1.82	0.37
150—400	1.01	1.59	0.64
400—1,000	1.16	0.40	2.90
1,000—1,750	2.34	0.31	7.55
1,750 and more	2.55	0.60	4.25

Source: Boyce and Evenson (1975).

other hand, very poor countries spend about three times as much on extension as do high-income countries. Developing countries also spend 37 cents on research for each dollar spent on extension, compared with $4.25 spent by industrialized countries.

Why are developing countries spending more on extension and less on research than industrialized countries? There are at least four reasons. First, it may be perceived – rightly or wrongly – by the decision-makers in developing countries that a significant part of their research needs can be met through research results from the industrialized countries. On the other hand, extension services must necessarily be carried out in the agricultural areas themselves. Secondly, investment in research requires a relatively long time period for pay-off, while investments in extension may be perceived to have almost immediate benefits. Acute nutritional problems, risk of social unrest, short time horizons among politicians and related issues may place a very high premium on short-term benefits. Thirdly, benefits from research may be more difficult to identify than extension benefits, and fourthly, research requires much larger capital investment per person employed than does extension. Furthermore, scarcity of well-trained researchers is a serious constraint to expansion in agricultural research, and the time required to expand the pool of such researchers is extensive. Extention service, on the other hand, requires little capital per capita and is frequently carried out by persons with relatively little or no higher education.

It is not surprising that poor countries emphasize investment with expected short-term pay-off. Extreme capital scarcity implies high discount rates. Furthermore, as mentioned above, politicians faced with a situation of extreme poverty, starvation and related existing or prospective social and political unrest, may have little choice but to attempt short-term solutions, even with the certainty of high costs in the longer term.

However, placing primary emphasis on extension in countries where effective technology is unavailable is a very short-sighted and mistaken policy. Although some increase in agricultural production may be achieved, such increase will tend to be very limited and not associated with significant improvements in resource utilization and productivity. Appropriate technology is an essential element of successful extension. But appropriate technology for the predominant production systems is very scarce in many of the poorest countries. Some technology may be imported; however, only a very small part of the technology needed is likely to be available from outside. Thus, expanded research in or for the poorest countries is urgently needed. It is possible that such research could be partially financed through temporary reductions in the extension service.

A proper balance between investment in research and extension is important to ensure the highest possible social benefits from the total effort. It is clear that the poorest developing countries place too little emphasis on research relative to extension. The result is that the extension service has little or nothing to extend. There are also cases where appropriate technology is available, but is not used by farmers because of a deficient extension service. However, such cases are not nearly as common as was earlier believed. It is true that a large part of the results from agricultural research in developing countries is not adopted by the farmers. But this is primarily because it is inappropriate for the existing production environment. Effective, appropriate technology for farmers in the poorest developing countries is very limited. Consequently, the results of the extension services in these countries are very limited.

However, the extension service should not be limited to facilitating the flow of results and information from research to farmer. It should also extend information in the opposite direction. Development of effective, appropriate technology depends to a large extent on a good knowledge and understanding of the existing production environments and related factors surrounding the individual farmer. An effective extension service should speed the flow of relevant information from the farmer to the researcher and policy-maker. Unfortunately, there are only few examples of extension activities in developing countries that promote such information flows. Rural development programmes and related activities have made some contributions in this regard.

The result of lack of knowledge and understanding regarding existing production environments, or lack of ability or desire to use such knowledge and understanding as a basis for agricultural research, is that a large part of the agricultural technology in developing countries is inappropriate. Fortunately, even the best extension service has severe difficulties in convincing farmers to adopt such technology. The relatively large extension service in the poorest developing countries should be used to facilitate the flow of information from the farmer to the research institutions for use in the design of technology. If appropriate technology is made available, it is usually not difficult to convince the farmer of its usefulness.

RESEARCH INVESTMENT OVER TIME

Investment in agricultural research has increased considerably during the last 30 years. The increase has exceeded the expansion in agricultural production (Fig. 3.1). The largest absolute increases have occurred in industrialized countries while the poorest developing countries show the largest relative increase. Thus, countries with per capita GNP of less than $150 per year have tripled their research expenditures from 1951 to 1974 when measured as a percentage of the value of agricultural

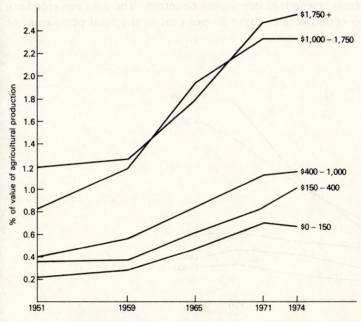

Fig. 3.1. Agricultural research expenditure in per cent of the value of agricultural production, 1951–74, by national per capita income level (based on data from Boyce and Evenson, 1975).

production. The absolute level, however, is still very low when compared to higher-income countries.

The poorest countries have experienced even larger relative increases in extension expenditures (Fig. 3.2). High-income countries, on the other hand, have maintained a growth rate in extension expenditure only slightly above that in agricultural production. The research : extension expenditure ratio fell slightly among the poorest countries, increased slightly for the second-poorest group of countries and increased considerably for the richest countries (Fig. 3.3). Falling relative emphasis on research in the poorest countries is undesirable. Attempts to solve the food and agricultural problems in these countries must aim at a reversal of this trend by expanding research and possibly reducing extension temporarily.

DISTRIBUTION OF RESEARCH EXPENDITURE AMONG DEVELOPING COUNTRIES

Table 3.4 provides a closer look at selected indicators of the extent of agricultural research in developing countries. The data presented are from 65 countries and cover 87 per cent of the total population of

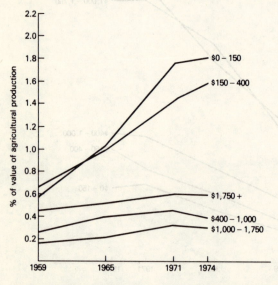

Fig. 3.2. Agricultural extension expenditure in per cent of the value of agricultural production 1951–74 by national per capita income level (based on data from Boyce and Evenson, 1975).

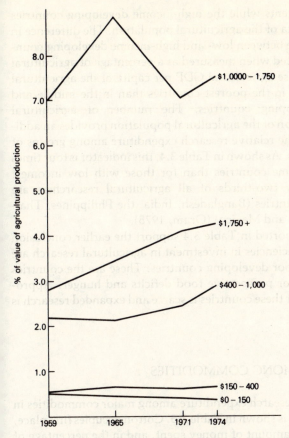

Fig. 3.3. The ratio of agricultural research expenditure to agricultural extension expenditure 1951–74 by national per capita level (based on data from Boyce and Evenson, 1975).

developing countries (Oram, 1978). Total agricultural research expenditure for these countries was estimated at $458 million for 1975. Adjusting for the countries not included, Oram (1978) estimates that the total agricultural research expenditure in developing countries for that year might be of the order of $520 million.

While representing 74 per cent of the population of the 65 countries, the poorest group accounted for only 46 per cent of the agricultural research expenditure. Thus, agricultural research expenditure per capita is much lower in the poor than in the better-off developing countries. This relationship is further illustrated by estimates of research expenditure per capita of the agricultural population. The poorest countries spent 26 cents while the high-income developing countries spent $1.57 per capita of the agricultural population. The difference in research expenditure between low- and high-income developing countries is less pronounced when measured as a percentage of agricultural GDP.[1] This is because agricultural GDP per capita of the agricultural population is lower in the poorest countries than in the middle and high-income developing countries. The number of agricultural researchers per million of the agricultural population provides an additional indicator of the relative research expenditure among groups of developing countries. As shown in Table 3.4, this indicator is four times larger for high-income countries than for those with low incomes. Furthermore, nearly two-thirds of all agricultural researchers are located in seven countries (Bangladesh, India, the Philippines, Thailand, Nigeria, Brazil and Mexico) (Oram, 1978).

Thus, the data reported in Table 3.4 support the earlier conclusion that the greatest deficiencies in investment in agricultural research are found in the very poor developing countries. These are the countries faced with existing or prospective food deficits and hunger. Appropriate technology for these countries is scarce and expanded research is urgently needed.

DISTRIBUTION AMONG COMMODITIES

The distribution of research expenditure among major commodities in developing countries is shown in Table 3.5. Cotton occupies first place, both in terms of the amount of money spent, and in the percentage of the value of production. The heavy research emphasis on this crop is partially caused by its importance in the export earnings of many developing countries, and the need to ensure supplies for a domestic textile industry. Other commodities receiving considerable research attention include cattle, wheat, rice and sugar-cane.

PUBLIC V. PRIVATE FUNDING

Research externalities and their impact on the distribution of research between public and private sources were discussed in Chapter 2. Because of large externalities, a great part of the agricultural research is carried out with public funds. The private sector is most important in North America and least important in Asia and Africa (Table 3.6).

Table 3.4 Selected indicators of agricultural research in 65 developing countries, 1975.

Groups of countries	Ag. res. exp. ($ ml.)	Population (%)	Ratio of % of ag. res. exp. and % of population	Agricultural research expenditures as % of agricultural GDP	Research expenditures $ per capita agricultural population	Number of research scientists	Research scientists per million agricultural population
Low income	210.5	73.9	0.62	0.26	0.26	13,752	16
Middle income	173.2	18.1	2.09	0.42	1.30	6,611	50
High income	74.0	8.0	2.03	0.33	1.57	2,957	62
All income levels	457.7	100.0	–	0.31	0.44	23,320	23
Asia	100.0	58.4	0.37	0.16	0.15	10,210	16
North Africa/ Middle East	54.3	9.2	1.29	0.31	0.64	2,116	25
West Africa	91.6	7.1	2.83	0.57	1.14	3,464	43
East Africa	29.5	7.3	0.88	0.43	0.30	864	9
Latin America	182.3	18.0	2.21	0.45	1.80	6,666	60

Source: Oram (1978).

Table 3.5 Estimated national research expenditure by commodity in developing countries, 1971.

Commodity	$ m.	% of the commodity value
Cotton	60.1	3.50
Cattle	54.8	0.88
Sorghum	12.2	0.77
Maize	29.6	0.75
White potatoes	8.2	0.68
Wheat	35.9	0.65
Barley	9.4	0.62
Sugar-cane	30.2	0.50
Coffee	8.5	0.40
Grapes	6.9	0.35
Olives	5.0	0.33
Rice*	34.7	0.26
Dry beans	4.0	0.25
Chick peas	3.0	0.18
Groundnuts	4.0	0.13
Sweet potatoes	3.4	0.09
Cassava	4.0	0.07

* Research expenditure as percentage of commodity value varied by system of production: shallow water 0.40%, upland rainfed 0.16% and deep-water rice 0.05%.

Source: National Research Council (1977a: 51–2).

There is a clear correlation between the proportion of total agricultural research carried out by the private sector and the national income level (Table 3.7). Thus, in the richest countries, the private sector accounts for about 25 per cent of total agricultural research, and only 2.8 per cent in countries with average national per capita incomes of $150–400 annually. The private sector finances a larger proportion of agricultural research in the poorest countries than in the second-poorest group of countries. This is probably explained, at least in part, by the very low

Table 3.6 Percentage of total agricultural research carried out by the private sector by continent, 1974.

	(%)
North America and Oceania	25.4
Western Europe	10.8
Eastern Europe and USSR	8.3
Latin America	5.1
Africa	2.9
Asia	2.2

Source: Boyce and Evenson (1975).

Table 3.7 Percentage of total agricultural research carried out by the private sector by income level, 1971.

GNP per capita 1971 (US$)	(%)
Less than 150	5.2
150—400	2.8
400—1,000	7.4
1,000—1,750	7.0
1,750 and more	24.0

Source: Boyce and Evenson (1975).

public investment in such research in many of the poorest countries.

The greater importance of the private sector in agricultural research in high-income countries is due in part to the greater use of purchased inputs by the agricultural sector. These inputs embody research results and it is primarily through the production and sale of such inputs that the private sector obtain economic gains from research. This is particularly pronounced for chemical and mechanical inputs to agriculture. In low-income countries, the agricultural sector uses purchased inputs to a much lesser extent. As a result, unless increased use of such inputs can be expected, the prospects of economic gains from private sector research may be unattractive.

NOTES

1. As shown in Table 3.4, Oram (1978) estimated that developing countries spent about 0.3 per cent of the agricultural GDP on agricultural research in 1975. This is considerably below the estimates by Boyce and Evenson (1975) for 1971 and 1974 mentioned earlier. The principal reason for the difference between the two sets of data is that Oram used the agricultural GDP for 1975 evaluated at current (1975) prices, while Boyce and Evenson used the value of agricultural commodities evaluated at 1971 prices. Under normal circumstances, this would not cause a large difference in the estimates. But because of the drastic increases in agricultural commodity prices between 1971 and 1974 mentioned above, the denominator (value of agricultural production) differs vastly between 1971 and 1975. A second reason for the difference may be that the estimates by Oram are limited to research directly for agriculture, while Boyce and Evenson also include 'agricultural-related' research.

4 International agricultural research for developing countries

Some of the most important issues arising from international agricultural research for developing countries will be discussed in this chapter. Issues needing international agricultural research are discussed first. Then, the development, organization, areas of work and special characteristics of the international agricultural research institutes are described. While issues that influence the size and magnitude of the economic benefits from international research are discussed in this chapter, the actual estimated economic benefits are dealt with in Chapter 5.

THE NEED FOR INTERNATIONAL AGRICULTURAL RESEARCH

As mentioned in Chapter 2, certain research needs are best met through international research institutes. This is particularly the case for research producing results applicable in a number of countries, i.e. research with large external economic benefits for the individual country. Furthermore, if such research requires large amounts of resources or special types of resources – whether these resources are financial, technical or human – there is an even greater reason for carrying out such research in international institutions, because it may be difficult for the individual country to obtain sufficient economic benefits to cover the research costs. Furthermore, the individual country may be incapable of mobilizing the necessary research capacity. Thus, the presence of large external economic benefits to any individual country is the most important reason why international research may be more advantageous than national research. However, there are other reasons why there is a need for international agricultural research. As mentioned in Chapter 3, there is a tendency in developing countries, particularly those with the lowest income, to invest available public funds in activities which are regarded as certain to pay off within a very short period of time. Investment in activities which may require a reasonably long period before producing benefits are postponed. Postponement is also frequently the outcome for activities where the amount of the return is uncertain. Both the requirements for a long period between investment and return, and uncertainty associated with the amount of such return are characteristic of a large part of agricultural research.

Thus, even though investment in agricultural research may present expectations for extremely high benefits in the long run, such research is postponed in the poorest countries. Instead, emphasis is placed on solving the most immediate problems, even though such a strategy may imply lower benefits to society in the longer run. This, of course, makes good sense in the short run. The immediate problems may be of such magnitude and involve such severe consequences that the solution of longer-run problems must necessarily be postponed. However, a long-run and self-sustaining solution to the food problems in these countries can only be obtained through development of the appropriate technology. Since, in many cases, these countries cannot and probably should not choose the long-run solutions over the more immediate, there is a need for the more long-run, time-consuming development of agricultural technology outside the country, or at least outside the budgets of the individual country.

Agricultural research is frequently very resource demanding. Not only does research require considerable financial resources, but it also places specific demands on the human resource. To meet these requirements a long period of training is necessary. Even though there has been considerable emphasis on the development of groups of people with such training in developing countries, the number of well-trained and sufficiently experienced agricultural researchers is still very low in many developing countries, particularly those with the lowest income levels. Thus, if the research programme in many of these countries has to start with investment in research training, the time requirement becomes even greater.

Effective development of technology requires collaboration among a certain minimum number of well-qualified researchers within the various areas of research. But many developing countries do not have such a critical number of well-trained researchers. This is another reason why a certain part of the technology development is carried out outside the individual developing country. In countries where sufficient agricultural researchers do in fact exist, obstacles to the development and interaction of the necessary research groups also frequently exist. Lack of understanding among politicians regarding the necessity for agricultural research, existing priorities regarding the solution of immediate versus longer-run problems mentioned above and bureaucratic problems such as low salaries to researchers relative to those in the private sector are only some examples of such obstacles.

Finally, it should be mentioned that government support for effective agricultural research in developing countries is often deficient or absent because it does not meet all the goals of society or of those in power. The development of technology which might be very effective in increasing yields of a certain crop produced primarily in one or a few geographical regions within an individual country, may be politically unacceptable because it implies geographical redistribution of income. Instead of utilizing the possibilities offered by the technology, and simultaneously introducing political measures to correct the undesired secondary effects, the technology is not developed. This problem is not only found in geographical distribution of the expected economic benefits. Expected undesirable distribution among other groups within the individual country may have a similar impact.

Of course, whether modern technology is acceptable in any individual country from the point of view of distribution should be determined by the individual country, not by outsiders. Each country must necessarily decide on its own path of technological development. The problem is that there is a tendency within the individual country to assess the consequences of modern agricultural technology in isolation and not as a part of a development strategy. Viewing agricultural technology as a part of the total strategy, any undesirable secondary effects of individual parts of the strategy, such as technology, may be corrected by means of other parts, such as price and income policies. But if agricultural technology is assessed in complete isolation, the specific potential contributions that such technology can make may not be realized because of undesirable side effects. Such a narrow view of agricultural technology is, of course, only found in some developing countries. It may also be found outside these countries. In all fairness, it should be added that the necessary policy measures may be difficult to introduce and maintain in some developing countries. Because of these difficulties there may be reason to avoid certain types of technology because correction of the undesirable side effects is not feasible.

Because of the above-mentioned conditions it may be difficult for national research institutions to obtain public research funds for certain research activities, even though such activities would be expected to result in very great benefits to society. Such activities must, to a large extent, be funded outside the individual country or the individual country's budget. This may be done either through external long-term support earmarked for certain technology development activities in the individual country, or through research outside the country. In the latter case, international agricultural research has been shown to be very effective. Certain research activities related to developing countries may also be effectively carried out by national research institutions in industrialized countries. However, the value to developing countries of such research may be very limited because of the dependence of these results on climatic, geographic and other conditions, which vary greatly between industrialized and developing countries. The limitations on effective direct transfer of research results from industrialized to developing countries are particularly important for the more applied types of research because the results of basic research tend to be less location specific. It should also be mentioned that although direct transfer of technology may be of limited value, industrialized countries may provide very useful assistance to developing countries through special research facilities, equipment and competence.

In addition to the above-mentioned reasons for the need for international agricultural research, it should also be mentioned that international research institutes normally have easier access to the benefits of inter-country communication and collaboration. This may be extremely important in certain areas such as plant breeding, where the international institute may benefit from a collection of plant material that far exceeds those available in any individual country. Access to a large genetic variation within the individual crop has been of very great importance for plant breeding in international agricultural research institutes. Likewise, these institutes frequently have access to the best qualified people for the particular job, whether these be long-term staff or short-term consultants. The creation of an interesting and stimulating work environment, competitive salaries and prestige assist in obtaining and motivating scientific staff of high quality. In comparison, researchers in a number of national agricultural research institutes frequently work in isolation where motivation is lacking.

International agricultural research does not and should not replace national agricultural research. The great majority of agricultural research should be carried out by national or local research institutes in collaboration, where necessary, with international agricultural research institutes. As discussed in Chapter 2, a very large proportion of modern agricultural technology is location specific. This implies that the efficiency of the technology depends on the production environment. Therefore, it is necessary that new technology is adapted to existing production environments. This should obviously be done by national and local institutions. The comparative advantage of international agricultural research is found in areas where the results can be used by several countries. But this does not imply that these results may necessarily be appropriate for the individual farmer. Even though this may be the case, it is common practice for results from international agricultural research to be subjected to further research and local testing before they are confirmed as suitable for the existing production process.

Thus, we may view the results from a large part of international agricultural research as raw material for research within the individual developing country. The development of improved genetic lines for use in attempts to develop improved varieties is but one example. The development of such raw material implies an increasing return to the developing country's own agricultural research. It also implies an increasing demand for research in these countries in areas where national and local research is most advantageous. Close collaboration between national and international institutes may also contribute to greater efficiency in countries where critical number of national researchers is not present, because such collaboration may ensure the individual researcher in such countries of a large portion of the potential advantages associated with working within such a critical number.

In summary, it may be stated that international agricultural research can be particularly advantageous for the solution of research problems where the results may be useful for a number of developing countries and where research demands are difficult to meet by the individual country, either because sufficient economic benefits cannot be obtained or because the necessary resources are unavailable. International research is capable of establishing a critical number of highly qualified scientific staff for development of technology for a long-run solution of some of the more important food production problems without regard to narrow group interests in the individual developing country. Finally, international agricultural research usually has easier access to existing knowledge, expertise and materials across country borders. However, the comparative advantage of international agricultural research is limited to certain research areas. The majority of the required agricultural research is best carried out in individual countries. Close collaboration between international and national research and between research and technology distribution is essential to obtain the economic benefits which the total research effort may make available.

THE INTERNATIONAL AGRICULTURAL RESEARCH INSTITUTES

HISTORIC DEVELOPMENT AND CURRENT SITUATION

Up through the 1950s and the beginning of the 1960s it was generally believed that the most effective way of increasing food production in developing countries was by development of the extension service and other activities in these countries aimed at the diffusion of modern technology developed in the industrialized countries. As a result of this belief, a large part of external assistance in agriculture was concentrated within those areas. However, the tendency of food production technology to be location specific implied narrow limits to the advantages associated with direct transfer of such technology from industrialized countries. Climatic, geographic and many other differences implied that much of the technology which had served the industrialized countries so well, frequently failed in developing countries.

The need for more research on food production in these countries, was advocated by a few institutions, including the Rockefeller Foundation, which supported its arguments with financial and human resources. Research assistance was offered to a number of countries including Mexico, Colombia, Chile, India and Thailand. As early as 1943, the Rockefeller Foundation initiated collaboration with the Mexican Ministry of Agriculture regarding research on grains with primary emphasis on wheat. The primary purpose of this initial research was to expand wheat production in Mexico. This was successfully achieved. When the research was initiated, Mexico imported about half of its wheat. For the first time in recent history, the country became self-sufficient in this commodity around 1957, in spite of a large increase in population and resulting increases in wheat demand during the prior period. The results of this and related programmes are further analysed in Chapter 5.

Motivated by the results of the Mexican wheat programme, the Rockefeller and Ford Foundations considered, towards the end of the 1950s, the possibility of initiating something similar for rice in Asia. The tremendous importance of that crop in the diet of the population, along with existing low rice yields and lack of food, meant that increasing the production of rice could have enormous implications. However, with some exceptions such as India, where extensive research on food production was taking place, the establishment of research programmes of sufficient magnitude in each of the individual Asian countries was unrealistic, partly due to the associated large resource requirements and partly because most of these countries had very few well-qualified agricultural researchers at the time. Instead, it was decided by the two foundations to establish the International Rice Research Institute (IRRI) in the Philippines in 1960.

The success of the Mexican wheat research programme created great interest in the research results – primarily those concerning improved wheat varieties – outside Mexico. In order to encourage this interest and to contribute to increased wheat production elsewhere, it was decided to change the programme from a collaborative national programme to an international research institute for wheat and maize. The institute, which was established in 1966, was organized along similar lines as the IRRI under the name Centro Internacional de Mejoramiento de Maíz y Trigo (CIMMYT). Success within IRRI and CIMMYT established the basis for the so-called 'green revolution' which has contributed to large increases in the production and yield of rice and wheat in many developing countries since the middle of the 1960s (see Ch. 5).

The increases in yield were made possible through effective multi-disciplinary agricultural research with a well-defined goal. The research attempted to remove yield-limiting factors of great importance in wheat and rice production. The most important of these was undoubtedly the lodging problem. Traditional varieties tended to be tall with relatively soft straw. Efforts to expand grain yields were normally unsuccessful because of early lodging. Thus, the benefits from the use of measures for increasing productivity, such as fertilizers, was low. This problem was in the forefront of the research programme of the two institutions. Successful plant breeding resulted in the development of semi-dwarf varieties that did not lodge, even at high grain yields. Means of increasing productivity could now be used with great economic advantage, and the new varieties, together with the accelerated use of other yield-increasing methods contributed to large increases in yield and productivity.

In addition to the incorporation of genes which brought about the semi-dwarf type variety, attempts were made to incorporate resistance and tolerance to other yield-limiting factors such as plant diseases and pests. Furthermore, efforts were made to develop additional knowledge to improve production systems as a whole, i.e. cropping methods, optimal fertilizer quantities, application times, optimal methods for disease and pest control, etc. One additional important objective, particularly in wheat research, was to develop varieties with high yield capacity under varying climatic and geographical conditions in order to reduce the location specificity and thus reduce the number of varieties required and the need for adaptive research at local level.

On the asssumption that an effective method for expanding food production in developing countries had now been realized, two additional institutes were created in 1968. These were the International Centre for Tropical Agriculture (CIAT) in Colombia and International Institute for Tropical Agriculture (IITA) in Nigeria. As opposed to the two initial institutes, CIAT and IITA were responsible for research on number of commodities including cassava, certain grain legumes and, in the case of CIAT, beef cattle (the commodities of the individual institutes will be discussed in greater detail later in this chapter), as well as certain activities, such as farming systems research, which were not commodity specific.

These four institutes covered only a small number of the agricultural products of importance for developing countries, although those covered were very important in terms of quantity of total food output. Therefore, there were strong desires to create more institutes along the same lines. These desires were supported by offers of financial assistance from a number of potential donors. However, the growth in the number of institutes and donors, as well as the increasing financial needs of these institutes, made it difficult to continue the loose and informal structure which was used initially to obtain financing and coordination of their work. On the other hand, it was strongly argued by many that the success of these institutes depended on precisely such a loose and decentralized structure.

Taking into consideration both the need for a more formal structure and to maintain a somewhat loose and decentralized structure, it was decided to create the Consultative Group on International Agricultural Research (CGIAR) in 1971. The CGIAR is a group of donor countries, development banks, foundations and other institutions. Its primary purpose is to provide and coordinate the financing of the international agricultural research institutes. A more detailed discussion of CGIAR will be presented later in this chapter.

Following the creation of CGIAR, a number of new institutes were formed. The International Potato Centre (CIP) and the International Crops Research Institute for the Semi-Arid Tropics (ICRISAT) were established in 1972 in Peru and India respectively. The family of international agricultural research institutes grew further in 1974 with the establishment of two animal research institutes in Africa. These were the International Laboratory for Research on Animal Diseases (ILRAD) in Kenya and the International Livestock Centre for Africa (ILCA) in Ethiopia. One additional institute, the International Centre for Agricultural Research in the Dry Areas (ICARDA) was created in 1976.

Through the 1970s the need for additional assistance to national research programmes became more apparent. As further discussed in Chapter 10, these needs motivated the Rockefeller Foundation to create the International Agricultural Development Service (IADS) in 1975. While IADS is concerned with providing assistance to agricultural research, as well as other areas within the overall agricultural development programme of individual countries, a new institute – with a narrower focus on assistance to research – was founded in 1979 within the auspices of CGIAR. The location of the headquarters of the institute, the International Service for National Agricultural Research (ISNAR) is in The Netherlands.

Two international research institutes, with overall objectives similar to those mentioned above, were established in the United States in 1975. These were: the International Fertilizer Development Centre (IFDC) and the International Food Policy Research Institute (IFPRI) with headquarters in Muscle Shoals, Alabama and Washington, DC respectively. While the formation of these two institutes should be viewed as an integral part of the overall efforts to provide effective agricultural research and research assistance for developing countries, they were not initiated under the auspices of CGIAR. The International Food Policy Research Institute became a member of CGIAR in 1979; IFDC applied for CGIAR membership, but has not been included in the group.

In addition to the above, three other activities are included in the work of CGIAR. These are: the West African Rice Development Association (WARDA) located in Liberia; the International Board for Plant Genetic Resources (IBPGR); and the Current Agricultural Research Information Service (CARIS), the last two being located in Rome. The role of IBPGR is further discussed in Chapter 9.

There are a number of other international institutions carrying out agricultural research. However, those mentioned above form a well-defined group in that they are all established with the same basic ideas and philosophy and – except for IFDC – they all receive financial support through CGIAR. One other institute established on the same lines, but which does not receive financial support through CGIAR is the Asian Vegetable Research and Development Centre (AVRDC) formed in 1971 and located in Taiwan. Finally, two international institutes working in collaboration with CGIAR without receiving CGIAR financial support and differing to some extent from the above institutes should be mentioned. These are the International Soybean Programme (INTSOY) located in the United States, and the International Centre for Insect Physiology and Ecology (ICIPE), located in Kenya.

Overview of the individual institutes
A listing of the year of establishment, location, product responsibility and primary geographical focus of each of the institutes and other activities mentioned above is presented below. The location of each institute is shown in Fig. 4.1. Budgets and staff sizes of the institutes are discussed in a subsequent section of this chapter.

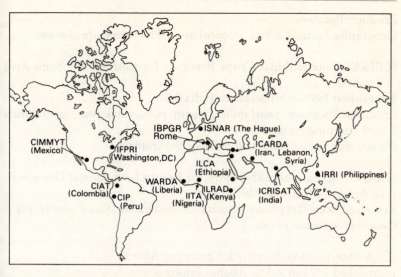

Fig. 4.1. The geographical location of the CGIAR-supported institutes.

IRRI (International Rice Research Institute)
Established 1960 in Los Banos, the Philippines
Products: Rice and multiple cropping
Geographic focus: Global with emphasis on Asia

CIMMYT (Centro Internacional de Mejoramiento de Maíz y Trigo)
Established 1966 in El Batan, Mexico
Products: Wheat, maize, triticale and barley
Geographic focus: Global

CIAT (Centro Internacional de Aqricultura Tropical)
Established 1968 in Cali/Palmira, Colombia
Products: Cassava, beans, beef cattle and pastures, rice and maize
Geographic focus: Lowland tropics with emphasis on Latin America

IITA (International Institute for Tropical Agriculture)
Established 1968 in Ibadan, Nigeria
Products: Cropping systems, grain legumes (cowpeas, soybeans, lima
   beans, pigeon peas), cassava, sweet potatoes, yams, rice and maize)
Geographic focus: Lowland tropics with emphasis on Africa

CIP (Centro Internacional de la Papa)
Established 1972 in Lima, Peru

Product: Potatoes
Geographic focus: Global, tropical as well as temperate climate

ICRISAT (International Crops Research Institute for the Semi-Arid Tropics)
Established 1972 in Hyderabad, India
Products: Sorghum, pearl millet, pigeon peas, chick peas, groundnuts and cropping systems
Geographic focus: Semi-arid areas of the tropics

ILRAD (International Laboratory for Research on Animal Diseases)
Established 1974 in Nairobi, Kenya
Research focus: Trypanosomiasis and theileriasis (East Coast fever)
Geographic focus: Africa

ILCA (International Livestock Centre for Africa)
Established 1974 in Addis Ababa, Ethiopia
Research focus: Livestock production systems
Geographic focus: Selected ecological zones in tropical areas of Africa

ICARDA (International Centre for Agricultural Research in Dry Areas)
Established 1976 in Lebanon, Syria and Iran
Research focus: Mixed animal-crop production systems with emphasis on sheep, durum wheat, barley and beans
Geographic focus: The Mediterranean area and North Africa

IFDC (International Fertilizer Development Centre)
Established 1975 in Muscle Shoals, Alabama, United States
Research focus: Chemical fertilizers
Geographic focus: Developing countries

IFPRI (International Food Policy Research Institute)
Established 1975 in Washington, DC, United States
Research focus: Food policy
Geographic focus: Global with emphasis on developing countries

AVDRC (Asian Vegetable Research and Development Centre)
Established 1971 in Shanhua, Taiwan
Research focus: Beans, tomatoes, cabbage and potatoes
Geographic focus: Asia

WARDA (West African Rice Development Association)

Established 1971 in Monrovia, Liberia
Research focus: Adaptive rice research through regional collaboration activities
Geographic focus: West Africa

IBPGR (International Board for Plant Genetic Resources)
Established 1973 in Rome, Italy
Activity focus: Conservation of genetic plant material with emphasis on grains
Geographic focus: Global

ISNAR (International Service for National Agricultural Research)
Established 1980 in The Hague, Netherlands
Activity focus: Assistance to national agricultural research
Geographic focus: Developing countries

The Consultative Group on International Agricultural Research
The CGIAR consists of representatives of a number of countries, foundations, development banks and other national and international institutions which together finance the international institutes and activities under its auspices. In addition to donor countries, two countries from each of the five major developing regions of the world participate in CGIAR as representatives designated for a two-year term. The CGIAR was established by the World Bank, FAO and UNDP, and its membership as of December 1979 includes 19 donor countries, of which 3 are developing countries, 5 foundations, 11 international institutions and 1 representative from each of 10 countries representing 5 regions: 1) Asia, 2) Africa; 3) Latin America; 4) South and East Europe; and 5) the Near East and South Asia. The composition of CGIAR is as follows.

Donor countries:

Australia	Ireland	Saudi Arabia
Belgium	Italy	Sweden
Canada	Japan	Switzerland
Denmark	The Netherlands	United Kingdom
France	New Zealand	United States
Germany	Nigeria	
Iran	Norway	

International organizations:
African Development Bank
Arab Fund for Social and Economic Development

Asian Development Bank
European Economic Communities
Food and Agriculture Organization
Inter-American Development Bank
International Bank for Reconstruction and Development
International Fund for Agricultural Development
Organization of Petroleum Exporting Countries Special Fund
United Nations Development Programme
United Nations Environment Programme

Foundations:
Ford Foundation
International Development Research Centre
Kellogg Foundation
Leverhulme Trust Fund
Rockefeller Foundation

Fixed-term members representing the five regions:

Costa Rica	Peru
Egypt	Philippines
Greece	Romania
India	Senegal
Kenya	Syria

The membership of CGIAR normally meets twice annually. The individual institutes are allocated funds on the basis of progress, financial needs, the interests of the individual donors and possibly recommendations from the Technical Advisory Committee (TAC) (this Committee is further discussed below). Each of the donors allocate financial support to one or more of the institutes and not to CGIAR as such. Thus, the financial assistance is of a direct nature. This does not prohibit donors from offering financial support for institutes that would not otherwise obtain sufficient funds to meet their needs. One of the primary purposes of CGIAR is to coordinate the available financial support in such a way that the needs of all the institutes are met to the fullest extent possible. The CGIAR is supported by a secretariat financed by the World Bank. Emphasis is placed on ensuring that the work of CGIAR is carried out without unnecessary bureaucratic procedures and without large costs. Furthermore, the independence of each of the institutes is given due consideration.

The CGIAR is advised by the TAC. The primary purpose of TAC is to advise CGIAR regarding gaps and priorities within agricultural research for developing countries and assess completed, proceeding and proposed agricultural research activities, with primary emphasis on those carried out or proposed to be carried out by the international agricultural research institutes under CGIAR. Such assistance includes assessments of proposals for possible new institutes. The TAC consists of 13 highly qualified scientists from various parts of the world. One of the primary tasks of TAC is to carry out overall periodic assessments of the individual research programmes and institutes in order to contribute to the best possible allocation of available research resources. The interaction between, and coordination of, national and international agricultural research for developing countries are important elements of such assessment. The membership of TAC meets when necessary. The Committee is administered by a secretariat financed by, and housed at, FAO in Rome.

THE SPECIAL CHARACTERISTICS OF THE INSTITUTES

The international agricultural research institutes described above present certain common characteristics which together separate these institutes from other international agricultural research activities. A description of these characteristics follows below.

An international agricultural research institute is an institute established and financed by donor agencies in close collaboration with the host country of the institute. Even though the institute is international the majority of its activities is usually carried out in a single country – in most cases a developing country. The institute is non-profit-making and each has its own board of directors, which has the final decision-making power regarding all aspects of the institute. Normally, the land required for the individual institute is made available by the host country free of charge or at nominal costs. The composition of the research staff is determined by the research priorities and the qualifications of the individual researcher, with little or no regard to nationality. Each of the institutes is dedicated to the solution of serious agricultural production problems within developing countries. Typically, these problems are identified by a committee prior to the establishment of the institute. Each committee is composed of the best available experts at the international level. The interests of the governments of the developing countries are considered in this initial priority setting. Of course, once the institute is established, periodic assessments and revisions of research priorities are carried out.

As mentioned above, the board of directors of the individual institute makes the final decision in regard to the areas of work, priorities, etc. Such decisions are made with due respect to the financial possibilities, because financial support is usually obtained only for one year at a time and is, of course, controlled by the donors. In addition to the individual boards and donors, TAC may have a significant influence on the research areas of the individual institutes through its advice to CGIAR which, in reality, is a meeting-place for donors, representatives from developing countries and the international institutes. It follows that the final research priorities and activities are in fact determined by inter-action between the institutes and the donors. Furthermore, neither of the two groups is represented by a central decision-making body.

Such decentralized decision-making is essential for the continued effective operation of the institutes. However, at the same time it is important that the research areas and priorities of each individual insti-tute are assessed within the world agricultural and food situation as a whole. This is the responsibility of TAC. Finally, it is obviously neces-sary that the interests of donors are taken into account. It should be mentioned that a very large part of the financial assistance made avail-able to international agricultural research institutes is on the basis of the most pressing needs of developing countries, and only to a very limited extent on that of the narrow internal political interests of the donors. There need not be a conflict between the priorities for developing coun-tries and the political interests of the donors, but this does occur in some cases. In such cases, the international agricultural research institutes seem to suffer less than many other international institutions. The ability to avoid narrow national political interests influencing decisions regarding financing, research areas and hiring of staff within the insti-tutes is of paramount importance for their effective operation.

Research within the individual institute is frequently limited to one or a few food commodities. One institute (IFDC) is concerned with a single input. Some of the institutes carry out research on multicrop produc-tion systems. Agricultural products that are not used as food, such as rubber and cotton, are not included in the work of the institutes. Research on animal feed and fodder commodities is included to the extent necessary to carry out integrated livestock research pro-grammes. In the majority of the institutes the research is carried out within multidisciplinary groups. These groups are frequently organized around a single commodity or commodity system. The primary purpose of research on a single commodity is to develop a package of technology expected to contribute to increased yields, reduced produc-tion risk or changed product characteristics in a number of developing countries. The research is purpose-oriented, and in many cases plant breeding and selection play a key role because emphasis is placed on the development of varieties with well-defined characteristics.[1]

Even though the results from the work of the institutes are made available to all countries, most institutes concentrate on serving the region where they are located. This implies in some but not in all cases that the results of the work of the institutes are best suited to the region where the individual institute is located.

In addition to its own research, institute activities include the development of effective collaboration with national research institutes in developing countries and improvement of the capacity of these institutes. Training of agricultural researchers, conferences, seminars and advice through visits by institute staff to individual developing countries are examples of activities with the primary objective of developing and maintaining an effective national research capacity and close contact between the international institute and research developments in the individual country. Furthermore, collaborative research among a number of national, as well as one or more international, institutes is developed and promoted by the international institutes. Closely related to collaborative research is the development of international networks for testing of experimental crop varieties. Such networks enable widespread testing for disease and pest resistance in new plant materials and other yield- and risk-related factors. During the 1970s more than 130 developing countries joined in such networks (Hanson, 1979). By 1979 the wheat network involved 106 collaborating countries, the maize network 82 and the rice network over 60 (Hanson, 1979).

It is important to point out that the international agricultural institutes were not established with the purpose of replacing national research institutions. On the contrary, they were to complement and stimulate such institutions in developing countries. As mentioned elsewhere in this book, only a relatively small proportion of the total need for agricultural research for developing countries can be advantageously carried out by international institutes. However, although it is a small proportion, it is a very important one.

RESEARCH EXPENDITURE AND DISTRIBUTION

The total core operating and capital expenditure of the institutes under CGIAR during the period 1960–80 is estimated at US$663 million in current prices. Expressed at the 1977 price level, this is close to US$700 million (Table 4.1). Operating expenses account for almost 80 per cent of the total. Following a capital expenditure of about US$7 million to

Table 4.1 Total core operating and capital expenditure for all CGIAR institutes 1960—80 ($US m.).

Year	Current prices			Constant prices (1977 dollars)
	Operation	Capital	Total	Total
1960	0.2	7.2	7.4	16.7
1961	0.2	—	0.2	0.4
1962	0.4	—	0.4	1.0
1963	0.5	0.4	0.9	1.8
1964	0.6	—	0.6	1.1
1965	1.1	0.2	1.3	2.4
1966	1.8	0.1	1.9	3.6
1967	3.0	—	3.0	5.5
1968	2.9	2.9	5.8	10.1
1969	5.6	4.6	10.2	16.9
1970	7.6	5.6	13.2	20.8
1971	9.9	8.0	17.9	26.7
1972	13.4	6.2	19.6	28.0
1973	18.1	7.6	25.7	34.7
1974	24.9	6.8	31.7	39.0
1975	32.9	10.8	43.7	49.3
1976	43.8	11.8	55.6	59.8
1977	58.2	26.7	84.9	84.9
1978	75.2	21.8	97.0	90.3
1979	94.3	14.9	109.2	94.2
1980	116.9	15.6	132.5	106.7
Total	511.5	151.2	662.7	693.9

Source: CGIAR (1977a, 1979).

cover the construction and initial development of IRRI in 1960, expenditure up to 1968 was very modest. Since 1968, however, a rapid increase in the number of institutes and expansions in existing ones have caused a large growth in total expenditure (Fig. 4.2).Expenditure for 1979 was about US$110 million, and an increase to US$133 million is expected for 1980.

Two comparisons might be useful here to place the above amount in an overall foreign assistance perspective.

Total official development assistance and assistance from private voluntary agencies to developing countries for 1978 (the latest year for which data are currently available) are estimated at US$25.2 billion (OECD, 1979), Thus, for that year, assistance to the CGIAR system amounted to less than 0.4 per cent of total development assistance. The financial requirements of the CGIAR institutes are also small relative to foreign assistance in the areas of agriculture and food. Total official

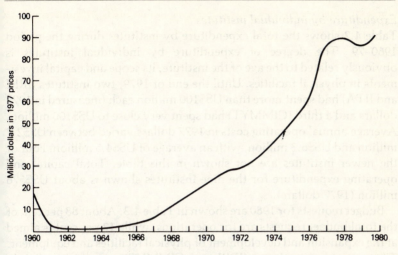

Fig. 4.2. Annual core expenses of the CGIAR-supported institutes 1960–80.

development assistance in agriculture and agro-industry from DAC member countries[2] in 1977 was US$2.4 billion, while food aid accounted for US$1.5 billion (OECD, 1979). The CGIAR institute expenditure amounted to about US$85 million for that year or about 2.2 per cent of the total foreign assistance from OECD Development Assistance Committee member countries in the areas of agriculture, agro-industry and food aid. One additional comparison might be of interest: CGIAR expenditure relative to expenditure on armaments. Total armament expenditure in 1976 amounted to about US$356 billion (Sivard, 1978). Of this total, US$275 billion were spent in the industrialized countries and US$81 billion in developing countries. In comparison, CGIAR expenditure for 1976 was US$55.6 million. Thus, for each dollar spent on international agricultural research within CGIAR, US$6,500 were spent on armaments, the share of the developed countries being almost US$5,000, and that of the developing countries about US$1,500. An irrelevant comparison? Maybe, but together with the above comparisons, it nevertheless gives some indication of how modest is CGIAR expenditure in the broader perspectives. However, a more important question regarding the appropriate amount of funds to be allocated to the CGIAR institutes is how large economic returns are obtained from the activities of these institutes, in particular the returns obtained at the margin, i.e. the pay-off from the last dollar invested. This question will be discussed in Chapter 5.

Expenditure by individual institutes

Table 4.2 shows the total expenditure by institutes during the period 1960–79. The degree of expenditure by individual institutes is obviously related to the age of the institute, its scope and capital investments in physical facilities. Until the end of 1979, two institutes (IRRI and IITA) had spent more than US$100 million each (measured in 1977 dollars and a third (CIMMYT) had spent very close to US$100 million. Average annual operating costs in 1977 dollars varied between US$2.7 million and US$6.3 million, with an average of US$4.5 million. Four of the newer institutes are not shown in this table. Total capital and operating expenditure for the nine institutes shown is about US$576 million (1977 dollars).

Budget requests for 1980 are shown in Table 4.3. About 88 per cent of the total budget requests are for operations, while 12 per cent is aimed at the expansion and development of physical facilities and equipment. The two oldest institutes (IRRI and CIMMYT) account for slightly more than one-fourth of the total budget requests.

Expenditure by commodity

Annual research and research support expenditure by commodity for the period 1971–80 are shown in Fig. 4.3. Cereals have traditionally accounted for a large portion of the annual budget of the CGIAR institutes. Among cereals, rice and maize are responsible for large shares.

Table 4.2 Total core operating and capital expenditure by institutes from the initiation of each institute to the end of 1979 (constant prices — 1977 dollars in millions).*

	Capital expenditure	Operating expenditure	Age of institute in years	Average annual operating expenditure
IRRI	32.7	78.6	20	3.9
CIMMYT	10.6	88.5	14	6.3
IITA	37.6	76.6	15	5.1
CIAT	15.7	62.4	12	5.2
CIP	4.4	25.5	8	3.2
ICRISAT	25.1	32.3	8	4.0
ILRAD	10.5	16.1	6	2.7
ILCA	10.7	23.4	6	3.9
ICARDA	8.3	17.1	4	4.3
Total	155.6	420.5	93	4.5†

* Expenditure for 1979 is estimated.
† Average per institute-year.

Source: CGIAR (1977a).

Table 4.3 Core operating and capital budget requests by institutes for 1980 (US$ m.).

Institute	Operation	Capital	Total
IRRI	16.0	0.8	16.8
CIMMYT	17.2	1.0	18.2
IITA	14.4	1.5	15.9
CIAT	14.8	0.9	15.7
CIP	7.8	0.4	8.2
ICRISAT	10.7	2.9	13.6
ILRAD	9.2	2.5	11.7
ILCA	8.5	1.3	9.8
ICARDA	8.8	3.5	12.3
IBPGR	3.1	0.0	3.1
WARDA	2.7	0.7	3.4
IFPRI	2.5	0.1	2.6
ISNAR	1.2	0.0	1.2
Total	116.9	15.6	132.5

Source: CGIAR (1979).

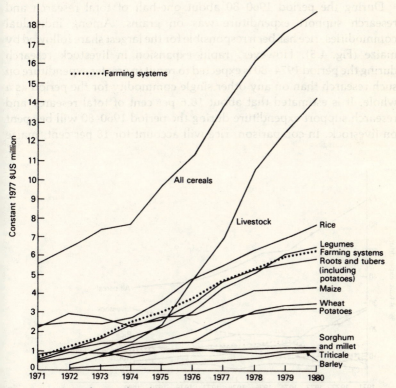

Fig. 4.3. Annual research and research support expenditure by commodity 1971–80 (in terms of constant 1977 dollars) (CGIAR, 1977a).

95

Rapid expansion in livestock research since 1975 has made annual expenditure on that commodity larger than that on any other single commodity

Initially, the international agricultural research institutes were limited to grains, primarily rice, maize and wheat. As more institutes were created and more commodities included in the system, the relative share of total expenditure on grains was obviously reduced. By 1971 the share had diminished to 69 per cent and has continued to decrease to current levels of about 36 per cent (Fig.4.4). Among grains, the largest decrease in the budget share has been experienced in maize which fell from 27 per cent in 1971 to 8 per cent in 1980. The largest budget share expansion was in livestock which increased from 11 to 28 per cent from 1971 to 1980. The budget share allocated to legumes has also increased considerably, while the budget shares allocated to roots and tubers and farming systems increased during the period 1971–74 followed by a slight decrease up to 1980.

During the period 1960–80 about one-half of total research and research support expenditure was on grains. Among individual commodities, rice has been responsible for the largest share followed by maize (Fig. 4.5). However, rapid expansion in livestock research during the period 1974–80 is expected to result in greater expenditure on such research than on any other single commodity for the period as a whole. It is estimated that about 18.6 per cent of total research and research support expenditure during the period 1960–80 will be spent on livestock. In comparison, rice will account for 18 per cent, maize

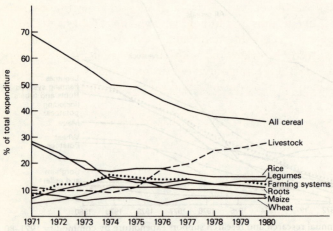

Fig. 4.4. Relative share of total institute expenditure by commodity.

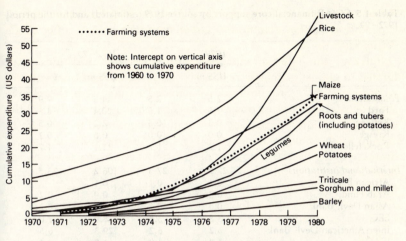

Fig. 4.5. Cumulative research and research support expenditure by commodity, 1960–80 (in constant 1977 dollars) (CGIAR, 1977a).

11.5 per cent and farming systems research 11.4 per cent.

About 60 per cent of the core operating expenditure of the institutes is used for research, while roughly one-fourth is used for general administration and operations (Table 4.4). The distribution between research and operations may be arbitrary in a number of cases and the allocation of budgets and expenditure between the two items may be correspondingly arbitrary. Training and conferences account for 8 per cent of the 1979 core operating expenditure and library and documentation is responsible for about 5 per cent.

The CGIAR institutes receive financial support from foundations, international institutions and individual countries (Table 4.5). Initial financial support for the international agricultural research institutes (IRRI and CIMMYT) originated with the Rockefeller and the Ford Foundations, and these foundations were responsible for a large part of the total financial support of these and subsequent institutes through

Table 4.4 Percentage distribution of core operating expenditure for all institutes.

Research	60.0
Training and conferences	8.1
Library and documentation	5.3
General administration and operations	26.6
Total	100.0

Source: CGIAR (1979).

Table 4.5 CGIAR financial core support by source 1979 (estimated) and for the period 1972—79.

	1979		1972—79	
	US$ m.	%	US$ m.	%
Foundations	2.5	2.5	44.5	9.9
Ford	1.0	1.0	20.4	4.5
Kellogg	0.3	0.3	2.2	0.5
Kresge	0.0	0.0	0.8	0.2
Rockefeller	1.2	1.2	21.1	4.7
International institutions	27.2	27.3	106.2	23.5
African Bank	0.1	0.1	0.1	—
Arab Fund.	0.3	0.3	0.9	0.2
Asian Devl. Bank	0.3	0.3	1.1	0.2
EEC	3.8	3.8	8.9	2.0
Inter-American Devl. Bank	6.2	6.2	29.3	6.5
IFAD	1.8	1.8	1.8	0.4
UNDP	4.1	4.1	19.0	4.2
UNEP	0.4	0.4	2.2	0.5
World Bank	10.2	10.3	42.9	9.5
Individual countries	69.7	70.2	300.6	66.6
Australia	2.7	2.7	11.1	2.4
Belgium	3.0	3.0	11.3	2.5
Canada (incl. IDRC)	7.1	7.2	45.0	10.0
Denmark	1.1	1.1	4.2	0.9
France	0.7	0.7	2.6	0.5
West Germany	9.2	9.3	34.6	7.7
Iran	0.0	0.0	4.0	0.9
Italy	0.1	0.1	0.4	0.1
Japan	5.0	5.0	13.5	3.0
Netherlands	2.4	2.4	9.8	2.2
New Zealand	0.1	0.1	0.2	—
Nigeria	0.6	0.6	3.1	0.7
Norway	2.0	2.0	8.0	1.8
Saudi Arabia	0.0	0.0	2.0	0.4
Sweden	3.0	3.0	15.2	3.4
Switzerland	1.9	1.9	6.2	1.4
UK	6.0	6.0	23.5	5.2
USA	24.8	25.0	105.9	23.5
Total	99.4	100.0	451.3	100.0

Source: CGIAR (1979).

the 1960s. As late as 1972, close to one-half of the total financial support of the institute system came from these two foundations. Since then, a number of international institutes and most Western developed countries have joined in financing the institutes, and the overall financial share of the two foundations had fallen to 3.7 per cent by 1979. Therefore, the initial foundation outlays have been extremely successful in attracting funds for international agricultural research.

Financing one-fourth of the total cost of the institutes for 1979, the United States is the biggest single contributor (Table 4.5). The World Bank provided more than 10 per cent of the 1979 budget. Other large donors include Germany, Canada, the United Kingdom the Inter-American Development Bank and Japan.

The decreasing budget share of the foundations is being compensated for by increasing the shares of individual countries and international institutions. Individual countries now account for more than 70 per cent of total financial support compared to less than 20 per cent in 1972.

As mentioned earlier, the informal structure used during the 1960s became insufficient to ensure an efficient allocation of funds among institutes as more institutes were developed and more financial donors were found. The CGIAR was created to facilitate effective communication between donors and institutes. In developing CGIAR, great care was taken to avoid a large and ineffective superstructure. As the system grows there is a danger that the flexibility and efficiency characteristic of the system will be stifled by a bureaucratic superstructure aimed more at control than at the facilitating of effective research. Increasing emphasis on excessive programme and budget reviews and other bureaucratic requirements, and attempts from various sources to centralize control and decision-making are danger signals which should not be ignored.

NOTES

1. See CGIAR (1979) and annual reports of the individual institutes for details on programme focus and accomplishment.
2. Development Assistance Committee of the Organization for Economic Cooperation and Development (OECD).

5 Economic returns to agricultural research and modern technology

The extent of agricultural research in developing countries was dealt with in Chapters 3 and 4. But what are the economic returns to society from such research? This chapter attempts to provide at least a partial answer to that question.

Estimation of the value of agricultural research and technology is difficult and associated with large uncertainties. In spite of these disadvantages, some information is available regarding the economic returns from a series of research programmes. The reasons why such information may be useful are discussed in the first section of this chapter. Then follows analyses of economic returns from national and international agricultural research. The distribution of economic returns from research and technology is discussed in Chapter 6. Economic returns to application of fertilizers are dealt with in Chapter 7.

REASONS FOR ESTIMATING ECONOMIC RETURNS

Public funds are scarce and are usually insufficient to meet the needs of public spending. Accordingly, some allocative mechanism is required for the distribution of these scarce funds among various types of public investment and spending. Agricultural research must compete for funds with other publicly financed projects.

In principle, the efficient allocation of scarce public funds should aim at the largest possible contribution to the achievement of a set of objectives. The expected relative contribution of each of the alternative public undertakings to the achievement of the various goals plays an essential role in efficient allocation of public funds. However, in practice, knowledge of the relative contributions is generally insufficient and expectations may be wrong or severely biased. As a result, the allocation of public funds may not be in the best interest of society. There are a number of other potential reasons for inefficient allocation of public funds such as poorly defined goals, conflict of interest among groups in society and uneven distribution of political and economic power.

As discussed in Chapter 2, the primary aims of most societies may be classified as either growth and efficiency aims or equity, or a combination of the two. Thus, other things being equal, an increase in the expected contribution of a particular public undertaking to the achievement of growth and/or equity goals would result in an increase in the amount of public funds allocated to that undertaking. The contribution of agricultural research to the twin objectives of growth and equity is difficult to estimate. The causal relationship between public research and agricultural production may be difficult to identify and even more difficult to quantify. The research institution cannot sell its research results at a price that corresponds to the future economic value of these results. This is so partly because the future economic value to society of such results is unknown, and partly because it may be difficult or impossible to prevent its use by non-buyers. Once the results of research are released to some, they would also usually be available to others at no cost. But if the future value to society could be estimated, the extent of public spending on agricultural research could be determined on the basis of relative benefits. Furthermore, estimates of the distribution of the benefits of research among groups in society would assist in selecting the correct policy measures to ensure that equity goals were achieved to the fullest extent possible.

Without information on the contribution of agricultural research to growth and equity, the optimal allocation of public funds will occur only by chance. A similar situation is, of course, found for investment in other public undertakings such as transportation, education, etc. Public investment in infrastructure is frequently based on elaborate calculations of internal rates of return as well as estimates of the distributional effects. Allocation of public funds to agricultural research is not usually based on such estimates. Owing to lack of information it has been implicitly or explicitly assumed that the return of public investment in agricultural research has been low. However, a number of analyses carried out recently have shown that it has in fact been extremely high in many cases. High returns from past research are a strong indication that public investment in agricultural research has been far below the optimal magnitude in so far as the growth objectives are concerned.

ECONOMIC RETURNS TO NATIONAL AGRICULTURAL RESEARCH

Following the study of Griliches (1958) of the economic return from research on hybrid maize in the United States, a number of analyses have been carried out to determine economic returns from selected agricultural research programmes. The primary purpose of these analyses has been to estimate the rate of return obtained by society from public spending on such programmes. Most of these analyses have dealt with past or present research programmes, and very few explicitly with the planning of future research. Nevertheless, estimated rates of return from past and present research provide guidelines for the future.

The estimated rates of return from 50 research programmes are shown in Table 5.1. Average annual rates of return for these programmes are slightly less than 50 per cent, only four showing returns of less than 20 per cent. Expected rates of return from investment of public funds in other activities are typically 10–20 per cent. Furthermore, interest rates in the international capital market have traditionally been below 10–15 per cent. Thus, public investment in agricultural research appears to be a very profitable undertaking.

Table 5.1 Estimated rates of return from investment in agricultural research.

Commodity	Country	Period	Annual rate of return (%)	Source
Aggregate	India	1953–71	40	Evenson and Jha (1973)
Aggregate	India	–	63	Kahlon et al. (1977)
Aggregate	Japan	1880–1938	35	Tang (1963)
Aggregate	USA	1949–59	35–40	Griliches (1964)
Aggregate	USA	1949–59	47	Evenson (1969)
Aggregate	USA	1937–42	50	Peterson and Fitzharris (1977)
Aggregate	USA	1947–52	51	Peterson and Fitzharris (1977)
Aggregate	USA	1957–62	49	Peterson and Fitzharris (1977)
Aggregate	USA	1967–72	34	Peterson and Fitzharris (1977)
Aggregate	USA	1938–48	30	Lu, Cline and Quance (1979)
Aggregate	USA	1949–59	28	Lu, Cline and Quance (1979)
Aggregate	USA	1959–69	26	Lu, Cline and Quance (1979)
Aggregate	USA	1969–72	24	Lu, Cline and Quance (1979)
Hybrid maize	USA	1940–55	35–40	Griliches (1958)
Maize	Chile	1940–77	32–34	Yrrarrazaval, Navarrete and Valdivia, (1979)
Maize	Peru	1954–67	35–40	Hines, (1972)

Table 5.1 *cont.*

Commodity	Country	Period	Annual rate of return (%)	Source
Maize and sorghum	Mexico	1943—64	26—59	Ardito-Barletta (1970)
Hybrid sorghum	USA	1940—57	20	Griliches (1958)
Wheat	Mexico	1943—64	69—104	Ardito-Barletta (1970)
Wheat	Colombia	1953—73	11—12	Hertford et al. (1977)
Wheat	Bolivia	1966—75	−48	Wennergren and Whitaker (1977)
Wheat	Chile	1949—77		Yrarrazaval Navarrete and Valdivia, (1979)
Rice	Colombia	1957—72	60—82	Hertford, et al. (1977)
Rice	Colombia	1957—74	94	Scobie and Posada (1978)
Rice	Japan	1915—50	25—27	Akino and Hayami (1975)
Rice	Japan	1930—61	73—75	Akino and Hayami (1975)
Rice	Asia	1950—65	32—39	Evenson and Flores (1978)
Rice	Asia	1966—75	73—78	Evenson and Flores (1978)
Rice	Tropics	1966—75	46—71	Flores-Moya et al. (1978)
Rice	Philippines	1966—75	27	Flores-Moya et al. (1978)
Cash grains	USA	1969	36	Bredahl and Peterson. (1976)
Soybeans	Colombia	1960—71	79—96	Hertford et al. (1977)
Potatoes	Mexico	1943—64	69	Ardito-Barletta (1970)
Sugar-cane	South Africa	1945—62	40	Evenson (1969)
Sugar-cane	Australia	1945—58	50	Evenson (1969)
Sugar-cane	India	1945—58	60	Evenson (1969)
Cocoa	Brazil	1923—74	16	Monteiro (1975)
Cocoa	Brazil	1958—74	60	Monteiro (1975)
Cotton	Brazil	1924—67	77[+]	Ayer (1970)
Cotton	Colombia	1953—72	Negative	Hertford et al. (1977)
Rubber	Malaysia	1932—73	25	Pee (1977)
Rapeseed	Canada	1964—75	95—105	Nagy and Furtan (1978)
Pastures	Australia	1948—69	65—80	Duncan (1972)
Poultry	USA	1915—60	21—25	Peterson (1967)
Poultry	USA	1969	37	Bredahl and Peterson (1976)

Table 5.1 *cont.*

Commodity	Country	Period	Annual rate of return (%)	Source
Sheep	Bolivia	1966—75	44	Wennergren and Whitaker (1977)
Dairy	India	1963—75	29	Kumar, Maji and Patel (1977)
Dairy	USA	1969	43	Bredahl and Peterson (1976)
Livestock	USA	1969	47	Bredahl and Peterson (1976)
Tomato harvest	USA	1958—69	37—46	Schmitz and Seckler (1970)

A note of caution may be useful at this point. The estimating procedures used to obtain the rates of return shown in Table 5.1 (production functions, index number and economic surplus analyses[1]) provide crude approximations rather than exact estimates, primarily because of insufficient data and difficulties in separating research and extension contributions. Therefore, the choice of assumptions to substitute for data deficiencies, and analytical short cuts, may bias the results, and it is possible that some estimates reported in Table 5.1 are severely biased one way or the other. Lindner and Jarrett (1978), Jarrett and Lindner (1977), and Scobie (1976) provide further information on this issue.

Not all public investment in agricultural research results in very high economic returns. Owing to the nature of research it is impossible to ensure a consistently high, or for that matter a positive, economic return from all research activities. There is undoubtedly a tendency to select the more successful research programmes for evaluating returns, those with no apparent success being of little interest to the analyst. If, in fact, the results shown in Table 5.1 consist of a selection of the more successful programmes, the average return to agricultural research may be considerably below the estimates shown. While such an argument is likely to have some validity, studies of complete national agricultural research systems have shown economic returns similar to those obtained from more limited research programmes. Thus, the upward bias caused by a possible biased selection of programmes to be analysed may not be great, and there is reason to believe that the very high economic returns shown in Table 5.1 provide a good indication of those from efficiently organized agricultural research in general.

The high economic returns from agricultural research relative to return from other public investment indicate that public investment in agricultural research has been too limited. An inverse relationship between the amount of investment in research and the rate of return, would be expected beyond a certain investment level. This would imply that marginal returns are below average returns. Such a relationship is documented for agricultural research in the United States (Lu, Cline, and Quance, 1979; Peterson and Fitzharris, 1977). On the other hand, it appears that the rate of return has increased over time in Columbia (rice), Japan (rice), Asia (rice), Brazil (cocoa) and the United States (poultry). In addition to the investment level, the marginal return to research is influenced by a number of factors such as the quality of the research resources, interaction with other research programmes, e.g. interaction between national and international institutions, and the rate of adoption and use of research results. Thus, increased financial support to agricultural research in isolation is likely to result in decreasing returns. However, the information available clearly shows that increased investment in agricultural research in developing countries is likely to provide very high returns. These will be even higher if supported by a series of other agricultural development activities. Therefore, from the view point of effective utilization of public funds for economic growth, public investment in agricultural research should be increased, both in absolute terms and relative to investment in other publicly financed projects.

ECONOMIC RETURNS TO INTERNATIONAL AGRICULTURAL RESEARCH

As mentioned earlier, research carried out by IRRI and CIMMYT have facilitated large increases in the production of rice and wheat in many developing countries. The return from this research and rice research carried out by CIAT is analysed in this section. It appears premature to attempt an assessment of the return from investment in the other international institutes.

The central element of the green revolution was, as mentioned earlier, improved wheat and rice varieties with high yield capacity. The degree of increase of production is determined partly by the size of the area on which these new varieties were adopted and partly on the resulting yield increase per unit area. The increase in yield, in turn, is determined by the yield capacity of the individual variety, together with the availability and management of water, the amount of fertilizer used and a series of other production-related factors. Distribution of modern rice and wheat varieties, their impact on yields and the resulting effect on production are analysed below.

AREA WITH MODERN TECHNOLOGY

Modern wheat varieties developed by the Mexican Wheat Research Programme were introduced in large areas in Mexico during the early 1950s. At the time of the establishment of CIMMYT in 1964, these varieties were used on 95 per cent of the total wheat area in Mexico. The foundation of CIMMYT made it easier to distribute these varieties to other countries. Testing of varieties from the Mexican Wheat Programme was initiated in India and Pakistan in 1964. In 1965, India imported 250 tons and Pakistan 350 tons of seed material from Mexico. The following year India imported an additional 18,000 tons from Mexico, and a very large proportion of India's and Pakistan's own production of these varieties was used as seed. The result was that the Mexican varieties were planted on roughly 3,000 ha in India and 5,000 ha in Pakistan in 1965/66. However, although considerable, this amounted to less than 1 per cent of the total wheat area in the two countries. From this modest beginning, the area with modern wheat varieties increased during a 10-year period to around fifteen million ha in India and 4 million ha in Pakistan, or roughly 73 per cent of the total wheat area in the two countries (see Fig. 5.1). Thus, the distribution of these wheat varieties in two of the principal wheat-producing developing countries was dynamic. Similar developments took place in other developing countries (See Fig. 5.1), new wheat varieties being grown on 73 per cent of the wheat areas in Bangladesh and Nepal. However, it was India, Pakistan and Nepal who first took the initiative in a rapid introduction of the new wheat varieties outside Mexico.

It is estimated that high-yielding wheat varieties were used on about 44 per cent of the total wheat area in developing countries in 1976/77 (Table 5.2). This amounts to about thirty million ha. About twenty million ha, or two-thirds of this area, are found in Asia where more than 70 per cent of the wheat area is grown with high-yielding varieties. The remaining regions with high-yielding wheat varieties are almost evenly divided between Latin America and the Near East, while Africa accounts for a relatively small area.

The distribution of modern rice varieties developed by IRRI was also dynamic. The area planted with new rice varieties in Asia and North Africa is approximately the same as that planted with new wheat varieties (Table 5.3). However, the total rice area is considerably larger than that of wheat in those regions. This implies that modern varieties are planted on a smaller percentage of the total rice area. It is estimated that about 30 per cent of the total area in rice in Asia is planted with varieties originating from IRRI research, while the distribution of these

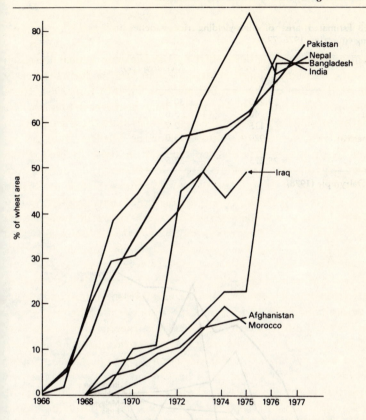

Fig. 5.1. Per cent of total wheat area planted with modern varieties in selected countries, 1966–77. (Based on data from Dalrymple, 1976 and 1978)

Table 5.2 Estimated area of high-yielding wheat varieties in developing countries, 1976/77.

Region	Hectares (1,000)	Wheat area (%)
Asia	19,672	72.4
Near East	4,400	17.0
Africa	225	22.5
Latin America	5,100	41.0
Total	29,397	44.2

Source: Dalrymple (1978).

Table 5.3 Estimated area of high-yielding rice varieties in developing countries, 1976/77.

Region	Hectares (1,000)	Rice area (%)
Asia	24,200	30.4
Near East	40	3.6
Africa	115	2.7
Latin America	920	13.0
Total	25,275	27.5

Source: Dalrymple (1978).

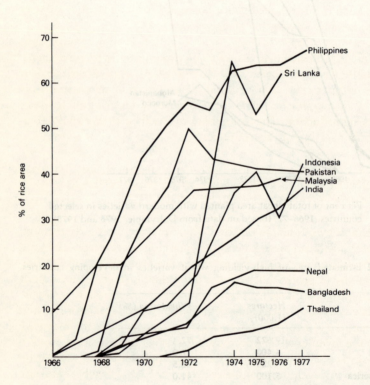

Fig. 5.2. Per cent of total rice area planted with modern varieties in selected countries, 1966–77 (based on data from Dalrymple, 1976 and 1978).

varieties in Latin America was limited to 13 per cent of the total in 1976/77.

The new rice varieties were first introduced in Malaysia, the Philippines and India. They were later introduced in a large number of other developing countries. The distribution of these varieties in a number of developing countries is shown in Fig. 5.2. In the Philippines, 68 per cent of the total rice area was planted with modern varieties in 1976/77. In Sri Lanka it was 63 per cent, in Korea 44 per cent and in Indonesia 41 per cent. Bearing in mind that these varieties were made available less than 10 years prior to 1976/77, the speed by which these varieties were distributed and adopted was highly unusual for agricultural technology in developing countries. Furthermore, it should be recognized that a large number of the farmers adopting these varieties are small landholders. Such farmers have traditionally and for a number of reasons tended to be slow to adopt new technology.

One example of an extremely rapid adoption of new rice varieties was found in Colombia. In a matter of three years the irrigated rice areas planted with modern varieties increased from 5 per cent to virtually 100 per cent. Such a rapid introduction of new varieties is unique in developing countries and obviously contributes to large increases in production. The Colombian case will be further analysed in a subsequent section of this chapter.

THE CONTRIBUTION OF MODERN RICE AND WHEAT TECHNOLOGY TO YIELDS AND PRODUCTION

New technology influences rice and wheat production partly through increases in yields on areas where the technology was introduced, and partly through an increase in the total area used for these crops, leading to an increase in profitability for the individual farmer. As a result of this increasing profitability, both in absolute and relative terms, previously unutilized areas may be drawn into production of rice and wheat. Similarly, a considerable amount of crop substitution may take place at the farm level. The area used for crops for which no modern technology is available may be reduced. Figure 5.3 illustrates such crop substitution in developing countries in the Far East. The wheat and rice areas were approximately unchanged during the period 1962–66, but introduction of new technology for these crops during the last half of the 1960s resulted in a dramatic increase in the wheat area during the period 1967–76 and in the rice area during the period 1966–69. The expansion of wheat and rice areas in the Far East since 1966 exceeded

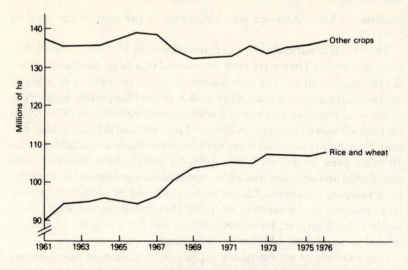

Fig. 5.3. Area with rice and wheat and other crops in developing countries in the Far East, 1961–76 (based on data from FAO, *Production Yearbooks*).

that of the total agricultural area in that region. Thus, this area increased by 11.3 million ha from 1961/65 to 1972/76, while those under wheat and rice increased by 12.1 million ha (FAO, 1976). The area with other crops was reduced by 0.8 million ha. Wheat and rice areas increased from 40.9 per cent of the total agricultural area in 1961/65 to 44 per cent in 1972/76.

As a result of the above-mentioned expansion, production increased more than yields for these two commodities. Yield increases for developing countries in the Far East are shown in Fig. 5.4. Wheat yields were roughly constant until 1967. After 1967 yields increased considerably. This yield-increasing trend was interrupted during the period 1972/74 primarily because of bad weather. The large increase in wheat yields corresponds closely to the introduction of new wheat technology in the Far East. Although wheat yields are determined by a number of factors, there is little doubt, that modern technology is responsible for a very large part of the increase after 1967. Rice yields were also roughly constant during the period 1961–67. After 1967 a considerable increase took place. However, this increase was less dramatic. This was partly to a somewhat more limited distribution of the new rice varieties (when measured as a percentage of the total rice area) and partly to a somewhat lower percentage increase in yields where the varieties were introduced.

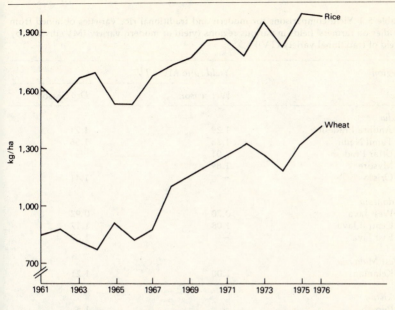

Fig. 5.4. Rice and wheat yields in the Far East, 1961–76 (based on data from FAO, *Production Yearbooks*).

The yield capacity of modern rice and wheat varieties is heavily influenced by a number of production-related factors such as water supply, use of fertilizer, climate, length of photo period, geographic conditions, etc. Likewise, the yield difference between modern and traditional varieties may vary considerably from one region to another, and even from one farm to another, within the same region. Results from a large number of farm level analyses show yield advantages of modern wheat varieties from 23 to 270 per cent. Those for modern rice varieties were found to vary from 10 to 158 per cent (Dalrymple, 1977). Farm level yield comparisons have been carried out by IRRI and national agricultural research institutions in a number of Asian countries. Results from some of these comparisons are shown in Table 5.4. In some cases, the introduction of modern rice varieties has greatly increased yields. However, the variation is large and in a few cases modern varieties have yielded less than traditional varieties. On the basis of a literature search, including 102 citations of the relative yield of modern versus traditional varieties in rice and 37 in wheat, Scobie (1979b) concludes that the yield superiority of modern varieties was about 100 per cent for wheat and 40 per cent for rice. Such average figures cover very large variations, as shown above.

Table 5.4 Yield comparisons for modern and traditional rice varieties obtained from studies on farmers' fields in various regions (yield of modern variety (MV) divided by yield of traditional variety (TV)).

Region	Yield ratio MV : TV	
	Wet season	*Dry Season*
India		
Andhra Pradesh	1.29	1.71
Tamil Nadu	1.56	1.56
Uttar Pradesh	2.01	—
Mysore	1.89	—
Orissa	—	1.41
Indonesia		
West Java	0.70	0.92
Central Java	1.08	1.17
East Java	—	1.07
West Malaysia		
Kelantan	1.00	1.21
Pakistan		
Punjab	—	1.6
Thailand		
Suphan Buri	1.43	—
Philippines		
Nueva Ecija	1.25	—
Leyte	1.31	1.36
Cotabato	1.06	—
Camarines Sur	1.04	—
Iloilo	1.08	—
South Cotabato	1.33	—

Source: IRRI (1975), Mangahas and Librero (1973) and Evenson and Flores (1978).

The estimated impact of modern rice and wheat varieties on output of selected countries and regions is shown in Table 5.5. Although modern rice varieties were initially developed for Asia, it appears that their largest percentage impact on output is found in parts of Latin America. Among Asian regions, modern rice and wheat varieties have been particularly well suited to the Punjab region.

Each of the countries where modern rice and/or wheat varieties have been introduced has its own interesting story to tell. Four countries will be singled out for further discussion. For two of these, India and the Philippines, only yield and production impacts will be discussed. For the others, Colombia and Mexico, a more detailed analysis will be pre-

Table 5.5 Estimated percentage increase in the output of selected regions and countries due to modern rice and wheat varieties.

Country/region	Year	Increase (%)
Rice		
Colombia (irrigated)	1974	68
Central America	1974	43
Mexico and Caribbean	1974	27
Latin America		
excl. Brazil	1974	40
incl. Brazil	1974	14
Latin America and Africa	1974—75	12—18
India	1974—75	8—12
Philippines	1974—75	9—24
Developing countries	1974—75	7—12
Asia	1972—73	5
Philippines	1968	3.9
	1973	7.2
Wheat		
Asia	1972—73	18
Indian Punjab	1967—68	23—45

Sources: The first five from above are from Scobie and Posada (1977), the next four are from Evenson, Flores and Hayami (1978), the next is from Dalrymple (1975b) and the last two estimates for rice are from Atkinson and Kunkel (1976). The two wheat estimates are from Dalrymple (1975) and Rao (1975) respectively. The table is taken from Scobie (1979b).

sented. Following this discussion, an analysis will be made of the global impact of modern rice and wheat varieties.

MODERN VARIETIES IN INDIA AND THE PHILIPPINES

Following the above-mentioned import and field testing of modern wheat varieties from Mexico and the subsequent import of relatively large quantities of seed, Indian wheat yield began a dramatic increase in 1966/67 (see Fig. 5.5). By 1976 this amounted to 68 per cent of the 1961/65 yield levels. As wheat yields increased, more land was devoted to that crop. As a result, 1976 wheat production was two and a half times the average annual production during 1961/65, or an increase of 150 per cent over approximately 10 years. In the case of rice, the introduction of modern varieties had a much more limited impact when measured at the national level (see Fig. 5.5). However, modern rice varieties had a very significant impact on yields and production in some regions, as discussed in Chapter 6.[2]

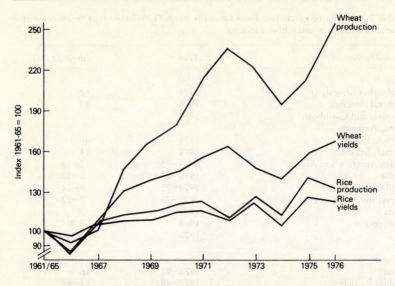

Fig. 5.5. Production and yields of wheat and rice in India, 1961/65–76 (based on data from FAO, *Production Yearbooks*).

The impact of new varieties on rice yields in the Philippines is another interesting case in point. As shown in Fig. 5.6, rice yields increased considerably from 1968 to 1970. This period corresponds to the introduction of new rice varieties over a considerable area. As opposed to a number of other countries, the higher yield level in the Philippines was not maintained. Rice yields fell considerably after 1970 and the 1970 level was not regained until 1975. The decrease after 1970 may be explained, at least in part, by adverse weather, reduced increases in fertilizer use and too little emphasis on improved water management. Improvements in these factors have contributed to a considerable increase in yield after 1974.[3]

MODERN RICE VARIETIES IN COLOMBIA[4]

The Colombian rice research programme was initiated in 1957 as a cooperative programme between the Colombian Agricultural Ministry and the Rockefeller Foundation. However, until 1967, more than 90 per cent of Colombian rice farmers used rice varieties developed in the United States. In 1964 rice varieties from the Colombian research programme were used on approximately 5 per cent of the area under rice, but, the yield capacity under Colombian conditions was relatively low.

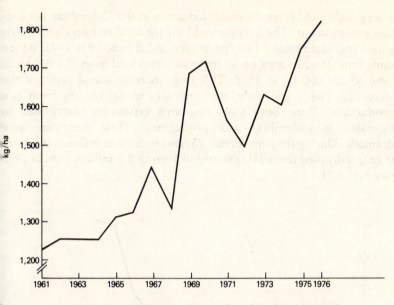

Fig. 5.6. Rice yields in the Philippines 1961–76 (based on data from FAO, *Production Yearbooks*).

A new variety developed by the Colombian research programme was made available to Colombian rice producers in 1966, and grown on 7 per cent of the total rice area in 1967, increasing to 42 per cent in 1968. In 1969 the variety was grown on only 36 per cent, falling to 26 per cent in 1970, 14 per cent in 1971, after which time it disappeared. The decreasing trend in the use of this variety after 1968 was caused by competition from a new variety imported from IRRI. This new variety (IR8) was introduced on 5 per cent of the rice area in 1969 and increased to around 30 per cent in the following year. Although IR8 yielded considerably more than earlier varieties, certain grain-quality and disease-resistance issues made the variety less suited for Colombian conditions.

Close collaboration between the National Research Institute and CIAT was initiated soon after the latter was developed in 1968. The focus of the collaboration was the development of rice varieties better suited for Colombia. The research programme was based on improved material from IRRI and resulted in new varieties which were very quickly introduced among Colombian rice producers. In 1973 the total rice area under irrigation was planted with varieties developed from the collaborative Colombian programme. The primary reason for the rapid distribution and adoption of these rice varieties was to be found in

115

a very high yield capacity under irrigation in the Colombian production environment. The average yield for the total rice area under irrigation increased from 3 tons/ha in 1966 to 5.3 tons/ha in 1973. At the same time, the rice area under irrigation increased from 114,000 ha in 1966 to 274,000 ha in 1975. This large increase was a result of the increasing yields and associated increases in net returns from rice production. Thus, both yield and area expansion contributed to increases in Colombian rice production. These increases were dramatic. During the period 1966–75 rice production in Colombia more than quadrupled from 341,000 tons in 1966 to 1.5 million tons in 1975 (see Fig. 5.7).

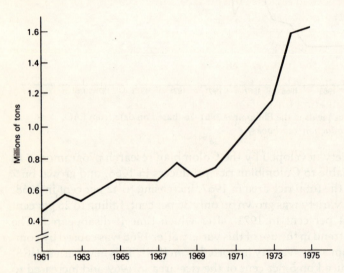

Fig. 5.7.   Rice production in Colombia, 1961–75 (Jennings, 1976).

The high yield capacity of the new varieties could only be obtained by irrigation. But only one-third of the total rice area in Colombia had access to irrigation in 1966. The remainder could not obtain significant gains from the new varieties, and yields on unirrigated land remained constant around 1.5 tons/ha (see Fig. 5.8). The dramatic increase in production in areas where irrigation water was available resulted in a chaotic market situation with drastic price decreases, the average deflated producer price for rice falling by 28 per cent from 1965/69 to 1970/74. This price decrease, together with price increases for most other food commodities made rice much cheaper than before relative to other foods. In 1965 the market value of 1 kg of beans was equal to the market value of 1.82 kg of rice. In 1974 1 kg of beans could buy 3.47 kg of rice. The decrease in rice prices came about in spite of government intervention aimed at prohibiting too drastic a decrease. With the same aim, a considerable amount of rice was used as animal feed and efforts were made to export rice. While farmers who introduced the new rice varieties were capable of reducing unit costs of production by around 30 per cent, such cost reductions could obviously not be obtained by non-adopters. Thus, farmers controlling land suitable for rice production and with access to irrigation obtained large benefits, even though prices fell. On the other hand, rice producers without access to irrigation experienced considerable losses. As a result the area planted with rice was reduced in regions with no access to irrigation. The area under upland rice production fell from 236,000 ha in 1966 to 95,000 ha in 1975, i.e. from 50 to 9 per cent of the total rice area.

It may be concluded that the introduction of new rice varieties in Colombia had the following effects:

1. Substitution of existing varieties by new ones on the total rice area under irrigation during a period of four years.
2. Almost a doubling of yields per hectare on these areas.
3. A large increase in the rice area under irrigation.
4. A large reduction in the area used for upland rice production.
5. An increase in the national average yield of rice from 1.9 tons/ha in 1966 to 4.4 tons/ha in 1975, i.e. more than a doubling of national rice yields.

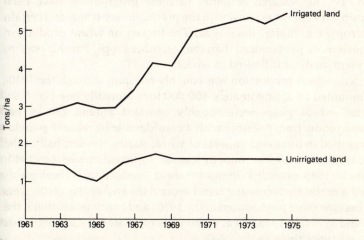

Fig. 5.8. Rice yields on irrigated and unirrigated land in Colombia, 1961–75. (Jennings, 1976).

117

6. A quadrupling of national rice production during the same period.
7. A reduction in rice prices, both in absolute terms and relative to the prices of most other food commodities.

The value of the increased rice production due to the introduction of new varieties to 1974 has been estimated to be about US$350 million. If the additional costs of production and rice research in Colombia are deducted, the annual internal rate of return to rice research in Colombia was estimated to be about 94 per cent. The cost of IRRI research is not included. These costs should be distributed over all countries benefiting from new rice varieties and the amount that should be charged to Colombia will be sufficiently small as to be unimportant for this purpose. Thus, given the very high rate of return from rice research in Colombia, it is difficult to visualize any better investment opportunity. Distribution of the benefits obtained from rice research in Colombia is discussed in Chapter 6.

WHEAT IN MEXICO

Another example of the dramatic impact of agricultural research and modern technology on food production is taken from Mexico. As mentioned earlier, the Mexican Ministry of Agriculture and the Rockefeller Foundation initiated a joint agricultural research programme in 1943. This programme existed for 16 years and was then replaced by that of the current National Agricultural Research Institute and CIMMYT. The research activities of these programmes have been responsible for a large expansion in the production of wheat and certain other crops, e.g. maize, since 1950. The impact on wheat production was much more pronounced than that on other crops. For this reason, the present analysis is limited to wheat.

Mexican wheat production was roughly constant through the 1940s and amounted to approximately 400,000 tons annually (see Fig. 5.9). Likewise, wheat yields were roughly constant around 750 kg/ha. Stagnant production, together with a considerable increase in population, resulted in increased imports of wheat during the first half of the 1940s. While Mexico was more or less self-sufficient in wheat in 1940, imports in 1945 exceeded domestic wheat production. Wheat yields showed a modestly increasing trend around the end of the 1940s. This trend became more pronounced in the 1950s and continued through the 1960s and 1970s. In 1976 wheat yields were estimated at 4,200 kg/ha or five to six times those in the 1940s.

As a result of these increases in yield and some expansion in the wheat

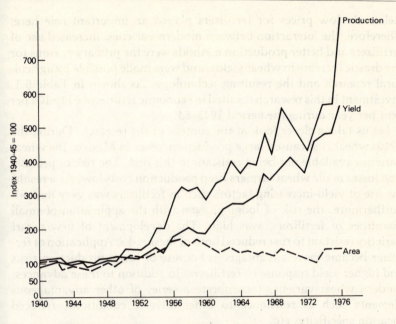

Fig. 5.9. Wheat production, area and yields in Mexico, 1940–76 (based on data from FAO, *Production Yearbooks*).

area, Mexican wheat production increased to more than 3 million tons or seven to eight times that in the 1940s. As a result, Mexico not only became self-sufficient but actually became a net exporter of wheat in 1963. The net exporting position was maintained until 1971, at which time a reduction in the wheat area, together with a constant increase in demand, made it necessary for Mexico to return to being a net importer. Expansion of the area under wheat during the period 1973–76, together with a constantly increasing yield, returned Mexico to the position of net exporter in 1976.

But which factors were primarily responsible for the above-mentioned large increases in yield? Edwin Wellhausen, former Director of CIMMYT, believes that three factors are of principal importance (Wellhausen, 1976).

These are:

1. Development and use of new varieties.
2. Development and use of better production methods, in particular better pest and wheat control and soil preparation as well as increased use of fertilizers.
3. Favourable price relations for production factors and agricultural inputs.

Relatively low prices for fertilizers played an important role here. Therefore, the interaction between modern varieties, increased use of fertilizers and better production methods were the primary reasons for the drastic increase in wheat yields, and were made possible by agricultural research and the resulting technology. As shown in Table 5.1, investment in this research resulted in economic returns of 61 to 104 per cent per year during the period 1943–64.

Let us take a closer look at the content of the research. During the 1940s wheat rust caused large production losses in Mexico, the wheat varieties available not being resistant to this pest. The risk of production losses made wheat farmers keep production costs low. As a result, the use of yield-increasing factors such as fertilizers was very limited. Furthermore, the risk of lodging, even with the application of small quantities of fertilizers, was high. The development of new dwarf varieties resistant to rust reduced both of these risks. Application of fertilizer became more advantageous because of lower production risks and higher yield response to fertilizers. In addition to these advances, modern wheat varieties incorporate a series of other advantageous elements such as resistance to other adverse conditions, reduced location specificity, etc.

Mexico utilized foreign trade to maintain the desired price level. Large quantities of wheat were exported at prices considerably below the domestic price level. These relatively high domestic producer prices for wheat were maintained in order to promote increased production. When this price level resulted in production in excess of domestic demand, the surplus was exported with a subsidy. This policy was changed towards the end of the 1960s and the beginning of the 1970s. The above-mentioned reduction in the wheat area between 1969 and 1973 was undoubtedly caused largely by this policy change. The interaction between government policy and technological change is extremely important not only for the extent of economic benefits obtained but also for the distribution of such benefits. This topic will be further discussed in Chapter 6.[5]

THE GLOBAL IMPACT ON PRODUCTION

Results from a somewhat superficial assessment of the impact of modern varieties on the 1976/77 production of wheat and rice in developing countries as a whole are shown in Table 5.6. According to these results, the use of modern varieties added about twenty one million tons of wheat and ten million tons of rice to the world wheat and rice production in that year. This amounts to 22 per cent of the total wheat production and 5 per cent of the total rice production in developing countries. If these quantities are valued at US$120 per ton of wheat and US$270 per ton of rice (these prices are rough guidelines for international prices at that time), the value of the additional output was US$5.3 billion. This total value was divided almost exactly between the two crops with a slight edge to rice.

About 95 per cent of the additional rice and close to 60 per cent of the additional wheat supply came about in the Far East. The additional wheat output in the Far East accounts for one-third of the total 1976/77 wheat production of that region. The expansion of output due to modern wheat varieties is also of great significance in Latin America and to a lesser extent in the Near East.

Increased output due to modern rice varieties was found to play a more moderate role when measured as a percentage of total production. However, because of higher rice prices, the value of the additional

Table 5.6 Estimated impact of modern varieties on wheat and rice production, 1976/77.

	Average yields 1961–65* (kg/ha)	Estimated increase on MV areas 1976/77† (kg/ha)	Estimated impact of MV on 1976/77 production		
			1,000 tons‡	% of total prod.§	Value// (US$ m.)
Wheat					
Far East	844	633	12,453	33.0	1,494
Latin America	1,430	1,073	5,472	28.0	657
Near East	994	746	3,282	10.5	394
Africa	700	525	118	1.8	14
Total			21,325	22.4	2,559
Rice					
Far East	1,596	399	9,656	6.0	2,607
Latin America	1,730	433	398	2.6	108
Near East	3,412	853	34	0.7	9
Africa	1,274	319	37	0.7	10
Total			10,125	5.4	2,734

*   FAO Production Yearbook 1975.
†   Based on the assumptions of 75% increase for wheat and 25% for rice.
‡   This is an estimate of the difference between actual production in 1976/77 and the production that would have been obtained in the absense of modern varieties (MV).
§   The estimated impact as a percentage of total wheat or rice production in the individual regions. Data for total production are from FAO (1975).
//   The value is estimated on the basis of the following prices: wheat US$120/ton; rice US$270/ton.

rice output exceeded that of the additional wheat output.

The results reported in Table 5.6 are at best rough approximations. Estimation of the impact on global production is difficult because crop yields are influenced by a large number of factors which vary among countries and over time. Data describing these factors and their effects on yield are scarce or non-existing. The results reported above were obtained simply by assuming that modern varieties, wherever used in 1976/77, caused overall average yield increases over average 1961/65 yields of 75 per cent in wheat and 25 per cent in rice. Thus, the total effect on production of area expansion is not included, only the effect of the yield differential. Yield advantages of 75 and 25 per cent are somewhat below those found by Scobie (1979b) and reported elsewhere in this chapter. As the area under modern varieties increases, a reduction in the yield advantage would be expected. The estimates surveyed by Scobie refer to a somewhat earlier period and the yield advantages may overstate those valid for 1976/77. However, it is possible that the figures used here underestimate the effect on production. It should be clear that both sets of estimates are very rough approximations only.

The estimated effect on wheat production is consistent with estimates by CIMMYT (1978) of between 19.9 and 26.7 million tons. Dalrymple (1977) estimated the output effect of modern wheat and rice varieties in Asia for the year 1972/73 under various alternative assumptions about the yield advantages of these varieties. Using a 75 per cent yield advantage for wheat and a 25 per cent yield advantage for rice, Dalrymple found that 27.4 per cent of Asian wheat production in that year, or 11.8 million tons, was due to modern varieties. In the case of rice, the estimates were 4.9 per cent and 7.7 million tons. Likewise, comparing these estimates with those given in Table 5.6, it appears that the annual output effect of modern varieties has increased considerably during the period 1972/73–1976/77. This is consistent with findings elsewhere.

A few attempts have been made to estimate the internal rate of return to international agricultural research. Thus, Flores-Moya, Evenson and Hayami (1978) estimated an internal rate of return to international rice research for the tropics of 46–71 per cent. Later estimates by Evenson and Flores (1978) are in the region of 82–100 per cent. However, while it is beyond reasonable doubt that the return from investment in international wheat and rice research has been very high indeed, it may be difficult to distinguish between the return from international research and that from related national research. It follows that the output effects reported in Table 5.6 are brought about not by international research in isolation but by an integrated international and national effort. Similarly, the high rates of return to Colombian rice research reported by Scobie and Posada (1977) and shown in Table 5.1 are due to an integrated national and international research effort. It is unlikely that such high returns would have been obtained by either national or international institutions in isolation. Other similar cases could be mentioned. In fact, the return from international research depends very much on effective national collaboration, and the mere fact that it is difficult or impossible to separate the contribution of one or the other should be of no serious concern as long as the overall outcome is successful.

NOTES

1. A description of estimating procedures may be found in Hertford and Schmitz (1977), Lindner and Jarrett (1978) and Schuh and Tollini (1979).
2. A more detailed analysis of the green revolution in India may be found in Mellor (1976) and Rao (1975).
3. A more detailed analysis of the green revolution in the Philippines may be found in Palmer (1975) and a number of IRRI papers.
4. Parts of this section is based on Scobie and Posada (1977).
5. For additional detail on the technological change in Mexican agriculture, see Hewitt de Alcantara (1976) and Wellhausen (1976).

6 Distribution of economic benefits from agricultural research and technology

As shown in Chapter 5, agricultural research and modern technology may be extremely effective in the expansion of food production. Likewise, returns to public investment in agricultural research are frequently very high. Thus, we may conclude that agricultural research and modern technology greatly contribute to the achievement of efficiency and growth objectives. This chapter addresses the distribution of the gains obtained.

Agricultural research and modern technology leading to the green revolution have been and still are severely criticized from a distributional viewpoint. It is argued that modern technology primarily benefits better-off groups in society and consequently contributes to a worsening of an already very skewed distribution of incomes, assets and power in developing countries (Griffin, 1972 and 1979; Frankel, 1976). In this chapter an attempt will be made to analyse whether and to what extent such criticism is supported by empirical evidence and what means might be available to correct undesirable distributional consequences.

Five factors are of major importance for the distribution of economic gains from agricultural research and technology. These are: (1) the nature of the technology; (2) the structure of the agricultural sector; (3) the structure of the market for factors of production and the possibilities of changing factor combinations; (4) the market for agricultural products; (5) agricultural policy. The influence of each of these five factors on the distribution of economic benefits from agricultural research and modern technology will be analysed in the following sections. As part of such analysis, available empirical evidence regarding the distribution of benefits from past agricultural research and technology will be presented and attempts will be made to point out which policy measures are available for modifying or removing undesirable distributional consequences.

TECHNOLOGY CHARACTERISTICS

PRODUCTION ENVIRONMENT AND TECHNOLOGY INTERACTION

As mentioned earlier, a large proportion of agricultural technology is location specific. The efficiency of such technology is largely determined by the production environment. Likewise, the distribution of economic benefits from a given technology among farmers will be greatly influenced by the distribution of control over the production environments. If modern technology is useful for certain regions but not for others, its introduction may produce severe changes in regional distribution of incomes.

Modern rice and wheat technology is responsible for such changes in a number of developing countries. The regional distribution of modern rice technology and associated economic benefits in India is a case in point. Modern rice technology was most suited for North and South India, while it was much less suited for the eastern parts of the country. The difference in regional suitability was to a large extent due to differences in water control. Consequently, new rice technology was introduced much more extensively in North and South India than in the eastern parts. Thus, in 1974 the technology was used on 71 per cent of the rice area in North India, 62 per cent in South India, but only 29 per cent in East India. The result was a drastic change in relative rice yields for the three regions (Fig. 6.1). The average rice yields in North India increased from about 1.6 tons/ha in the first half of the 1960s to around 3.0 tons/ha in the middle of the 1970s, e.g. almost a doubling of rice yields in 10 years. During the same period, rice yields in East India remained almost unchanged at 1.4–1.5 tons/ha. Although the rice area in North India was considerably smaller than that in East India (9 million ha as opposed to East India's fifteen million ha), North India produced 27 million tons of rice in 1974, as compared to 21 million tons produced in East India (Barker, 1977). Increasing yields in North and South India resulted in large increases in incomes in those regions. Therefore, modern rice technology has contributed to a considerable change in regional income distribution.

A somewhat similar case was found in Colombia. As is the case for most recently developed high-yielding rice varieties, the varieties developed for Colombia depended for their high yield potential on access to sufficient water and good water-management practices. As a result of the introduction of these varieties, large economic benefits were obtained in regions with access to sufficient water, while rice producers without such access experienced severe losses.

The introduction of high-yielding hybrid maize in Colombia shows similar distributional characteristics. These hybrids were introduced on almost all maize-producing farms in the Valle del Cauca region, while only a very small proportion of other maize producers in the country introduced hybrid maize or any other improved plant material. Partly

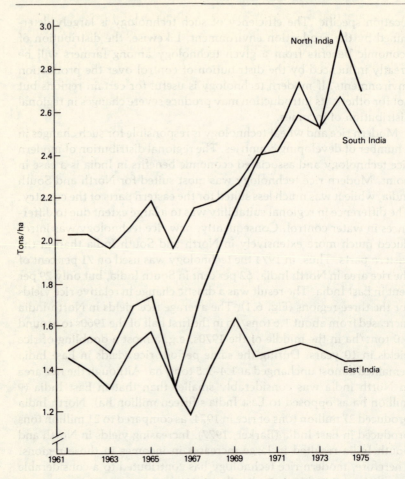

Fig. 6.1. Rice yield in three areas of India, 1961–75. (Barker, 1977).

because of the introduction of hybrid maize, average yields in Valle del Cauca were three to four times larger than the national average. The primary reason for the regional differences in the introduction of hybrid maize was that the yield capacity of the hybrids is determined to a very large extent by climatic and geographical conditions. A very large part of the maize improvement research took place in Valle del Cauca. Therefore, it is not surprising that the hybrids developed were best suited for that region. A number of hybrids were developed for other agro-climatic zones, but the yield capacity under existing conditions was much lower.

Another constraint to the introduction and use of hybrids in general, a constraint that was also observed in Colombia, is the need to purchase seed every season in order to maintain the yield capacity of the hybrid. This is a particularly important problem for producers with small land-holdings in areas where transportation facilities are very limited. The need to purchase seed before every planting also contributed to the above-mentioned regional difference in adoption rates. Farms in Valle del Cauca tend to be larger than other maize-producing farms in the country. Likewise, transportation facilities were much better in Valle del Cauca than in most of the other agro-climatic zones.

The end result was that considerable economic benefits were obtained by large maize producers in Valle del Cauca, while smaller maize producers elsewhere obtained relatively little or no economic gains from the development of hybrid maize.

The above examples clearly illustrate the need to determine explicitly for which production environments a given technology will be suited, before specifying the desired technology and establishing research priorities. Furthermore, information should be available on the distribution of the control over these production environments in order to determine *a priori* which groups of producers are likely to benefit from alternative technological developments.

If increasing production and low unit costs are the primary goals within agricultural research, attempts should be made to develop technology for production environments where such objectives are expected to be achieved to the greatest extent possible. The choice will most likely fall on those environments that are optimal for the production of the individual crop and where the most important yield-limiting factors can be removed by means of new technology. Modern rice and wheat technology, which triggered the green revolution, were in fact developed for production environments considered optimal for these commodities. In addition to the efforts aimed at increasing yield capacities within such environments, a number of other objectives entered into rice and wheat research. Some of these goals were aimed precisely at reducing the location specificity of the varieties developed. However, as mentioned earlier, with respect to soil quality, water control and use of production factors, most of the plant improvement and selection of the best-suited varieties took place on the basis of optimal production environment.

Such an approach is not unique for the research leading to the green revolution. In fact, the great majority of the world's agricultural research stations are located on soils considered optimal for the particular crop, and field research – including the evaluation of yield capacity of new varieties – frequently takes place under optimal production conditions.[1] This is undoubtedly the best approach, if increasing production and improved productivity are the only objectives. However, it should not be surprising that new technology produced by means of such an approach will benefit those farmers controlling optimal production environments, while others may benefit little or actually incur losses.

If such distribution of research benefits is undesirable, attempts must be made either to change research priorities or introduce public policy measures which correct the distributional pattern or compensate groups unable to achieve sufficient economic benefits. However, great caution should be exercised when aiming agricultural research priorities at distributional goals if it implies the forgoing of large potential increases in production and productivity. In cases where there is considerable conflict between desired growth, e.g. increases in production and productivity, and desired distribution, when planning future agricultural research it is probably advisable to place major emphasis on growth. Agricultural research and technology may be very effective in promoting growth and efficiency, but questions of distribution are often more effectively dealt with through public policy measures of various types. Coordination between research, technology and policy measures is essential to ensure the most effective utilization of research resources. In cases where policy measures aimed at distributional issues cannot be introduced or are ineffective, it is important that such issues are considered at the time of establishing research priorities. Also, there are many cases where these considerations can be included in decision-making on research priorities without any significant negative effect on efficiency and growth.

On the basis of the above, it may be concluded that in most cases new agricultural technology will benefit farmers who control optimal production environments or have access to such environments. Empirical evidence strongly supports such a conclusion. In some developing countries, not least in Latin America, optimal production environments are frequently controlled by the larger and more affluent landholders. In other areas, particularly those where good soil has been distributed through land reform, they may be controlled by smaller landholders. The interaction between farm size and technological benefits is further discussed in a subsequent section.

RISK AND CAPITAL REQUIREMENT

The influence of technological change on production risk and capital requirement is another important characteristic of technology that may influence the distribution of benefits. Low-income farmers may be very reluctant to accept increases in production risk, because the consequences of crop failures may be unacceptable. However, modern agricultural technology may be effective in reducing production risk. This is particularly the case for varieties with built-in genetic resistance or tolerance to certain diseases, insects, variation in water supply and other adverse conditions. Such technology meets the requirements of reduced production risk. A similar case could be made for technology which contributes to a better control over the water supply, such as the provision of pumps.

However, the introduction of modern technology frequently requires additional capital for purchase of fertilizers, irrigation equipment and other factors necessary to ensure optimal or near-optimal production conditions. These additional capital requirements frequently make it difficult for low-income farmers in developing countries to introduce modern technology. Small landholders are often reluctant to seek credit, particularly in cases where the perceived element of risk is large. For good reason, many of these farmers prefer current low levels of income if higher levels are associated with additional risk. Such risks may be partially or totally removed by means of public policy measures or modifications in agricultural technology. In cases where it is seen that technological change is associated with increasing risk, it is usually the larger farmer who first adopts the technology. The time lag between adoption by the larger farmers and adoption by the smaller greatly depends on the perceived increase in production risk. Thus, agricultural technology with high yield potential and high perceived risk will tend to benefit the more affluent landholders.

PRODUCTION ENVIRONMENT AND FARM SIZE

Results from a number of studies carried out during the last half of the 1960s on the adoption pattern of new rice and wheat technologies showed that adoption was strongly biased towards larger farms. On the basis of these results, it was widely believed that only the larger farmers would benefit from this technology. However, studies carried out during the 1970s clearly show that a large number of low-income landholders had introduced modern rice and wheat technology. The earlier results merely measured the relationship between farm size and early adoption, and the time lag between adoption by large and small farmers appears to be much shorter than originally expected (Ruttan, 1977). This, of course, is true only in cases where large as well as small farmers controlled favourable production environments.

The relationship between absolute farm size and the adoption of six modern practices in rice production was studied in 30 villages of five Asian countries (IRRI, 1978). The results are shown in Fig. 6.2. The percentage of farms in each of three size groups that had adopted each of the practices in the years indicated are shown. Small farmers adopted improved varieties, fertilizers and insecticides before those with medium and large farms. On the other hand, labour-saving technology (herbicides, tractors and mechanical threshers) was adopted first and primarily by the larger farmers.

The effect of relative farm size on adoption behaviour within the individual village was also studied. Villages were grouped into three categories according to the 'gini' coefficient (a measure of the degree of dispersion in the farm size within each village). Then, within each village, farms were grouped into small and large on the basis of the median farm size in each village. The cumulative adoption of improved rice varieties over the period 1966–72 for each group is shown in Fig. 6.3. Results from one region with a very skewed distribution of farm sizes are also shown. In all the groups, larger farmers adopted improved varieties sooner than smaller farmers. However, except for the region with a very skewed land distribution, the time lag was not large.

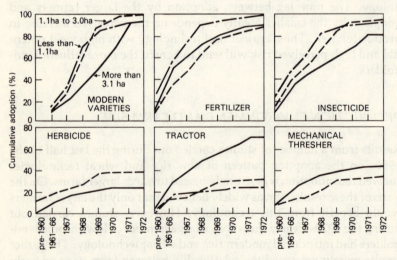

Fig. 6.2. Cumulative percentage of farms in three sizes classes adopting specific innovations. Farms in 30 selected villages in Asia (IRRI, 1978b).

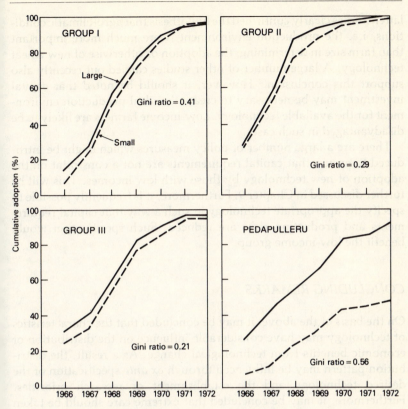

Fig. 6.3. Gini coefficients, farm size and year of adoption of modern varieties in groups of villages in Asia (IRRI, 1978b).

On the basis of the findings from the 30 villages, the authors conclude that

> while labour-saving technology is more likely to be found on large farms, in many locations the adoption of yield-increasing technology appears to be constrained by *relative* not *absolute* farm size. Hence a person's access to the new technology and to the associated modern input is dictated by his power position relative to his neighbors within the village (IRRI, 1978: 89).

Studies in Turkey, Kenya, and Mexico showed that early adopters of modern wheat varieties in most cases were found among the larger farmers. However, smaller farmers followed in adopting these varieties within a relatively short time (Winkelmann, 1977). Results from these latter studies clearly confirmed the hypothesis that agro-climatic conditions, i.e. the production environment, were much more important than farm size in determining; the adoption or otherwise of new wheat technology. A large number of other studies carried out recently also support this conclusion.[2] However, it should be noted that capital investment may be necessary to create the ideal production environment for the available technology. Low-income farmers are likely to be disadvantaged in such cases.

There are a large number of policy measures which might be introduced to ensure that capital requirements are not a constraint on the adoption of new technology by those with low incomes. This will be further discussed in Chapter 9. Furthermore, it is frequently possible to specify the appropriate technology in such a way that capital requirements and production risks are reduced. Such specification would benefit the low-income group.

CONCLUDING REMARKS

On the basis of the above, it may be concluded that the characteristics of technology may have considerable influence on the distribution of economic benefits from technological change. As a result, the distribution pattern may be influenced through *ex ante* specification of the desired technology and the establishment of research priorities. Furthermore, it may be concluded that extreme care should be taken when establishing research priorities on the basis of distributional goals, if this implies that large potential yield increases must be forgone. Modern agricultural technology may be extremely effective in expanding production and improving productivity. Questions of distribution may often be more effectively dealt with by other policy measures. In order to achieve the objectives of both growth and distribution, it is important that agricultural research, technology diffusion and other policy measures be integrated. Some adverse distributional effects may be most effectively corrected through changes in research priorities and technology specifications. Others may best be dealt with through correcting or compensatory public policy measures.

THE STRUCTURE OF THE AGRICULTURAL SECTOR

This may be important for the distribution of economic benefits from agricultural research and modern technology. Structural factors may make the introduction and use of new technology easy for some groups of farmers and difficult or impossible for others. These factors may also have great influence on the extent to which the potential production and productivity improvements are in fact obtained by those adopting new technology. Finally, the structure of the agricultural sector may be important in determining the distribution of economic benefits between landowners and tenants.

IMPACT OF SECTOR STRUCTURE ON BENEFIT DISTRIBUTION

The distribution of economic benefits from new agricultural technology may be greatly influenced by existing land tenure and differential access to capital and factors of production among various groups of farmers. Access to certain factors of production may be vital to guarantee benefits from the introduction of new crop varieties. In cases where certain groups do not have access to such factors of production, the distribution of benefits will obviously be affected.

Although technology characteristics and the structure of the agricultural sector are discussed in different sections, interaction between the two is of paramount importance. The relationship between technological change and the production environment on the one hand, and distribution of the economic benefits associated with technological change, both regional and among large and small farms, on the other, was discussed in the previous section. Clearly, farmers controlling production environments that are favourable to a particular technology are most likely to gain from its introduction.

Access to sufficient water and the possibility of controlling the water supply, as well as access to fertilizers, have been of enormous importance in obtaining economic benefits from the introduction of modern rice and wheat technology. As a result, the adoption of new crop varieties has been associated with a series of attempts to improve water supply. Similarly, fertilizer usage has been greatly expanded in areas where new rice and wheat varieties have been introduced.

However, the introduction of pumps and irrigation facilities as well as fertilizers requires capital. It is therefore important that the existing structure of the agricultural sector permits either accumulation of capital within agriculture or access to credit on reasonable terms. The existing structure of the agricultural sector in many developing countries hampers accumulation of capital among many farmers because of small farm size, lack of infrastructure and lack of political measures to prevent large outflows of capital from the agricultural sector. In some countries this is made worse by the presence of a small group of very large and affluent farmers, who contribute to production expansion and lower prices through the introduction of new technology. The price effect is further discussed in a subsequent section.

Separation of land-ownership and tilling rights through various kinds of tenancy agreements is common in a number of developing countries. The distribution of economic benefits from modern agricultural technology between tenants and landowners depends on the type of tenancy agreements. Tenants are frequently unable to provide the necessary security to obtain credit for the purchase of fertilizers and other factors of production. In some cases, landowners are willing to provide the necessary security. In other cases, tenants may own land of their own and thus be able to provide sufficient guarantee for credit required on both rented and owned land.

In cases where both costs and production are distributed between landowners and tenants in a given proportion, the economic benefit from new technology is likely to be distributed in similar proportions. Tenancy agreements of this nature are common in certain parts of India (Rao, 1975). Sharecropping and other tenancy arrangements implying a sharing of the production without cost-sharing make the introduction of modern technology less advantageous for the tenant, while it may be of great economic benefit for the landowner. Such arrangements are common in a number of developing countries and have undoubtedly reduced the rate of adoption of modern technology. While the tenant must pay the total costs associated with the introduction of the technology, he obtains only part of the gains. On the other hand, landowners wish to see a high degree of technology adoption because they obtain part of the benefits without sharing the costs. The conflict of interest between sharecroppers and landowners has resulted in the termination of many sharecropping and tenancy arrangements in order that the landowner may obtain the full benefit of the available modern technology.

There are several other reasons why tenancy arrangements have been terminated by landowners. Political issues aimed at the protection of tenants by means of ceilings on land rents have helped to make landowners less interested in renting out land. Similarly, mechanical technology, together with increasing yields brought about by new varieties and fertilizers, have contributed to increasing economies of scale. Thus, landowners have tended to terminate tenant arrangements and accumulate a number of small landholdings in order to reap the benefits from such economies.

The tendency to reduce the extent of rented land has been strong in

India (Rao, 1975). In the district of Ferozepur in the Punjab 37 per cent of the total agricultural area was tilled by tenants in 1954–55. In 1969–70 it was down to 12 per cent. Similar, although less drastic, decreases in the extent of rented land took place in certain other districts of India (Rao, 1975).

IMPACT OF TECHNOLOGICAL CHANGE ON SECTOR STRUCTURE

As discussed in the preceding section, the structure of the agricultural sector influences the rate of adoption of new technology and the distribution of associated economic benefits, and vice versa. It has been argued that recent technological change in developing countries has led to increasing polarization of rural communities (Griffin 1972 and 1979; Frankel 1976). It is argued that modern technology has been monopolized by the large farms. As a result of the higher earnings made possible by modern technology, large landowners have terminated land-rental arrangements and purchased land from smaller farmers who did not benefit from modern technology. Furthermore, the argument continues, the process of the concentration of land in fewer hands has made labour-saving mechanization more profitable. The net result is polarization of rural communities into those owning large farms and a landless, frequently unemployed, proletariat.

The argument gained considerable strength during the initial period of the green revolution, during which the adoption of modern technology was strongly biased towards larger farms. However, as mentioned earlier, current empirical evidence clearly shows that the observed bias reflected a time lag between adoption by large and small farmers, and not that small farmers would not adopt modern technology. However, early adopters have in many cases obtained large economic gains, a considerable portion of which has undoubtedly been used to purchase land from non-adopters. Thus, although the time lag in general appears to be much shorter than originally anticipated, there is a danger that by the time small farmers have overcome the obstacles to the adoption of modern technology and increase their productivity, the land resources under their control may be seriously reduced and the number of landless, low-productivity workers increased correspondingly (Berry and Cline, 1979).

While small farmers in general utilize available land more efficiently than those with large farms (Berry and Cline, 1979), policy-makers frequently see large farms as desirable. Therefore, instead of policy measures aimed at reducing the time lag between the adoption of modern technology on large and small farms and hampering the concentration of land-ownership during the lag period, governments may promote such land concentration.

A combination of rapid technological change and policies adverse to small farmers has no doubt led to larger farms and increasing numbers of landless farm workers. Such adverse development is most pronounced in regions where the ownership of land was very skewed prior to the introduction of modern technology, where institutional arrangements and factor markets favoured larger farmers and where public policy in support of small farmers was absent.

DISTRIBUTION OF BENEFITS AMONG FACTORS OF PRODUCTION

Modern agricultural technology may contribute to an increase in the efficiency of one or more factors of production. Likewise, the introduction of modern technology may facilitate increased production, reduced use of a given factor of production or a combination of the two. Unless the efficiency of all factors of production is increased in the same proportions, factor substitution is likely to be economically advantageous. Such factor substitution may have considerable impact on the distribution of economic benefits from technological change.

Resources used in agriculture may be grouped into labour, land, fuel energy, water, chemical materials and other capital inputs. As mentioned in Chapter 2, agricultural technology may be grouped into biological, chemical, mechanical and management technology.

Technological change may also be classified according to its resource bias. Technological change is resource-saving if it brings about greater production with the same amount of the resource, or maintains existing production with a reduction in the amount of the resource used. Similarly, technological change is resource-using if existing production can be maintained only if the quantity of the particular resource used is increased. Thus, if technological change increases production on a given area it is classified as land-saving. Labour-saving technological change refers to where either current output is maintained with a reduced labour input or an increase in output comes about with the current labour input.

The resource bias of technological change should not be confused with factor substitution due to changes in relative factor prices. Confusion may easily occur because such change tends to influence relative factor prices through changes in demand. The magnitude of change in demand for the individual factors of production and the resulting change in factor prices and quantities used depend on the resource bias of the technology, the institutional structure and a series of other variables. The distribution of benefits from technological change among owners of factors of production depends in turn on the change in factor prices and quantities used. Likewise, the factor bias, together with the institutional structure, the structure of the factor market and agricultural policies, greatly influences the functional distribution of benefits from technological change. This implies that in cases where a certain functional distribution is desired, e.g. a large share going to labour, research and technology strategies and related policies must be based on a sound knowledge of the expected factor bias of alternative paths of technological change.

BIOLOGICAL AND CHEMICAL TECHNOLOGY

Most biological technology, e.g. high-yielding varieties, has been labour, land and fuel energy saving and water, chemical resources and other capital input using. Chemical resources, particularly fertilizers, capital inputs and irrigation water, have been substituted for labour, land and, in some cases, fuel energy. But expanded output and higher productivity of labour and land have increased the demand for these resources. Thus, where the supply of agricultural land has been fixed, prices of land suitable for the particular biological technology have increased significantly. Such price increases have been particularly pronounced in areas where most or all suitable land was grown with the crop for which biological technology was introduced, e.g. many rice areas in Asia. In other areas, where suitable land was used for a number of crops, considerable crop substitution has occurred.

Accordingly, a large part of the economic benefits associated with the introduction of modern technology has been capitalized into land values. Those owning land during the period of rapid increase in land values have been major beneficiaries. Land prices have also increased dramatically in areas where the production environment was favourable to modern technology, while those in other areas may have been affected only a little, if at all. The result has been a change in the regional distribution of assets. Results from an analysis carried out in Nueva Ecija, the Philippines, illustrate how modern rice technology has contributed to changes in the regional distribution of assets (IRRI, 1975). Land prices in three regions within the area where the study was carried out were roughly equal in 1966, rice being the dominant crop in all three regions. Two of the regions had access to water for irrigation and thus provided a favourable production environment for new rice technology, but in the third region water supply was exclusively based on rainfall. Modern rice technology was introduced in all three regions, the economic benefits obtained being much larger in the two regions having access to irrigation water than in the one without. As a result, land prices in both these regions increased by 116 per cent while those in the third region during the same period increased by only 65 per cent.

Regarding the effect of biological technology on employment, it is now documented beyond reasonable doubt that the increase in the demand for labour due to increased output has been considerably larger than the labour-saving effect, the net result being an increase in labour demand. In areas with high unemployment and a highly elastic labour supply, this has resulted in a considerable increase in employment. Where there is little unemployment and an inelastic labour supply, whether existing prior to the introduction of, or brought about by, the technology, considerable wage increases have occurred. However, the availability of labour-saving mechanical technology tends to establish limits for such wage increases.

In the Punjab region of India introduction of yield-increasing biological and chemical technology caused an annual increase in the demand for labour of 6.5 per cent during the last half of the 1960s. However, because the rate of unemployment in the region was relatively low, the increase in labour demand was not paralleled by increases in labour supply, in spite of a considerable influx of labour from other regions. As a result, wages increased considerably and, together with a scarcity of labour in the region, contributed to the rapid introduction of mechanization. Introduction of yield-increasing technology in other areas of India has not resulted in similar wage increases, the introduction of labour-saving technology being much less in these regions.

A considerable part of new biological technology depends on fertilizers, irrigation and, to a lesser extent, pesticides to express its full yield-increasing capacity. Thus, the introduction of the kind of biological technology which led to the green revolution has greatly increased the demand for, and use of, fertilizers and other chemical inputs. The introduction of combined biological–chemical technology has been capital-intensive. The importance of this issue and access to inputs was discussed in Chapter 2. However, increasing capital requirements also imply that a considerable portion of the economic benefits associated with new technologies may be acquired by capital owners and producers of capital goods, such as fertilizers, pumps and chemical plant protection measures. Many examples could be cited where private sources of loans to agriculture have obtained enormous profits. Interest rates of 5–10 per cent per month, i.e. annual interest rates of 60–120 per cent, are not unusual for short-term credit in certain regions where modern technology is introduced. In all fairness, it should be noted that the security for these loans may have been very low. The extent to which private sources of agricultural credit are able to obtain such large profits is constrained by publicly supported credit programmes now in existence in many developing countries. The real interest rate on such programmes is frequently low or negative.

Economic gains obtained by the input supply sector, e.g. producers and distributors of fertilizer and other chemical inputs, irrigation equipment and other inputs, have undoubtedly been large, although accurate estimates are unavailable. To the extent that the production and distribution of these inputs were carried out in the individual developing countries, technological change in agriculture may have had a very significant positive impact on employment and incomes outside the agricultural sector.

Some biological technology is chemical resource-saving, both in a relative and in an absolute sense. Examples of such technology are biological nitrogen fixation from the atmosphere and biological insect control. If reduced usage of chemical technology or reduced rates of increase in such usage is a long-term objective of society, emphasis might be placed on developing such technology. One reason for such an objective might be to reduce foreign exchange requirements for import of fertilizers, fertilizer raw materials or fuel energy. Environmental considerations might be another reason. However, as long as fertilizer supplies are plentiful for the individual farmer at reasonable prices, he may have little interest in adopting fertilizer-saving technology. Public policy aimed at the above should consider the effect on output, as well as on the resource and the environment. The environmental effects of technological change are discussed in more detail in Chapter 8.

As mentioned above, the introduction of a considerable part of biological technology is closely linked with the simultaneous introduction of chemical technology. Introduction of chemical technology by itself would tend to have the same resource bias as biological technology. However, there is one important exception. Labour-saving chemical technology with little or no effect on output will reduce net demand for labour. Chemical weed control is an example of such technology.

MECHANICAL TECHNOLOGY

The impact of the introduction of mechanical technology on demands for land and labour depends on whether or not there is an increase in output. Introduction of mechanical technology with a considerable effect on output, e.g. irrigation equipment and mechanization which permits more crops per year on a given area, may cause a considerable increase in the demand for labour and land, although it is labour and land saving. The case is identical to that of biological technology in so far as land and labour are concerned. However, a large part of mechanical technology has little or no effect on output, while the labour-saving effect may be very great. Tractors and farm machinery of various types have reduced the demand for labour in certain regions of developing countries. While many of these technologies have significant effects on output through better land preparation, more timely planting and application of pesticides and reduced harvesting losses, as well as facilitating multiple cropping under certain circumstances, the majority of these effects are not reflected in the demand for labour, because the activities are already mechanized.

Results from a number of analyses show that the introduction of tractors reduced labour use per hectare by 12–27 per cent in parts of India. Introduction of threshing machines for wheat in Punjab reduced labour requirement per hectare by 13 per cent, while the use of combine harvesters caused a reduction in labour use per hectare of 25 per cent (Rao, 1975). A large number of other analyses for wheat and rice shows similar results. Thus, introduction of this type of mechanical technology has reduced employment in agriculture in developing countries.

However, it appears that the introduction of labour-saving technology has, to a very large extent, been a reaction to labour shortage at the local level and difficulties in labour management. In the future, increased mobility of available labour is likely to reduce the increase in labour-saving mechanization in many developing countries. It should be added that labour-saving technology has obviously increased the productivity of the remaining labour force. Thus, wage increases have been made possible and some part, although it is probably a relatively small part, of the economic benefits from labour-saving mechanization has been obtained by the remaining work force.

To the extent that farm machinery, irrigation equipment and other mechanical technology have been produced in the developing countries themselves, employment and capital formation outside the agricultural sector have increased.

THE MARKET STRUCTURE FOR AGRICULTURAL PRODUCTS AND THE PRICE EFFECT

Introduction of yield-increasing technology facilitates increasing production and market supply, which, in turn, may contribute to reduced market prices. The extent to which such price reductions actually occur, as well as the magnitude of such reductions, is of great importance in the distribution of the associated economic benefits.

DISTRIBUTION BETWEEN CONSUMERS AND PRODUCERS AND AMONG PRODUCERS

In a free market the price of a given product is determined on the basis of supply and demand. Assuming a constant demand function, additional food supplies can only be sold in the domestic market at lower prices. In percentage terms the price reduction is usually larger than the increase in supply. As a result, increased output caused by modern technology would result in a reduction in gross incomes to the producer sector, total spending by consumers being reduced correspondingly. Consumers may purchase more, but at a lower total outlay. In such cases, the total economic benefit associated with the introduction of modern technology will be obtained by consumers. This is one of the primary reasons why public funds are used to finance yield-increasing measures, including agricultural research, in countries where increased food supplies would be sold on the domestic market.

Empirical evidence of consumer gains from technological change in agriculture in developing countries is plentiful (e.g. Scobie, 1979b; Scobie and Posada, 1978; Evenson and Flores, 1978; Mellor 1975; Akino and Hayami, 1975). These consumer gains are expressed in terms of lower food prices relative to those expected in the absence of the particular technological change, and may be large. Thus, Scobie and Posada (1978) estimated that Colombian rice consumers gained about $500 million during the period 1957–74 because of the introduction and use of modern technology in Colombian rice production.

But if the agricultural sector loses by introducing modern technology, why is it introduced? The reason is that certain groups within the agricultural sector, such as those first adopting the technology, may obtain large economic benefits, while other groups adopting at a later period or not at all, incur losses. A farmer controlling a production environment for which modern technology is suitable is better off by introducing the technology than by not introducing it, although the sector as a whole may lose from such an introduction.

The above is valid for countries that are more or less self-sufficient in the particular commodity in question, provided that additional quantities of the commodity cannot be exported. The situation is different in countries that either meet part of their domestic demand through imports or have access to export markets. Importing countries may reduce the quantity imported as well as increasing domestic production. Such import substitution will result in smaller price reductions on the domestic market or none at all. A similar situation may be found in cases where production increases can be exported, particularly if the exported quantity occupies a very small proportion of the total world trade for that commodity. Exporting the additional production will not depress domestic prices. In cases of import substitution or increased exports, the agricultural sector may obtain large economic benefits from yield-increasing technology. On the other hand, domestic consumers will obtain little or no economic benefit.

When the introduction of new wheat and rice technology in parts of Asia contributed to large increases in production, import substitution was effective in avoiding large price reductions. Thus, during the period 1966–70, India reduced wheat imports by an amount equal to approximately one-half the increase in domestic wheat production. Similarly, during the same period, Pakistan reduced wheat and rice imports by an amount equal to approximately one-third the increase in domestic production in that country (Pinstrup-Andersen, 1970). Because of these reductions in imports, wheat and rice prices in India and Pakistan remained higher than they would have been had the expanded production been added to existing supplies. As a result, the agricultural sector gained considerably. Large economic gains were also obtained by the consumer sector, but may have been considerably more in the absence of import substitution.

As mentioned above, opportunities for the exportation of expanded production may also facilitate large gains to the agricultural sector. Research and new technology for cotton in Sao Paulo is a case in point. As shown earlier in Table 5.1, the associated annual internal rate of return on investment was estimated at 77 per cent. More than 90 per cent of the total economic gains was obtained by the cotton producers (Ayer, 1970). Research and new technology for rape in Canada is another example. Nagy and Furtan (1978) estimated that about one-half of the total associated economic benefits was obtained by the producers. A considerable proportion of Canadian rape is exported. Therefore, the price-reducing effect of increases in production was much less than it would have been in the absence of exportation. It is for these reasons that producers of export commodities are frequently willing to finance measures to increase yields, such as agricultural research, extension, etc. The above-mentioned research on cotton in Brazil was to a very large extent paid for by the producers themselves, and it is not difficult to find examples of producer associations financing research on export crops. Producers of basic food commodities aimed at the domestic market are not usually willing to finance agricultural research on their commodities, simply because they as a group are unlikely to benefit to any great extent.

As mentioned earlier, import substitution and export are not the only possibilities for avoiding price reductions when output-expanding technology is introduced. Food prices in developing countries are very often manipulated through government price policy. Such policy measures have been used in some countries to avoid excessive price reductions when successful yield-expanding technology was adopted. In fact, the nature of the price policy may greatly influence both the rate of adoption and the distribution of benefits.

DISTRIBUTION AMONG CONSUMER GROUPS

An analysis of the distribution of benefit between consumers and producers is useful in estimating the transfer of resources from one sector to the other in a comparative sense, and information on this issue may assist in deciding on possible corrective policy measures or preparing to deal with the consequences. However, the analysis does not explain the equity implications of new technology within the sectors. The income disparities within each of the two sectors may well be much larger than that existing between the sectors. Many developing countries have a large number of poor farmers; however, they also usually have a large number of poor consumers (non-farmers). Likewise, a relatively small number of very wealthy people may be found in both sectors. Hence, an analysis of the equity implications must look at the distribution of benefits by income group within each sector. The issue of principal interest here is: How large are the benefits obtained by the poor? Distribution of benefits among income groups within the producer sector was discussed previously. This section takes a look at the distribution among income groups within the consumer sector.

Relatively few analyses have been carried out on this topic. Two studies of the distribution of benefits from new rice technology (Scobie and Posada, 1977; Hayami and Herdt, 1977) estimated the distribution among consumer income groups as the relative price reduction multiplied by the budget proportion spent on rice. If all consumers are faced with the same market, and therefore the same decline in rice prices, the distribution of benefits is then proportional to the proportion of the budget spent by each income stratum. The proportion spent on rice in both cases was inversely correlated with per capita income, something that would generally be found for basic food commodities. Hence, a decline in rice prices would result in a percentage increase in real incomes, inversely correlated with income levels, and it was concluded that new yield-increasing agricultural technology for rice would provide larger relative gains to poor consumers than to those more affluent.

These findings were supported by the results of an analysis of the distribution of benefits associated with output expansion in each of a number of food commodities in Cali, Colombia (Pinstrup-Andersen, 1977). According to these results, low-income consumers obtained larger absolute gains than did higher-income consumers from output-expanding technology for the basic staple foods (cassava, maize and plantain). For all the other foods, the absolute gain obtained by low-income consumers was smaller than that obtained by those with higher incomes. However, for most of these foods, the gain expressed as a percentage of current incomes, i.e. relative real income improvements, was largest for the poor. Furthermore, the distribution of benefits from output-expanding technology was less skewed than existing income distribution for all foods. This means that in the absence of government intervention, new technology tends to modify existing income distribution in favour of those with low incomes. More empirical studies are needed to test the general validity of the findings of this study.

Calorie and protein deficiencies are a serious problem in many developing countries. Such deficiencies are closely correlated with income levels. Hence, the extent to which new technology can reduce these deficiencies might also be used as a measure of the equity implications of new technology. An analysis of this issue was carried out for the population of Cali, Colombia (Pinstrup-Andersen, Londono and Hoover (1976)). The study estimated the distribution of increases in each of 22 food commodities among consumer groups (nutrient-deficient and non-nutrient-deficient groups), the related adjustments in total food consumption for each group and the implications for calorie and protein intake. It was found that the relative increase in total nutrients was a poor indicator of the relative impact on nutrition. There are three principal reasons for this: (1) the proportion of the total increase in supply obtained by nutrient-deficient groups varies considerably among commodities; (2) the adjustment in the consumption of foods, other than those for which the supply is increased, is of considerable importance in determining the final nutritional implications; (3) the nutritional effects of changes in income may not be closely correlated with the magnitude of changes in the supply of nutrients.

Hence, the choice of commodity priorities in agricultural research may greatly influence the resulting distribution of benefits among consumer groups, as well as the effect on nutrition. The purpose of the above analysis was to assist in establishing commodity priorities in research and technology development, if improved nutrition is a goal. The analysis estimated the effect of a hypothetical expansion in supply rather than evaluating the effect after it had occurred.

Analyses of the nutritional impact of accomplished technological change in agricultural are scarce. Intuitively, one would expect that expanded food production would result in improved human nutrition. However, substitution among food commodities in production, consumption and/or foreign trade, as well as the actual distribution of the additional food between malnourished and well-nourished people may greatly influence the extent of nutritional improvement actually obtained. There has been some concern that the expansion of the area grown with rice and wheat brought about by the green revolution may have had adverse nutritional effects, because the area under other commodities, such as food legumes, has been reduced. A study of the position in India (Ryan, 1977) concluded that the net effect of the green revolution on the production of energy, protein and essential amino acids has in fact been positive and large, in spite of some substitution of wheat for food legumes on agricultural land.

THE SEMI-SUBSISTENCE FARMER

In the previous analysis it was assumed that the proportion of production retained by the producers for home consumption was small. Hence, the possible gains by producers in their capacity as consumers were ignored. But if a large part of the total farm production is used for home consumption, as in the case of semi-subsistence farming, these gains should not be ignored as consumer gains are partly acquired by the producers. Thus, new technology may influence the real income of the semi-subsistence farmer through changes in consumer as well as producer gains. This issue is of importance in many developing countries because semi-subsistence farmers account for a large proportion of the low-income population.

It has been estimated that the introduction of modern rice technology in the Philippines increased the incomes of semi-subsistence farmers, while reducing those in the commercial farming sector (Hayami and Herdt, 1977). The analysis concludes that modern technology has promoted a more equal income distribution within agriculture 'through downward pressures on prices and hence on the incomes of those farmers with a large proportion of marketed surplus' (Hayami and Herdt, 1977).

AGRICULTURAL POLICY

The relationship between various policy measures and the distribution of benefits from technological change has been discussed in the preceding sections of this chapter. Furthermore, policy measures needed to facilitate the desired distribution and correct and/or compensate for undesired distributional effects are discussed in Chapter 9. Thus, to avoid repetition, this section is limited to a brief summary of some of the policies that have had a significant impact on the distribution of benefits from past technological change.

In some countries, government policy aimed at facilitating access to modern factors of production, such as fertilizers, among small farmers, has greatly reduced the existing institutional and input-market biases against these farmers. Government credit programmes, improvements in input-distribution systems, intensive production programmes combining input-delivery schemes, credit, advisory services, input subsidies, and output price support, have been very effective in some countries, e.g. the Masagana 99 Programme in the Philippines (Alix, 1978). Price policies have greatly influenced this distribution of benefits between consumers and producers and among groups within each of the two sectors. In some cases, these policies have benefited the producers by avoiding drastic price reductions. In other cases, a continuation of a cheap food policy has been adverse to the sector while advantageous to consumers, at least in the short run. Some countries have maintained foreign trade and exchange-rate policies adverse to the producer sector. In other cases, such policies have been favourable to that sector. Some countries have introduced or maintained foreign trade and exchange-rate policies favouring the importation of labour-saving technology, while others have introduced import taxes on agricultural inputs such as fertilizers. The latter have been used for generating government revenue, reducing foreign exchange spending and protecting domestic fertilizer production.

In some countries, public investment in rural infrastructure and integrated rural development has been accelerated in an attempt to promote technological change and output expansion among small farmers in remote areas, and improve the standard of living in these areas. Public policy measures aimed at influencing the distribution of benefits from technological change between tenants and landowners have been introduced in some countries. However, measures to deal with one of the principal causes of biased distribution of benefits from technological change in many countries – skewed distribution of land-owner-ship – have been almost totally lacking in almost all developing countries. Instead, public policy has facilitated, or at least not hindered, trends towards increasing the concentration of land in fewer hands in some areas where technological change has been widespread and the landowner-ship bias severe. As a result of the lack of political will and the inability of governments to promote a more even distribution of resource ownership or avoid an even more uneven distribution, technological change has in fact contributed to a more uneven distribution of incomes and assets in some rural areas. The full blame for such developments should be accepted as being due to faulty economic policy and not to research and technology.

NOTES

1. However, international varietal testing networks maintained within the international agricultural research system facilitate a more widespread testing and evaluation of new plant materials, and efforts are also being made to carry out such testing and evaluation under non-optimal conditions.
2. References to such studies may be found in Scobie (1979b), Ruttan (1977) and Singh (1979).

7 *The role of fertilizers*

Fertilizers have contributed more to the improvement of crop yields in developing countries than any other individual factor of production during recent years. While the use of fertilizers is still responsible for only a small proportion of the total agricultural production in most developing countries, a large part of the increases in production and yield obtained during the last 25 years is associated with expanded fertilizer usage.

As mentioned in Chapter 2, the response to fertilizers depends on the extent to which other factors of production and modern technology are used. Similarly, the yield increase obtained from the use of such factors, for example improved crop varieties, irrigation, etc. depends on the quantity of fertilizers applied. Interaction between the use of fertilizers and other technology plays an important role in relation to the effectiveness of agricultural research and the resulting modern technology.

This interaction, together with the paramount importance of fertilizers in efforts to expand crop yields in developing countries, seem to warrant an analysis of some of the most important issues related to this factor of production. The purpose of the present chapter is to provide such an analysis. The extent of fertilizer usage and the contribution of fertilizers to food production are treated first. Then follows an analysis of factors expected to restrict the contribution of fertilizers to an accelerated rate of increase in food production, and a discussion of ways to remove these factors with emphasis on the role of public policy measures.

FERTILIZER CONSUMPTION IN DEVELOPING COUNTRIES

The consumption of chemical fertilizers in developing countries during the year 1977/78 amounted to 16.3 million tons of nitrogen (N), 7 million tons of phosphorus (P_2O_5) and 3.2 million tons of potash (K_2O) (Table 7.1). These amounts correspond to slightly more than one-third of the total world consumption of nitrogen, about one-fourth of the world consumption of phosphorus fertilizers and about 14 per cent of

Table 7. Fertilizer consumption by region 1977/78.

	Nitrogen (N)		Phosphorus (P$_2$O$_5$)		Potash (K$_2$O)	
	Million tons	% of world cons.	Million tons	% of world cons.	Million tons	% of world cons.
Developing ME*	9.7	20.3	5.2	18.4	2.6	11.1
Africa	0.5	1.0	0.4	1.4	0.2	0.8
Latin America	2.6	5.5	2.2	7.8	1.4	6.0
Near East	1.5	3.1	0.9	3.2	0.1	0.4
Far East	5.1	10.7	1.7	6.0	0.9	3.9
Developing CE†	6.6	13.9	1.8	6.4	0.6	2.6
Developed ME	19.7	41.3	13.1	46.5	11.5	49.4
Western Europe	8.8	18.5	5.6	19.9	5.2	22.3
North America	9.7	20.3	5.2	18.4	5.3	22.8
Others	1.2	2.5	2.3	8.2	1.0	4.3
Developed CE	11.7	24.5	8.1	28.7	8.6	36.9
Total	47.7	100.0	28.2	100.0	23.3	100.0
Developing countries	16.3	34.2	7.0	24.8	3.2	13.7
Developed countries	31.4	65.8	21.2	75.2	20.1	86.3

* ME = market oriented economies.
† CE = centrally planned economies.

Source: FAO, *Monthly Bulletin of Agricultural Economies and Statistics*, **2** (April) 1979, 25–6.

potash consumption. Among developing regions, the Far East is responsible for a large share of nitrogen consumption, while Latin America accounts for a relatively large proportion of the consumption of phosphorus and potash.

The consumption of fertilizers has increased substantially during the last 25 years (Fig. 7.1). The increase has been particularly spectacular for nitrogen fertilizers. Although the percentage increase in nitrogen consumption has been higher in developing than in developed countries, the latter show the largest absolute increase.

Fertilizer consumption per unit area for the various regions is shown in Table 7.2. On average, developing countries used less than 28 kg/ha in 1976/77. In comparison, developed countries used about 107 kg/ha, or about four times as much as developing countries. The use of fertilizers in developing countries quadrupled from the first half of the 1960s to 1976/77. In developed countries, on the other hand, fertilizer usage was slightly more than doubled during the same period. However, in absolute terms, the increase in developed countries (57.4 kg/ha) exceeded by far that in developing countries (20.7 kg/ha). Among developing regions, fertilizer usage per unit area is high in the centrally planned economies dominated by China.

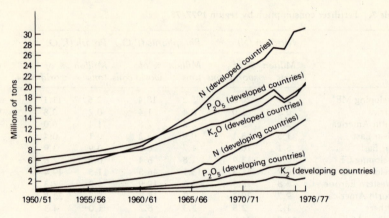

Fig. 7.1. Fertilizer consumption in developing and developed countries, 1950/51–1976/77. (Based on data from UNIDO, 1978).

The economically optimal quantities of fertilizers per unit area may be smaller in developing than in developed countries, as will be substantiated in a subsequent section. However, it is very unlikely that the large and increasing difference between fertilizer consumption in the two groups of countries can be explained exclusively on the grounds of differences in the optimal quantities. Thus, increasing fertilizer usage in developing countries would undoubtedly lead to economically sound increases in agricultural production. But how can fertilizer usage be expanded at an accelerated rate? To answer this question it is necessary to identify the factors limiting current fertilizer usage. Such identification will be attempted in subsequent sections of this chapter. But before turning to the limiting factors and ways of removing them, attention will be given to the projected increase in fertilizer consumption until the year 2000 and the impact of fertilizers on food production in the past.

FERTILIZER DEMAND FORECASTS

Fertilizer demand by developing countries in the year 2000 is projected to be about four times the 1977/78 consumption (Table 7.3). The relative increase is about the same for the three major types of fertilizers. In absolute terms, the projected increase in nitrogen demand is much larger than that in the other two types of fertilizer. During this period the annual percentage rate of increase is expected to fall, while the absolute annual increase is expected to rise. Thus, the annual rate of increase in nitrogen demand falls from 8.7 to about 5 per cent, while the

Table 7.2 Consumption of fertilizer per hectare of arable land and permanent crops (kg/ha).

	Nitrogen (N)		Phosphorus (P$_2$O$_5$)		Potash (K$_2$O)		Total		Increase in total 1961/65–1976/77	
	1961/65	1976/77	1961/65	1976/77	1961/65	1976/77	1961/65	1976/77	kg/ha	%
Developing ME	3.3	13.0	1.5	6.6	0.8	3.1	5.7	22.8	17.1	300
Africa	0.7	2.9	0.6	2.3	0.4	1.2	1.7	6.3	4.6	271
Latin America	5.1	15.8	3.4	13.1	2.1	7.6	10.6	36.6	26.0	245
Near East	4.8	20.2	1.7	11.5	0.2	0.6	6.6	32.4	25.8	391
Far East	3.8	16.3	1.2	4.7	0.6	2.8	5.7	23.8	18.1	318
Developing CE	8.8	35.5	3.6	11.7	1.0	3.5	13.4	50.7	37.3	279
Developed ME	24.0	50.7	24.0	33.9	18.9	29.3	66.9	113.9	47.0	70
Western Europe	39.9	87.6	40.0	57.0	36.9	51.1	116.8	195.7	78.9	68
North America	18.3	44.2	14.7	24.3	11.6	23.9	44.6	92.4	47.8	107
Developed CE	9.6	40.5	7.7	25.1	8.9	32.0	26.2	97.6	71.4	273
Total	10.8	30.3	9.1	17.8	7.4	15.5	27.2	63.6	36.4	134
Developing countries	4.3	16.9	1.9	7.5	0.8	3.2	7.0	27.7	20.7	296
Developed countries	18.0	46.5	17.1	30.3	14.7	30.4	49.8	107.2	57.4	115

Source: FAO, *Annual Fertilizer Review*, 1977.

Table 7.3 Fertilizer demand forecast for developing countries up to the year 2000.

	Nitrogen (N)		Phosphorus (P$_2$O$_5$)		Potash (K$_2$O)	
	Million tons	Index	Million tons	Index	Million tons	Index
1977/78 (actual)	16.3	100	7.0	100	3.2	100
1982/83	22.8	140	10.3	147	4.6	144
1987/88	32.7	201	14.5	207	6.6	206
2000/01	63.5	390	27.9	399	12.4	388

Source: UNIDO (1978: 261).

annual increase in quantity rises from about 1.1 to 2.2 million tons.

It is expected that demand for fertilizers by developing countries will increase rapidly during the next 20–25 years. Whether this increasing demand will be matched by a similar increase in supply depends on many factors. Although a fuller discussion of some of these factors is presented later in this chapter, it should be pointed out here that absolute scarcity of rock phosphate and potash is not a limiting factor at present and is not likely to become so in the foreseeable future. There are sufficient quantities of these raw materials readily available to meet demand for a long time to come. This point is made in an attempt to remove the widespread misunderstanding that the world is close to running out of these raw materials. However, the costs associated with the mining and processing of the raw materials are likely to increase over time because raw materials of the highest quality and which are most accesible will be used first. The future availability of natural gas for the production of nitrogen is somewhat less certain. Future availability and prices of fossil fuel and other energy sources may exercise a considerable influence on future fertilizer supply and production costs.

THE CONTRIBUTION OF FERTILIZERS TO FOOD PRODUCTION

DEVELOPING COUNTRIES

As mentioned at the beginning of this chapter, fertilizers have played a major role in the expansion of agricultural production in developing countries during the last 15–25 years. But exactly how important have fertilizers been? What proportion of the increase in production can be attributed to increased fertilizer usage? No precise answer can be provided because of the interaction between response to fertilizers and a series of other factors such as climatic variations, use of other inputs, etc. Attempts to isolate the output effects of fertilizers from those of improved crop varieties and better water management in a situation where the effect of either of the three depends on the other two, may enjoy only limited success and may in certain cases be irrelevant. What is of more practical interest is the aggregate output effect of the package of practices, not each one individually. However, where fertilizer is the limiting factor it does make sense to estimate the output effect of this factor of production alone.

In accordance with the law of diminishing returns, the response to fertilizers would tend to be inversely correlated with the quantity applied. Thus, the response would be expected to be greater in developing than in developed countries because fertilizer consumption is less in the former than in the latter. On average, this is likely to be true. However, the difference in response to fertilizers between the two groups of countries is much less than would be expected on the basis of the difference in the quantities of fertilizers applied. In other words, it cannot be assumed that the two groups of countries are operating on the same response function. For any given level of fertilizer consumption per unit area, the average response would be considerably higher for developed than for developing countries because the former generally operates on a higher response curve. This curve in developed countries is due to better crop varieties, production methods, disease and insect control, water management, soil characteristics and other factors which together facilitate a higher technological level of agriculture.

It should be pointed out that the above refers to averages for the two groups of countries. Within the group of developing countries, fertilizer usage is often concentrated in certain regions and on certain crops. In such regions and for such crops the quantity of fertilizer used per unit area may be as high as those used in developed countries. Thus, average usage in developing countries represents very high usage levels in some regions and crops, and very little or no usage in others.

An average response rate of 10 kg of grain for each kilogram of fertilizer (measured in N, P_2O_5 and K_2O) is frequently assumed for developing countries as a whole. This average figure is supported by a number of studies. On the basis of 385 observations from 20 Asian countries, Timmer (1976) concluded that the average response to nitrogen in rice was 12–13 kg of grain per kilogram of nitrogen (measured as N). Similarly, Herdt and Barker (1975) found that the average response to nitrogen in rice in Asia was 10–15 kg of grain per kilogram of N. Nitrogen accounts for about two-thirds of the total fertilizer consumption in Asia. Thus, if it is assumed that the above response rates to nitrogen can be obtained only if an amount of phosphorus and potash fertilizers equal to one-third of total fertilizer usage is added, the response to total fertilizer usage is 8–10 kg of grain per kilogram of fertilizers. Such estimates should, of course, be considered as crude approximations only, and may vary greatly from one region to another (Table 7.4). Similarly, crude estimates for developed countries would be about 4–7 kg of grain per kilogram of fertilizers (Pinstrup-Andersen, 1980).

The above average response rates may be used to estimate the contribution of fertilizers to food production. However, because of the uncertainty associated with these estimates, an additional or alternative approach is desirable. A production function approach provides such an alternative.

The contribution of fertilizers to increases in production and yield for grain in market-oriented developing countries during the period 1948/52–1972/73 was estimated using both a production function approach and a response ratio of 10:1 (Pinstrup-Andersen, 1976). The production function used was developed by Evenson (1974) for 20 developing countries for the period 1948–71. The results obtained from the two estimates are shown in Table 7.5. The total increase in annual grain production from the beginning to the end of the period was estimated to be about one hundred and fifty-five million tons. Using the ratio of 10:1 it was estimated that about forty-eight million tons, or 31 per cent of the total increase were due to increasing fertilizer usage. Using the production function, it was estimated that increasing fertilizer usage was responsible for about 30 per cent of the total increase in grain production. Thus, the two approaches produced virtually identical results. Fertilizers were responsible for about one-third of the total increase in Asian grain production, but only one-fifth in Africa.

The increase in grain production came about partly through an increase in the area under cultivation and partly through increasing yields per unit area. Although fertilizer may play an important role in facilitating economically sound expansion of the agricultural area, its production effects show up through increased yields per unit area. If we consider only that part of the increase in grain production due to improved yields, that due to the use of fertilizers amounted to more than one-half. Fertilizer usage was responsible for about 85 per cent of the improved yields in the Near East, about 65 per cent in Latin America and 43–49 per cent in the Far East.

It can be seen that increased use of fertilizers played a large part in the improvement of production and yield of grains in market-oriented developing countries. On the other hand, the use of fertilizer per unit area is still low in these countries. Therefore, the role of fertilizers in

Table 7.4 Estimated yield increases due to application of fertilizer on six crops in eight developing countries.

Crops	Country	Period	Quantity of fertilizers applied (kg/ha)*	Average yields increase %	Per kg fertilizers*
Groundnuts	Ghana	1961–65	22	33	15.7
	Senegal	1964–66	45	39	8.9
Maize	El Salvador	1962–65	90	38	10.8
Millet	Senegal	1962–66	42	40	5.6
Rice (paddy)	Bangladesh	1971	100	124	11.6
	Ghana	1963–65	22	43	29.4
	Philippines	1973–74	30	9–12	10.6–16.3
	Senegal	1961–66	45	30	7.4
Wheat (unirr.)	Morocco	1964–65	60	72	12.0
	Turkey	1962–66	60	58	8.9
Wheat (irr.)	Turkey	1964–66	60	77	17.6

* $N + P_2O_5 + K_2O$.

Source: FAO/FIAC, *Fertilizer Subsidies, Alternative Policies*, Rome 1976, p. 36.

Table 7.5 Estimated contribution of fertilizer to cereal grain production in developing market economies, 1948/52–1972/73.

Item	Africa	Latin America	Near East	Far East	Developing market economies
Total increase in annual cereal production ('000 tonnes)	12.339	40.527	21.000	81.518	155.413
Estimated increase due to fertilizer ('000 tonnes)*	2.523	10.779	9.240	26.226	48.243
Percentage of total production increase due to fertilizer*	20.4	26.6	44.2	32.2	31.0
Percentage of total yield increase due to fertilizer*	36.4	64.9	84.2	49.2	57.0
Percentage of total production increase due to fertilizer†	–	27.1	32.5	28.0	29.8
Percentage of total yield increase due to fertilizer†	–	66.1	85.1	42.8	54.8
Percentage of total production 1972/73 due to fertilizer‡	6.6	16.2	19.1	15.0	15.2

* Estimated on the basis of increases in fertilizer use for cereals and an average response rate of 10 kg of cereal grains per 1 kg of fertilizer (nutrients).

† Estimated on the basis of production function.

‡ Total production due to fertilizer estimated on the basis of the average response rate of 10 : 1.

Source: Pinstrup-Andersen (1976a).

total current grain production would be expected to be much less pronounced. This expectation is supported by the above estimations which showed that the effect of fertilizers corresponded to about 15 per cent of the total grain production in these countries in 1972/73. The importance of fertilizers in total grain production was highest in the Near East and lowest in Africa (Table 7.5).

The above estimates should be considered as crude approximations because of the estimation procedures used. However, the similarity of the results from the two approaches provides some indication (but by no means proof!) that the results are within an acceptable margin of error.

Further indication to that effect is provided by the results of other studies. Herdt and Barker (1975) estimated that 13.5 per cent of the total grain production in Asia and 51 per cent of yield increases were due to fertilizers (Table 7.6). The role of fertilizers in both total grain production and the production increase varied considerably among countries. Thus, in South Korea and Taiwan about one-half of the total grain production can be attributed to the use of fertilizers. On the other hand, it was a regligible factor in total grain production in Thailand and Nepal. Fertilizer usage was estimated to account for more than half of the increases in yield in India, Bangladesh, Pakistan and Nepal during 1970/71–1971/72, while in Sri Lanka and Thailand it was relatively unimportant.

Table 7.6 Estimated impact of fertilizers on rice production in a number of Asian countries.

Country	% of total rice production due to fertilizers 1971/72	% of rice yield increase 1970/71—1971/72 due to fertilizers
Bangladesh	3.1	60.0
India	11.4	69.9
Iran	7.0	22.7
Nepal	1.1	55.0
Pakistan	19.4	55.6
Sri Lanka	3.4	3.3
Indonesia	6.5	23.3
Philippines	13.5	41.5
Thailand	1.6	7.2
Japan	34.1	n.a.*
South Korea	56.1	n.a.
Taiwan	46.0	n.a.
Total for region	13.5	51.2†

* Not available.
† Japan, South Korea and Taiwan not included.

Source: Herdt and Barker (1975).

In another study, the US Department of Agriculture (1965) concluded that 20–66 per cent of the increase in agricultural production of 26 developing countries during the period 1949–63 was due to the use of fertilizers.

The elasticity of production with respect to fertilizers is another method of measurement of the importance of changes in fertilizer usage in agricultural production (elasticity of production expresses the percentage change in the production of the commodity in question caused by a 1 per cent change in the quantity used of a given input). Table 7.7 shows estimates for 11 Asian countries. According to these estimates, a 1 per cent increase in fertilizer usage in Japan would result in an expansion of the Japanese agricultural production equal to 0.75 per cent of current production. The same percentage increase in Nepal would result in an expansion of that country's agricultural production by 0.06 per cent.

Table 7.7 Estimated production elasticity for fertilizers in a number of Asian countries.

Country	Production elasticity
Japan	0.73
Taiwan	0.69
South Korea	0.41
Pakistan	0.20
Philippines	0.20
Thailand	0.19
Sri Lanka	0.18
Indonesia	0.18
Iran	0.16
India	0.15
Nepal	0.06

Source: Chujiro Ozaki (1975).

Fertilizer has played an increasing role in efforts to expand food production in developing countries. This point is illustrated by Mellor (1976) for India. Fertilizers accounted for 8 per cent of the increase in Indian food-grain production during the first half of the 1950s, increasing to 11 per cent during the second half. During the first and second halves of the 1960s, the figure had risen to 38 and 59 per cent respectively, and estimates of future potential increases in food-grain production indicate that the contribution of fertilizers will be as high as 79 per cent by 1983/84 (Mellor, 1976: 33)

COMPARISON WITH DEVELOPED COUNTRIES

Since fertilizer consumption per unit area is considerably higher in developed than in developing countries, the proportion of total grain production that could be attributed to fertilizers would also be expected to be higher. Results from studies in the United States support this expectation. Thus, the Council for Agricultural Science and Technology (1974) estimated that about one-third of the total US grain production was due to the use of fertilizers.

Both grain yields and fertilizer usage have increased more in developed than in developing countries during the last 25–30 years. Thus, fertilizer usage is assumed to have made a greater contribution to the growth in grain production in the former countries. However, there is no apparent reason why the *proportion* of the yield increase due to fertilizer should differ between the two groups of countries. Results from studies on US agriculture support the hypothesis that no such difference exists. Christensen et al. (1964) estimated that 55 per cent of the yield increases in US grain production during the period 1940–55 was due to increasing fertilizer usage. Estimates related to the total agricultural production rather than to grains alone are somewhat lower. Thus, Heady et al. (1965) estimate that about 45 per cent of yield increases in US agriculture were due to fertilizer while that of Ibach (1966) is as low as 36 per cent.

Looking finally at the effect of fertilizers on total world production of grain, it was estimated that between 28 and 47 per cent of the increase in world grain production during the period 1948/52–1972/73 was due to the use of fertilizers (Pinstrup-Andersen, 1976b).

Although the margin of error of the estimates reported in this section may be large, the evidence very strongly supports the argument that fertilizers have been of paramount importance in bringing about the increases in yields of grain in developing as well as developed countries during the last 25 years.

Most of the above estimates referred to average rather than marginal effects of fertilizers. A large average effect does not necessarily imply that expanded fertilizer usage result in large yield increases, i.e. the marginal effect may be small. In fact, it appears that in some cases the marginal effect of one or more fertilizers may be zero or negative. Such cases are mostly found in countries or regions with very high levels of fertilizer usage. In most countries with low usage, i.e. most developing countries, a high average effect will probably imply a high marginal effect. Thus, expanded fertilizer usage offers great opportunities to developing countries in their efforts to accelerate agriculture production in the future. But such expansion must be coordinated with other production-expanding programmes because of the close interaction between the response to fertilizers and other factors of production and technology. Futhermore, efforts to expand economically sound fertilizer usage must be based on knowledge and understanding of the factors determining or influencing such usage. The following section is focused on this issue.

FACTORS INFLUENCING FERTILIZER USAGE

Fertilizer use is determined primarily by fertilizer and agricultural product prices, the response to fertilizers and the presence or absence of constraints to fertilizer use, such as lack of knowledge, risk and uncertainty, lack of credit and limited fertilizer availability.

One condition that must always be met if fertilizer usage is to be extended in countries where the individual farmer is free to decide on the use of fertilizer and other factors of production is that it should be profitable. It follows that succesful government policy aimed at expanding the use of fertilizers must either provide the farmer with an economic incentive or remove or reduce the effect of existing constraints to obtaining the associated potential economic benefits.

Economic incentives may be provided through a reduction of fertilizer prices, an increase in agricultural product prices or an increase in the agronomic response to fertilizer through better balance of nutrients, better timing or placement and application and other inputs (water supply, improved varieties, etc.). Policy measures aimed at each of these three objectives are discussed in the following. Then follows a discussion of constraints (other than price) to expand fertilizer use, and possible policy measures to remove such constraints.

FERTILIZER PRICES AND SUBSIDIES

Lower fertilizer prices would normally increase fertilizer use unless the presence of certain constraints prohibits such increase. The relationship between price change and the corresponding change in the quantity demanded is measured by the price elasticity of demand. This term expresses the percentage change in quantity demanded caused by a 1 per cent change in the price. The magnitude of this term is extremely important in estimating the impact of price policies on fertilizer use. Although elasticity estimates are subject to varying degrees of error, it appears that, for each 1 per cent decrease in the fertilizer price in many developing countries, the quantity demanded would tend to increase by 0.5–1.0 per cent in the short run, and by 1–2 per cent in the long run.

The price elasticity of demand for fertilizer varies among locations, types of fertilizers and other variables. The nitrogen/rice price ratio and nitrogen usage per unit area is shown in Table 7.8 for a number of Asian countries. Although such a comparison covers a number of factors influencing nitrogen usage, the effect of the price level is sufficiently strong to show a clear relationship between the price ratio and the level of nitrogen usage. Similar findings are reported by Timmer and Falcon (1975).

The price responsiveness of fertilizer demand has led governments to subsidize fertilizer prices in order to expand usage. Direct price subsidies for fertilizer are very common in developing countries. Dalrymple (1975) lists 20 African, 12 Asian and 3 Latin American countries that had direct subsidies in the 1960s and early 1970s. As shown in Table 7.9, the level of subsidy varies considerably. It is not uncommon to find price subsidies that amount to about one-half of the retail price. Thus, even though the quantities of fertilizer may be small, government expenditure on these subsidies may be large.

Table 7.10 shows annual government expenditure on fertilizer subsidies in eight developing and five developed countries during the period 1969–75. This expenditure is compared to that on agricultural research in the same countries. As shown, public funds allocated to fertilizer subsidies in the developing countries exceed by far those allocated to agricultural research. Research expenditure in the largest of

Table 7.8 The interaction between the nitrogen/rice price ratio and rice yields in selected countries, 1973.

Country	Nitrogen/paddy rice price ratio	Paddy rice yield (tons/ha)
Burma	4.84	3.5
Thailand	4.03	4.3
India	3.73	11.1
Philippines	2.63	14.8
Pakistan	2.55	17.2
Indonesia	2.43	18.9
Malaysia	2.08	36.6
Bangladesh	1.82	13.9
Sri Lanka	1.23	25.9
Japan	0.77	145.4
South Korea	0.66	172.3

Source: Mudahar and Pinstrup-Andersen (1977).

Table 7.9 Fertilizer price subsidies as a percentage of retail prices without subsidy, 1969—71.*

Country	Nitrogen	Phosphorus	Potash
Bangladesh	56	55	65
Botswana	—	29	—
Cameroon	20	20	20
Chile	50	50	50
Gambia	—	24	—
Ghana	37	38	28
India†	25—50	25—50	25—50
Ivory Coast	33	33	33
Kenya	—	24	—
Khmer	34	—	34
Lesotho	11	24	—
Libya	50	50	50
Malagasy Republic	6	—	25
Mali	15	20	30
Nigeria	50	50	50
Pakistan	30	56	14
Senegal	48	46	27
Sierra Leone	30	40	—
Sri Lanka	50	50	50
Tunisia	20	50	—
Uganda	50	50	50
Uruguay	20	35	—
Zambia	34	29	50

* In some countries, the level of subsidy differs among type of fertilizer within nitrogen, phosphorus and potash. In these cases, the subsidy used for the most commonly used type is shown.
† The subsidy level varies among regions.

Source: Dalrymple (1975a).

these countries, Indonesia, is less than 5 per cent of that on fertilizer subsidies. Thus, much larger sums of money are used to reduce the price of existing technology (fertilizer) than to develop new technology through research. However, as mentioned in Chapter 2, the effect of fertilizer on agricultural production depends on improved crop varieties, better water management and other improved management practices, the greater part of which can be obtained only through research. Hence, it is important to maintain a proper balance between efforts to expand fertilizer usage and those to develop new and complementary technology.

The sustained effect of fertilizer subsidies may be very limited. If subsidies are discontinued, fertilizer usage will be reduced. On the other hand, investment in agricultural research is likely to have a much stronger sustained effect. A better crop variety or a more suitable type

Table 7.10 Fertilizer subsidy and agricultural research expenditure in selected countries (1969–75).

Country	Subsidy expd. (US$ m.)	Agric. res. exp. (US$ m.)	Subsidy as % of agric. res. exp. (%)
Developing			
Afghanistan	15.10	0.63	2,397
Bangladesh	14.63	1.40	1,045
Indonesia	71.90	3.42	2,102
Iran	36.08	16.66	217
South Korea	27.26	2.44	1,117
Pakistan	20.97	1.26	1,664
Philippines	36.77	7.96	462
Sri Lanka	5.25	2.44	215
Developed			
Australia	110.49	133.90	97
Austria	2.11	4.50	47
Greece	4.79	4.57	105
New Zealand	27.07	28.60	95
UK	75.38	60.20	125

Source: Muhadar and Pinstrup-Andersen (1977).

of fertilizer provide a more sustained and long-term effect on agricultural production than fertilizer price subsidies because government expenditure on the latter must be continued year after year to maintain the effect.

Therefore, while fertilizer subsidies may be an effective means of expanding agricultural production in the short run if fertilizers are a major limiting factor, they are unlikely to provide a long-term solution to the food and agricultural problem.

Subsidies may be paid directly to the farmer, to the distribution outlets or to the fertilizer manufacturers. If sufficient control is maintained to ensure that they are in fact being reflected in the fertilizer price to the farmer, direct subsidies may be a very effective means of expanding the use of fertilizers. However, if the subsidy is sufficiently large to have a significant impact on use, subsidy programmes tend to be very expensive. Furthermore, unless policies are introduced to expand supplies of fertilizers simultaneously with the subsidies, the latter will promote fertilizer scarcity and the potential increase in use due to the price subsidy will only be partially realized.

Subsidies may be successfully used to introduce fertilizer on farms with favourable crop response, but where no fertilizer is currently being used. As will be discussed later, the decision to use fertilizer for the first time may be greatly influenced by lack of knowledge and corresponding risk and uncertainty. To overcome such constraints, the fertilizer price may have to be lower for the first purchase than for subsequent ones.

Temporary subsidy programmes may also encourage the rapid expansion of fertilizer consumption in countries with excess productive capacity and resulting high domestic prices. As consumption increases, capacity utilization goes up and costs per unit of output may be reduced. This, in turn, would reduce the need for a continuation of the subsidy programme. The problem with such temporary subsidies is that, once introduced, they tend to be difficult to phase out.

Returning to Table 7.10, it is interesting to note that developed countries as a general rule use a much smaller amount of public funds for fertilizer price subsidies relative to research expenditure than do developing countries. Thus, many developed countries have no price subsidy for fertilizers, and those that do tend to spend less on such subsidies than on agricultural research.

What are the reasons for this stronger relative emphasis on fertilizer price subsidies in developing countries? The most important is undoubtedly that the time lag between government spending and the resulting production increase is much shorter for fertilizer price subsidies than for agricultural research. The food and agricultural problems in many of these countries are so urgent that investment in short-term effects takes high priority, even though the long-term benefits may be lower than those obtainable from investment in more long-term solutions, e.g. research. This corresponds with the great emphasis on extension relative to research in many developing countries, as discussed in Chapter 3. Furthermore, lack of knowledge and the resulting uncertainty associated with fertilizer usage is more pronounced in developing countries. Thus, temporary subsidies to obviate these factors are more relevant in these countries.

A third reason for the emphasis on fertilizer price subsidies in developing countries is that it may be politically more feasible to expand food production through fertilizer subsidies than through price support for agricultural products. In developing countries a relatively large share of the consumer budget is spend on food. This is, of course, particularly pronounced among low-income groups. Increasing food prices (through for example food price support to farmers) would have a significant and negative effect on consumer real incomes and may contribute to a lowering of the standard of living, inflation, reduced growth and political instability. Negative effects of input subsidies, on the other hand, would be less obvious for the individual consumer and might be distributed differently among income groups. Thus, while developed countries tend to place greater emphasis on output price support and long-term improvements in productivity, e.g. research, political reality and the urgency of food and nutritional problems may force developing countries to place greater emphases on input subsidies and other short-term, temporary solutions.

Indirect subsidies
The real price of fertilizers may be reduced in a number of ways other than direct subsidies. One of the most common is to make credit available to farmers at a subsidized interest rate. Subsidized credit programmes may be effective in increasing the use of fertilizers in cases where lack of credit with reasonable interest rates is a major constraint. Although the allocative mechanism of the free market system does not necessarily operate perfectly, there is nevertheless a tendency to allocate credit to projects where the highest return can be obtained. Hence, permanent subsidization of credit for the purchase of fertilizer may involve considerable cost to society because returns to limited capital are reduced. A less costly policy may be to remove the factors causing the high interest rates associated with such credit.

Risk and uncertainty in agricultural production and lack of credit security are probably the major factors causing such high interest rates and reluctance among commercial banks to provide agricultural credit. Government policy aimed at reducing the risk and uncertainty and providing additional security for the moneylenders in a way acceptable to the farmer is likely to provide higher benefits than subsidized interest rates.

It is difficult to ensure that subsidized credit is in fact used for fertilizer purchases over and above those that would have taken place in the absence of such subsidies. Hence, the impact of such programmes on fertilizer use tend to be much smaller than expected.

Other indirect subsidy programmes include tax concessions, preferential exchange rates, preferential freight rates, etc.

Other ways of reducing the fertilizer price
Subsidies are, of course, not the only way to reduce fertilizer prices. These prices are influenced by a number of factors such as the cost of production and distribution, existing and anticipated supply and demand, the structure and competitive situation of the fertilizer sector, etc. Thus, increasing efficiency in fertilizer production and distribution, improved competitive conditions and public subsidies to production and distribution could lower the price. Increased capacity utilization is one way of reducing unit costs and prices. The capacity

utilization in fertilizer production in developing countries is around 60 per cent, and it appears that an expansion could contribute significantly to reductions in unit costs.

The efficiency of fertilizer distribution in developing countries is low. The result is large distribution costs. There are also cases where exploitation of imperfections in the distribution system leads to excessive profits to middlemen. In both cases excessive marketing margins contribute to high prices to the farmer. The costs of distribution as a percentage of the fertilizer retail prices in a number of countries are shown in Table 7.11. It is not unusual for these costs to account for one-third to one-half of the price paid by farmers. Although the high distribution costs may be explained in part by the small quantities of fertilizers handled by the system, there is little doubt that these costs could be greatly reduced, even at current amounts.

In a number of developing countries, exchange rate and trade policies contribute to high fertilizer prices. Such policies may be aimed at the protection of national fertilizer production and/or saving of foreign exchange.

International fertilizer prices
International fertilizer prices play an important role in determining prices in the individual developing country, although the above-mentioned exchange rate and trade policies reduce this role in some countries. International fertilizer prices are largely determined by supply and demand. World supply capacity and projected demand for each

Table 7.11 Estimated distribution costs for three fertilizer types for selected developing countries (% of retail prices).*

	Year	Ammonium sulphate	Urea	Selected phosphate fertilizer
Brazil	1972	–	57.3	31.3
Colombia	1972	–	–	52.8
Ghana	1971	50.8	–	–
India	1972	10.0	8.3	–
Mexico	1970	19.0	11.4	19.5
Nepal	1971	27.7	24.5	–
Taiwan	1972	20.0	15.0	–
Thailand	1971	56.7	62.2	–
Zambia	1972	32.0	25.4	33.7

* The distribution costs reported here are the difference between c.i.f. price and the retail price for imported fertilizers, and that between factory and retail price for domestically produced fertilizers.

Source: FAO/FIAC (1972).

of the three major fertilizers are compared in Table 7.12 for the period 1980–83. Supply capacities exceed projected demand for all years and fertilizers. Heavy investment in nitrogen production capacity during the last half of the 1970s is expected to cause an increasing 'over-capacity' up to 1981/82. The 'overcapacity' for the other two fertilizers shows a decreasing trend during this period. Very limited new invest-ment in potash production capacity may result in 'undercapacity' before the middle of the 1980s unless current investment trends are reversed.

Table 7.12 Forecast balance between world fertilizer supply capacity and demand up to 1982/83.*

	1980/81		1981/82		1982/83	
	Million tons	% of supply capacity	Million tons	% of supply capacity	Million tons	% of supply capacity
Nitrogen	+3.36	5.5	+4.35	6.7	+3.59	5.3
Phosphorus	+3.03	8.3	+2.64	6.9	+1.97	5.0
Potash	+1.30	4.4	+0.91	3.0	+0.40	1.3

* Supply capacity less estimated demand.

Source: UNIDO/FAO/IBRD Working Groups on Fertilizers (1978a).

'Over' or 'excess capacity' implies either a supply reduction or a downward pressure on prices. In fact, a combination of the two is the likely outcome. Whether a downward pressure on prices will in fact result in lower prices depends on a number of factors, including the trends in costs of production and the competitive structure of the fertil-izer industry. Increasing oil prices are likely to cause increases in fertil-izer production costs, particularly in so far as nitrogen is concerned, although the role of energy in the total production costs for fertilizers is much less than generally believed. It follows that a reduction of fertil-izer prices in absolute terms is unlikely. Rather, the supply will pro-bably be adjusted to ensure some price increase.

The fertilizer sector is subject to cyclical fluctuations in prices and supply. Falling prices during the 1960s resulted in the termination of less efficient production units, while new investment was very limited. The industry was therefore unprepared to meet a large increase in fertilizer demand at the beginning of the 1970s. The result was drastic price increases in nitrogen and phosphorus (Fig. 7.2). These resulted in large investments in fertilizer production capacity. But the construction of fertilizer plants is time consuming. It is not unusual for the time lapse

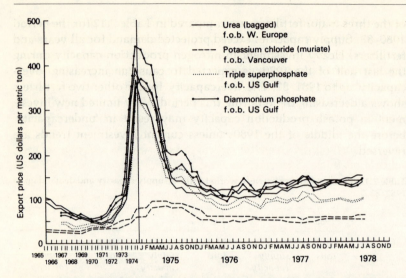

Export price (US dollars per metric ton)

Urea (bagged)
f.o.b. W. Europe

Potassium chloride (muriate)
f.o.b. Vancouver

Triple superphosphate
f.o.b. US Gulf

Diammonium phosphate
f.o.b. US Gulf

Fig. 7.2. Export Prices for some major fertilizer materials (US dollars per metric ton of product) (Commission on Fertilizers, Fifth Session, Rome, 22–25 January, 1979. FERT/79/3, Nov. 1978).

between the initiation of construction and new production to be four to six years, although varying considerably for the various fertilizer materials and locations.

The long time lapse, together with uncertainty associated with future demand projections and lack of coordination among firms, contribute to excess or deficient investment over time. As a result, cyclical price and supply fluctuations are maintained. The reaction to the large price increases in 1972–74 appears to have caused excess investment resulting in future excess supply capacity, as shown in Table 7.12. Such investment was due in part to overestimation of the actual fertilizer deficit and lack of coordination among fertilizer producers. It was also heavily influenced by the desires of many developing countries to expand fertilizer production for domestic use irrespective of the future world supply – demand balance. The issue for these countries was food security and less dependence on foreign sources for their fertilizer requirements, although saving of foreign exchange obviously was also an important consideration.

AGRICULTURAL PRODUCT PRICES

Agricultural price-support policies are common in developing and developed countries. While some such policies aim at price stabilization, others attempt to maintain agricultural product prices above free market prices and/or increase incomes to farmers. Increases in product prices will make it profitable for the farmer to increase fertilizer usage. However, while policies resulting in reduced fertilizer prices promote more agricultural products at lower prices, policies aimed at increasing product prices promote more, but also more expensive, agricultural products. When prices are above free market equilibrium between demand and supply, the latter policies tend to create a surplus of agricultural products. Such surplus must be removed from the market to maintain the higher price. While the higher prices are passed on to the consumer, the cost to government of surplus removal can be very high, as experienced by the United States during the 1950s.

Many developing countries are faced with severe nutritional deficiencies among a large part of the population, mainly due to lack of purchasing power. Furthermore, as mentioned earlier, even where malnutrition is not a major problem, food costs account for a large part of the family income and the level of food prices is of extreme importance in the development process. The implications for trade-offs between input subsidies and output price support were discussed earlier and need not be repeated here.

AGRONOMIC RESPONSE

The agronomic response to fertilizer depends on a number of factors including: (1) soil characteristics; (2) climatic variables such as rainfall pattern; (3) irrigation; (4) plant variety; (5) disease and insect attacks; (6) the type and nutrient balance of the fertilizer; (7) timeliness and form of application.

The agronomic response to fertilizers may be improved in a number of ways. The interaction between fertilizers, and agricultural research is mentioned frequently throughout this book. The interdependence among the various factors of production and technological change is a key issue in efforts to expand agricultural production and productivity. In the case of fertilizers, the potential contribution to food production is realized only to the extent that the factors limiting fertilizer response are removed or their effects are reduced.

New crop varieties with high fertilizer response rates, varieties capable of utilizing a larger proportion of applied fertilizer, varieties resistant or tolerant to certain diseases, insects and stresses, better cultural practices, including better soil and water management to reduce nutrient losses, better fertilizers and irrigation are but a few examples of what might improve the efficiency of fertilizers and thus increase agricultural production and/or save resources. Agricultural R&D plays an important role in ensuring improvements along these lines. But the importance of related public policy should not be underestimated. Public investment in irrigation infrastructure and related policy measures to facilitate effective resource utilization, land reform and credit policies and a series of other measures may be of great importance in enhancing the contribution of fertilizers to agricultural production.

CONSTRAINTS TO FERTILIZER USE

In addition to fertilizer and crop prices and agronomic response, the use of fertilizers is determined by the presence or absence of a large number of constraints. Such constraints may either reduce the profitability to the farmer of using more fertilizer, or prohibit him from obtaining – or make it unattractive to him to seek – such potential profits.

The type of constraints and their relative impact on fertilizer use vary among geographical regions and among farm groups within regions. In general, small farmers tend to be faced with more severe constraints than larger farmers, for a number of reasons to be further discussed.

While the presence and impact of individual constraints are location specific, a number of constraints appear to be present in most developing countries. These include: (1) unavailability of fertilizers where and when needed; (2) lack of knowledge; (3) risk and uncertainty; (4) lack of credit; (5) land tenure; (6) lack of the most appropriate complementary inputs. Each of these constraints, and measures aimed at reducing their impact, are discussed below.

Unavailability of fertilizer
Lack of fertilizer where and when needed is a serious problem in many developing countries. On the basis of a survey of 46 developing countries, FAO found that the use of fertilizer was seriously hampered in 75 per cent of these countries because of unavailability at the local level (Mathieu and Vega, 1978). Unavailability at the local level may be a result of poorly developed and/or inefficient distribution networks. Large distances between distribution outlets and difficult transportation facilities make it difficult or practically impossible for many farmers to obtain the desired fertilizer.

Fertilizer distribution systems based on private firms tend to place the principal emphasis on regions with large fertilizer demand and well-developed infrastructure. This, of course, is perfectly rational behaviour. However, the result is – or may be – that small farmers in regions where infrastructure is lacking may not have easy access to fertilizers. In order to remedy this problem a number of developing countries have establised public distribution systems. Such systems have in fact made fertilizers available to many farmers who would otherwise be denied access. But the very reason why private firms are less interested in these regions – high distribution costs per unit of fertilizer – may require large subsidies to the public distribution systems to avoid excessive fertilizer costs to the farmer. This relates to the much broader question of public subsidies to farmers in remote areas, a question that is beyond the scope of this book.

Casual observation indicates that in many cases public distribution systems are considerably less effective than private systems in getting the right kind of fertilizer to their distribution outlets at the time needed. Thus, although outlets are within the reach of the small farmer, the fertilizer needed may arrive too late in relation to the cropping season, or the kind of fertilizer may not be that which is needed. There are, unfortunately, very many examples of this kind. As the infrastruture improves and the fertilizer demand increases among small farmers, the need for public intervention in fertilizer distribution is likely to change from direct ownership and management of the system to regulation of the private sector to ensure acceptable levels of competition and prices.

Shortages or unavailability at the local level may be a result of shortages at the national level. In many developing countries, fertilizer production is far less than the demand. Thus, a large part of domestic demand must be met through imports. But importation requires spending of foreign exchange – a very limited commodity in most developing countries. Foreign exchange considerations may, therefore, place constraints on fertilizer imports. At the same time, domestic fertilizer prices may well be subsidized. This, in turn, tends to expand domestic fertilizer demand. The net result may well be excess demand, i.e. shortages at the national level. Such shortages are frequently dealt with by means of some forms of allocative or rationing policy.

The level of self-sufficiency for the three principal fertilizers in the developing countries is shown in Table 7.13. Currently, fertilizer production in developing countries amounts to 70–80 per cent of their nitrogen consumption, 75–90 per cent of their phosphorus consumption and about 9 per cent of the potash consumption. Growth in fertilizer production has exceeded consumption growth during the last 25

Table 7.13 Estimated and projected rates of self-sufficiency for the three major fertilizers in developing countries for selected years.*

	N	P_2O_5	K_2O
1955/56	39.3	54.5	6.8
1965/66	52.0	68.3	−†
1976/77	71.3	74.9	−†
1980/81	81.4	94.5	9.5
1982/83	83.7	99.6	13.3

* The rate of self-sufficiency is defined as the supply capacity divided by the demand and multiplied by 100.
† Reliable data unavailable.

Source: UNIDO (1978), and FAO/UNIDO/World Bank Working Group on Fertilizer (1978b).

years, a trend that is expected to continue. It is projected that developing countries as a group will be virtually self-sufficient in phosphorus fertilizers by 1982/83. The degrees of self-sufficiency for nitrogen and potash for the same year are projected to be 84 and 13 per cent respectively.

The increasing degree of self-sufficiency is expected to reduce the occurence and severity of fertilizer shortages, save foreign exchange and increase the security of food supplies through less dependence on developed countries for fertilizer. However, it should be noted that a high degree of self-sufficiency for developing countries as a group does not guarantee this for the individual country. Some countries will continue to rely heavily on imports while others will produce exportable surpluses.

Lack of knowledge
There are still farmers in developing countries who have never heard of fertilizers. However, effective promotion by many local and national institutions, often supported by international agencies, during the last 25 years has greatly reduced the number of such farmers. But it is not sufficient to know only that fertilizers exist.

Farmers – and for that matter extension workers – are frequently poorly informed about the kind and quantity of fertilizer to use and how and when it should be applied. Government measures are needed to support agronomic research and to generate information adequate to guide farmers as to type of fertilizer needed, optimum quantities and timing, placement, etc. under various climatic, environmental, economic and soil conditions. Such research should be carried out by, or in close collaboration with, farmers and extension agents. Individual on-farm experiments should be used to demonstrate to the farmer the economic return from increasing fertilizer use and to assist farmers in using improved practices and inputs other than fertilizers.

Response to fertilizers is location specific and influenced by many factors which, in turn, differ among regions and even among individual farms. Thus, sound fertilizer recommendations must be based on results from local trials carried out under production conditions relevant for the farmer.[1] However, owing to lack of resources for such work, and possibly in some cases a lack of appreciation for the location specificity of the response to fertilizers, such trials are often not carried out. Instead, fertilizer recommendations are based on results from trials carried out under a completely different set of production conditions. This contributes to poor or faulty recommendations, economic losses to the farmer and increased uncertainty associated with fertilizer use. The latter is particularly important in cases of first usage. Erroneous recommendations reduce the farmer's confidence in the extension agent. Such lack of confidence is likely to carry over into advice and recommendations on other technology which may, in fact, be based on correct information.

Risk and uncertainty
Risk and uncertainty may be caused by natural or environmental factors or by market factors. Rainfall patterns and disease and insect attacks are the most important natural or environmental factors. These may be reduced through better management practices, including the use of pesticides and irrigation, or through the development and use of resistant varieties.

Government policy aimed at facilitating irrigation, developing and/or distributing resistant varieties, making pesticides available and improving crop-management practices in general may have considerable impact on the use and efficiency of fertilizers though a reduction in risk and uncertainty. Hence it is important that government policy aimed at increasing the use of fertilizers be established in the broader context of agricultural production.

While fertilizer price fluctuations may affect the quantity of fertilizer used, they do not add much to the risk because in most cases the farmer knows the actual price before purchasing, and hence can react accordingly. Agricultural product price fluctuations, on the other hand, introduce considerable risk and uncertainty because the investment in fertilizers must be made before the actual crop price is known. The economic optimum quantity of fertilizer varies according to the crop price and it is to be expected that the farmer, faced with the experience of large crop price fluctuations, will tend to limit fertilizer use to correspond with optimum quantities at relatively low crop prices. Government policies aimed at crop price stabilization may be very effective in increasing the use of fertilizers. The government cost of price stabilization programmes for agricultural products need not be high if price levels are established at the right level. However, this is difficult to specify because of uncertainty in future supply. Too high price levels will result in market surpluses, while those which are too low result in scarcities.

Lack of credit

Lack of credit is probably the one single constraint to fertilizer use most frequently mentioned by farmers. While this factor is undoubtedly important, it is argued here that this is grossly overstated in results from farm surveys. A large proportion of the farmers who state that lack of credit is the reason for not using, or not increasing the use of, fertilizers would probably not utilize the credit for this purpose, even if provided. Lack of knowledge, risk and uncertainty, and the unwillingness to risk the consequences of being unable to repay the credit from the income generated by the crop to which the fertilizer was applied, are frequently the real reasons why credit is not sought and obtained.

Subsidized credit programmes were discussed previously. It appears that in many countries government measures are needed to provide sufficient guarantees to lenders of money to avoid excessive interest rates and limit the liability of the farmer in case of crop failure. Government-supported crop and credit insurance programmes might be effective.

Land tenure

If the same person or family owns both the crop and the land on which it is produced, the use of fertilizers tends to be larger than where they are separately owned. Tenant farmers in some countries may be required to pay for all inputs including fertilizers, and deliver a portion of the crop to the landlord. Hence, the tenant gains only part of the return on his fertilizer investment which, in turn, means that the economic optimum quantity of fertilizer is smaller than where the farmer is also the landowner. Government policy aimed at encouraging or compelling cost as well as output sharing between tenants and landlords would be expected to increase fertilizer use and agricultural production. Likewise, of course, land reform policies resulting in a shift from tenancy to ownership by the grower would expand fertilizer use, other things being equal.

The benefits of fertilizers usually extend beyond one cropping season. Hence, short-term tenancy arrangements and uncertainty about future arrangements tend to reduce fertilizer use because of the uncertainty as to who will reap the benefits beyond the cropping season for which the fertilizer was initially applied. This same problem exists where government plans call for land reform and redistribution in the near future. Whether or not such plans in fact materialize, they tend to create sufficient uncertainty among larger landowners to reduce investment in fertilizers and other land-improving measures. Government policy aimed at facilitating longer-term tenancy arrangements and reducing the uncertainty concerning land-ownership would probably result in expanded fertilizer use and increased agricultural production.

Lack of complementary inputs

The importance of irrigation, pesticides, herbicides and other production inputs and management practices to reduce risk and uncertainty and to increase the response to fertilizers was mentioned above. Lack of access to these inputs at the local level is a commonly encountered obstacle to obtaining potential production and productivity gains from fertilizer application. Thus, an integrated and well-balanced public policy focused on specific local situations with respect to fertilizers and other inputs is required. In such a policy, the main aim should be constant attention to the most limiting factor.

NOTES

1. FAO has assisted a number of countries in such efforts.

8 Environmental effects of modern technology

Increasing population and desires for higher real incomes place increasing demands on a finite natural resource base. In order to meet rapidly rising demand for food and other agricultural and forestry products, the agricultural resource base in developing countries is being exploited with increasing intensity. Furthermore, increasing amounts of non-renewable resources from outside the agricultural sector, e.g. fertilizer raw materials and fossil fuel, are being drawn into the production of food, animal feed and fibre.

Food shortages are acute and of great magnitude in many developing countries. As a result, projects aimed at immediate expansion of production take high priority. Some such projects may be very ineffective when viewed in a longer-term perspective, and some may make a long-term solution very difficult because of the deterioration of the resource base needed for future production. However, the more acute the food problem and the more serious the consequences if the problem is not resolved quickly, the less important the longer-term effects appear. A community or a family faced with a serious threat of starvation and death in the near future obviously place great emphasis on the immediate increase in food availability, while possible deterioration of the resource base and associated negative effects on future availability are likely to be of little concern.

But need there be a conflict between attempts to meet current and future food demands? Is it not possible to incorporate into the strategy for short-term agricultural development, elements that will ensure that the resource base does not deteriorate, but instead is made more productive for future generations?

Some non-renewable resources are necessarily consumed in the production process. Others need not be. Tractor fuel can be used only once. Land, on the other hand, may be used over and over again provided it is properly managed. Thus, in the first case the question is one of economizing in the consumption of a finite quantity of non-renewable resources over time with due consideration given to the possibilities for substitution. In the second case, the question focuses on the proper use and management of a finite quantity of resources in order to maintain or improve its productivity over time.

Serious concern has been expressed in various sources regarding the long-term effects of the current aims of technological change in agriculture. It is argued by some that while such aims may provide at least partial solutions to immediate problems, they cannot be maintained without high cost to future generations in terms of a reduced and degraded resource base. In other words, it is argued that the time horizon used in decision-making on technological change is too short.

A very short planning horizon may be found in public as well as private decision-making. Public policy usually places great emphasis on obtaining visible results in the short term. The reasons may differ from one political system to another. In those with some semblance of democracy, the politicians are concerned about the next election, while in dictatorships there may be disquiet about social and political unrest. In either case, long-term effects may be of little concern to the policy-maker. In private decision-making, market forces would be expected to make provision for both short- and long-term preferences of producers and consumers. However, input and output price distortions, institutional arrangements, as well as factors external to the individual firm, may imply that certain long-term social costs and benefits are inadequately reflected in private decision-making. Negative environmental effects not reflected in private costs represent such a case.

There are many examples of deterioration of the agricultural resource base in developing as well as developed countries. Some of these and the principal causes will be briefly discussed below. But the primary focus of this discussion is on the role of agricultural research and modern technology. A review will be made of the empirical evidence regarding the effects of modern technology on the resource base and the environment in developing countries. The effects on the environmental and resource base of current and expected future aims of the path of technological change in agriculture in developing countries will be discussed and the chapter terminates with an overall assessment of the impact of modern technology on environment and the resource base and how conflicts between technological change to meet short-term production goals and long-term resource and environmental goals may be minimized or eliminated.

LAND RESOURCES

Large areas of agricultural land are currently being degraded, allowed to deteriorate or lost for future agricultural production in developing countries. Soil degradation and deterioration are caused by physical environmental factors and by misuse and mismanagement of soil. The most common types of soil degradation may be discussed under two headings:

1. Desertification, wind and water erosion and general loss of nutrients and organic matter.
2. Waterlogging, salinization and alkalinization.

These headings will be briefly discussed below.

DESERTIFICATION, EROSION AND ORGANIC MATTER LOSSES

Kassas (1975) estimates that more than 6 per cent of the earth's land area has been transformed into what he calls 'manmade deserts', i.e. land that was not inherently desert in environmental character. The rapid desert expansion which took place in the Sahel region of Africa during the period 1968–73 received world-wide attention. But desertification is not limited to a period of drought in the Sahel. It is a continuing process in many parts of the developing countries (United Nations, 1977; Eckholm and Brown, 1977). The primary causes of desertification are climatic factors, e.g. severe droughts, as well as deforestation, over-grazing, burning and bad farming practices.

Deforestation is a result of increasing population pressures, increasing food demand, increased numbers of livestock and higher demand for wood and forestry products. Clearing of wooded areas for agricultural use is frequently followed by extensive erosion, losses of organic matter and desertification. Fuel-wood harvesting is a principal cause of deforestation. According to Eckholm (1975, 1979) household use of fuel wood accounts for at least half of all tree felling, and increasing prices of fossil fuel is causing an increase in fuel-wood demand. High wood prices and prospects of large short-term profits have contributed to excessive commercial tree felling, primarily for export. Replanting is frequently not done and the social costs associated with deforestation, land deterioration and the resulting damage to the future resource base are not usually borne by those who obtain the profits. The problem is not that the demands for fuel wood and other forestry products should not be met, but rather that the resource base necessary for future wood and/or agricultural production is not being maintained or improved through replanting and/or proper soil management. In the process of fulfilling current demands, the ability to meet future demand is being reduced.

Closely related to the above problem are the changes occurring in shifting cultivation practices. In regions where shifting cultivation has been practised for centuries, increasing population pressures have reduced the bush fallow period. As a result, soil degradation and reduced agricultural productivity occur.

Overcultivation, particularly overgrazing, and poor farming practices and soil management are causing severe soil degradation in many regions of the developing countries. The urgency of existing food and agricultural problems, together with lack of knowledge regarding long-term effects and the fact that the social costs of adverse effects on the soil resource base may not be borne – or perceived to be borne – by the individual farmer-decision-maker, or for that matter by the current government, result in an excessively high priority on providing short-term solutions irrespective of the longer-term implications. The result is that private decision-making as well as public policy may grossly underestimate the importance of adverse effects on the resource base. According to a survey of 69 countries with 1.8 billion people, over-grazing and overcropping, which result in heavy loss of soil by erosion, are serious problems in 43 countries with 1.4 billion people (Bente, 1977).

WATERLOGGING AND SALINIZATION

Salinity and drainage problems are serious in many regions of developing as well as developed countries. In a United Nations paper (1977) it is estimated that almost 125,000 ha of irrigated land are lost annually due to waterlogging, salinization and alkalinization. This amounts to more than 0.5 per cent of all irrigated land. If these rates of losses remain constant, approximately 2.75 million ha will be lost by the end of the century (Barney et al., 1980).

Problems of waterlogging and salinity are of great magnitude in a number of developing countries including Pakistan, India and Iraq. In Sind, one of Pakistan's major provinces, 49 per cent of all agricultural land was moderately or severely waterlogged in 1960, 50 per cent was highly saline and 25 per cent was moderately saline. In the Punjab, over 30 per cent of all agricultural land was suffering from salinization (United Nations, 1977). In India, over 6 million ha, or about 15 per cent of the total irrigated area have been severely damaged by waterlogging and salinity (Eckholm, 1976).

Soil degradation due to waterlogging and salinization need not be irreversible. Soil reclamation may bring agricultural productivity back to normal. While this is likely to be costly, there are examples of quite successful projects, e.g. those in Pakistan (Barney et al., 1980).

The above has been limited to a very brief summary of some of the most important issues related to the problem of land degradation and deterioration. Additional information may be found in a number of recent studies on the subject including Brown (1978), FAO (1978b), Eckholm (1976), Bently et al. (1980), Riquier (1978), Bente (1977), Biswas and Biswas (1979) and a series of documents from the UN Conference on Desertification, August 1977.

THE EFFECT OF TECHNOLOGICAL CHANGE

Private as well as public efforts to expand agricultural production through expansion of the agricultural land base is a major factor in degradation. Incorporation of marginal lands, clearing of forest land, shortening of the bush fallow period in shifting cultivation and excessive exploitation of land through overcultivation and overgrazing are mostly a result of increasing population pressures in agricultural areas and the increasing demand for food and other agricultural products. The supply of agricultural products may be increased either by expanding the land base or by increasing yields per unit area. Thus, technological change resulting in higher yields reduces the pressures for expanding agricultural production into marginal lands and excessive exploitation of the land base. There is little doubt that the development and use of high-yielding crop varieties, increased use of fertilizers, better production practices and other yield-increasing factors have been of great importance in limiting land degradation in developing countries.

This very significant positive environmental effect of modern technology is frequently overlooked. To further restrain land degradation, more – not less – yield-increasing technology must be developed and introduced.

In addition to its impact on yield, modern technology may contribute to the conservation of land currently under cultivation. Improved agricultural practice, including reduced tillage, more appropriate water management and a series of other methods may greatly reduce soil and water erosion and increase both current and future yields. A number of agricultural research institutions in developing countries, including the international institutes ICRISAT, IITA and CIAT, currently place considerable emphasis on developing improved soil and crop management systems for the combined purpose of increasing yields and conserving soils in danger of degradation. Such systems are of interest not only for land currently under cultivation but – perhaps more importantly – for new lands brought into agricultural production. The risk of land degradation associated with land expansion may be greatly reduced.

Inappropriate technology or inappropriate use of modern technology may accelerate land degradation. The most striking example is waterlogging and salinization caused by inappropriate irrigation and drainage, mentioned above. Chemical soil pollution has also been mentioned as a negative environmental effect of modern technology (Golubev, Shvytov and Vasiliev, 1978). Such pollution may result from the application of pesticides. Furthermore, waste materials applied as fertilizer may contain certain undesirable elements. However, the available evidence does not suggest that chemical soil pollution is, or is likely to be, a significant issue in developing countries. But, as discussed later, heavy application of chemical pesticides and certain waste products may cause water pollution and undesirable changes in the chemical composition of food commodities. Thus, effective testing and monitoring of the effects of the various chemicals followed by legislative action when appropriate is essential.

WATER RESOURCES

The water supply throughout the growing season is of great importance in crop production. The land-saving effect of improved water supply and management and the interaction between water supply/management and the yield response to fertilizers and varietal improvements are discussed elsewhere. This section discusses the impact of technological change on water resources and other water-related implications of modern technology.

Agricultural production practices may affect both the quantity and quality of water resources. Increasing water use by upstream farmers may reduce that available for downstream farmers. Similarly, increasing use of ground-water may lower the water table and thus reduce the quantity available currently and in the future. Thus, technological change which includes more irrigation may result in water shortages in certain locations and for certain periods. Although marked permanent falls in the level of the water table may have serious consequences for the future water supply in certain locations, either because of a slow replenishment or inflow of salt water, the principal issues are those associated with the allocation of water among farmers and between agriculture and other uses within a given time. It is seen that the problems associated with the quantity of water are frequently of a short-term nature and the risk of serious, long-term, irreversible environmental effects is probably not widespread, although it may be so in certain locations. However, available quantities of ground- and surface water pose serious limitations on the expansion of irrigation in many regions. In these regions the water-use efficiency should be increased. R&D is under way to achieve this, for example by drop irrigation methods.

Negative effects of technological change on the quality of ground- and surface water may be of a more long-term nature. It is feared by some that application of fertilizers may cause eutrophication of streams and lakes and nitrate contamination of drinking water supplies. Pesticides may contaminate ground- as well as surface water and use of sewage and waste products as fertilizers may result in water pollution.

The available empirical evidence suggests that the application of increasing quantities of fertilizers has had very limited – if any – harmful effect on the quality of ground- and surface water in developing countries (Pinstrup-Andersen, 1980b). A number of individual cases of high nitrate concentration in ground-water has been reported (Nightingale, 1970; Stout and Burau, 1967; Smith, 1967; Gruener and Shuval, 1970). These cases refer to industrialized countries and are explained either by the outlet of large quantities of sewage and wastes with high nitrogen content or by a sudden large increase in irrigation (Viets, 1971). Application of excessive quantities of nitrogen, i.e. in excess of that of economic interest to the farmer, and wrong timing of application may cause significant eutrophication and possibly ammonia toxicity in fish. But wrong methods of application and application of excessive quantities cause immediate economic losses to the farmer and are not widespread. Where a great deal of eutrophication does occur, it appears to be caused primarily by industrial and urban wastes.

Water pollution by pesticides has been of serious concern in a number of locations (Pimentel, 1978). Application by aircraft and poor handling of pesticides are the principal causes. An overall assessment of the magnitude of this problem is difficult owing to shortage of data. We have even less reliable information on the environmental effects of the application of sewage and wastes on agricultural lands.

The construction of dams for irrigation may have serious adverse effects on the eco-system, including drastic changes in the living conditions of wildlife and marine life. Dam construction may also cause serious hardships for local families through loss of land and homes and relocation. Expanded irrigation systems have contributed to the spread of water-borne diseases. In the tropics and subtropics, irrigation schemes have enhanced or created favourable ecological and environmental conditions for such parasitic and water-borne diseases as schistosomiasis, filariasis and malaria (Olembo, 1976).

The risk of increasing health problems should not be ignored. Neither should such risk be used as an argument for reducing the rate of increase in the development of economically sound irrigation systems. Rather, efforts to prevent the spread of water-borne diseases should be an integral part of overall irrigation schemes.

GENETIC RESOURCES

Genetic improvement in plants is the key to yield-expanding and risk-reducing research on crops. Selection and breeding are used to obtain varieties with certain desired characteristics. Resistance or tolerance to specific diseases, pests and a series of other characteristics may be sought to produce varieties with high yield potential and low production risk under certain growing conditions. The effects on yield and production of such research have already been discussed. This section deals with some important side effects: increasing genetic uniformity in crop production, potential reduction in genetic reserves and expanded areas under crops for which genetic research has been successful, at the expense of other crops.

Substitution of one or a few new varieties for a number of local varieties over vast geographic areas greatly enhances the likelihood of epidemics through increased genetic uniformity. Improved varieties for a given crop are likely to represent similar gene combinations. On the other hand, a large number of local varieties may represent great genetic diversity. Increased genetic uniformity for a given crop makes the crop more vulnerable to unexpected diseases and pests. This is not because improved varieties generally have a weaker natural resistance to pathogens and pests, as has been argued (Barney et al., 1980). Rather, the issue is that one or a few inbred varieties tend to have the same resistance or non-resistance characteristics, as opposed to a large number of local varieties with great gene diversity. If a serious disease or pest occurs for which the improved varieties have no resistance and if these varieties occupy a large proportion of the area grown with the crop in a given region or country, disaster may result. It is like a forest fire without fire-lanes. In the case of many local varieties, some may be resistant and thus serve as 'fire-lanes'.

The risk of extensive crop losses facilitated by high degrees of genetic uniformity is particularly high in areas dominated by a single crop. But the development of improved varieties with high yield capacity in some crops would tend to cause expansion of the area grown with these crops at the expense of those crops for which no such varieties are available. Thus, increased uniformity and greater domination of a single crop in a given geographical region may go hand-in-hand.

There are a number of examples of crop failures facilitated by genetic uniformity and/or high concentration of a single crop in a given region or country. The most dramatic example was the Irish potato blight around the middle of the last century. Among other examples are: coffee rust in many developing countries; corn blight in the United States; wheat rust in various countries; witches'-broom in cocoa in a number of tropical countries; downy mildew in pearl millet in India.

Some (most?) of the diseases and pests causing large crop failures in the past have been dealt with through the development of genetic resistance or tolerance. Others are controlled or avoided by chemical means. The critical issue here is that while genetic improvement may develop varieties with a series of desirable characteristics, such as resistance to specific diseases and pests, it may also exclude from these varieties other characteristics that may prove to be highly desirable, e.g. resistance to unexpected diseases and pests. A related issue is that genetic resistance frequently becomes less effective over time. Thus, plant breeding must continue.

The message conveyed by these two issues is clear: if current levels of benefits from genetic improvement are to be maintained in the future and if additional benefits are to be obtained, genetic improvement must continue and a high degree of genetic variability must be maintained.

As the genetic variability is reduced in agriculture, efforts must be made to preserve genetic resources elsewhere. Native strains developed and used by local farmers over centuries, as well as wild species, must be preserved when farmers shift to improved varieties. The success of future genetic improvement to develop better varieties and to avoid or fight potential or real new crop epidemics depends on the diversity of genetic material available. No one can predict which genetic materials will be needed and any reduction of current diversity would be unfortunate.

A great deal is being done to preserve genetic resources. Germ-plasm banks are maintained at various locations. The international agricultural research institutes play a major role in maintaining germ-plasm banks for crops on which they carry out research. As mentioned in Chapter 4, an International Board for Plant Genetic Resources (IBPGR) was created in 1973 under the auspices of CGIAR. The primary purpose of the Board is to facilitate germ-plasm preservation through a variety of seed collection, storage and documentation schemes. A more detailed description of national and international efforts to preserve germ plasm is given by Harlan (1975).

This author is not qualified to judge whether enough is being done to preserve genetic resources in plants. It is clear, however, that failure to preserve genetic material with potential future use may cause irreversible damage to the genetic resource base. It is equally clear that genetic improvement has greatly reduced crop losses caused by diseases and pests. At the same time, reliance on fewer varieties and a more homogeneous genetic material for our food production introduces some very undesirable risk elements. Awareness of the risk, effective warning systems, germ-plasm banks and agricultural research, continuous efforts to avoid unnecessary reduction in the genetic diversity in agriculture and improved plant protection methods will together provide insurance against disaster while yields are being increased. Failure to recognize the risk of epidemics and failure to take the proper precautions may have severe consequences. On the other hand, rejection of modern plant breeding and its ability to increase yields and reduce losses by diseases and pests on the grounds of genetic risk is absurd.

ENERGY RESOURCES

According to FAO (1979), the agricultural sector in developing countries accounted for 3.1 per cent of the total consumption of fossil fuel in these countries in 1975. In comparison, 24 per cent of the total output of these countries originated in agriculture. Furthermore, agriculture accounts for a small proportion of the energy used in rural households in many developing countries. Cooking is the dominant energy user in these households and fossil fuel plays a very limited role. Wood, charcoal, animal waste and crop residues account for more than 90 per cent of the fuel used in the rural areas of many developing countries (Leach, 1979).

Fossil fuel is used directly as tractor fuel, fuel for pumps, generators, etc. or it is embodied in fertilizers, pesticides and other farm inputs. Up until 1972, technological change in agriculture was influenced by sufficient supplies of fossil fuel at stable or gradually falling real prices. Therefore, it is not surprising that the resulting technology requires increasing quantities of fossil fuel. During the 1950s and 1960s, this general trend was questioned by few, although there were isolated warnings of approaching shortages of fossil fuel (Meadows et al.,

1972). However, the drastic oil price hikes beginning in 1972 raised some serious concerns about the path of technological change. Energy accounting procedures and energy budgets were developed for agriculture, and priorities in agricultural R&D were modified in the light of the new energy situation. During the initial phases of the so-called 'energy crisis', over-reactions were common. Previous technological change in agriculture was unjustly criticized, and suggestions were made for reductions in energy use in agriculture far beyond what could be justified on grounds of relative prices and impact on food supply.

There is little doubt that technological change has caused relatively large increases in the use of fossil fuel by the agricultural sector worldwide. In developing countries, nitrogenous fertilizers and irrigation account for a large part of the fossil fuel used in agriculture. However, these two inputs are also responsible for a large part of the recent increases in food production. Hence, reductions in the application of nitrogen and irrigation or, more realistically, attempts to reduce the rate of increase of application, might have unacceptable consequences for the food supply. However, as fossil fuel prices increase, alternative sources of nitrogen and energy become economically more attractive, and it is important that R&D priorities be adjusted to reflect future price relations. White (1978) reports that considerable adjustment of this nature took place in the US fertilizer sector during the period 1972-77. Thus, it is estimated that the energy use per unit produced of the principal fertilizers fell by 12 per cent, resulting in savings of about 4.5 million barrels of oil.

Since the beginning of the 'energy crisis', agricultural R&D priorities have placed more emphasis on such issues as nitrogen fixation by plants from the atmosphere, improved photosynthetic efficiency, use of organic wastes as fertilizers and a number of other related issues. Energy production in agriculture – either for its own use or for use in other sectors – is another area where additional measures are getting under way. Production of biogas from animal waste and of alcohol from sugar-cane, cassava and other crops are examples of such measures.

However, in spite of projects such as those exemplified above, the food supplies required can only be obtained through increasing use of fossil fuel for many years to come. However, overall strategies and policies for energy usage in the individual developing countries are made outside the agricultural sector. Depending on its political power, this sector may be short-changed in these strategies and policies. If this happens, severe effects may be expected on future food supply, and an increase in rural poverty. Adverse energy policies may severely restrict the ability of technological change to increase food supply and reduce poverty. Promotion of the use of energy budgets and energy input/output ratios, instead of economic relationships for resource allocation and production and policy decisions within agriculture, adds to the confusion and increases the probability of wrong policy decisions.

FERTILIZER RESOURCES

It has been argued that current trends in fertilizer usage cannot be continued because of insufficient quantities of fertilizer raw materials. In particular, serious concern has been expressed about future short-ages of rock phosphate. This was accentuated during the first half of the 1970s when prices of fertilizers and rock phosphate were drastically increased. However, as further elaborated in Chapter 7, known reserves of fertilizer raw materials including rock phosphate are suffi-ciently large to support current trends in fertilizer use for a very long time to come. There is thus no justification for general restrictions on fertilizer usage on the basis of expected future shortages of raw materials. The energy issue related to fertilizer usage is treated elsewhere.

AIR RESOURCES

A considerable amount of the nitrogen applied to crops may be lost through denitrification. Such losses to the atmosphere are believed to have an adverse effect on the ozone layer. It has not been possible to establish an empirical link between application of nitrogen fertilizer and changes in the ozone layer, and it is not clear whether this effect is significant or of theoretical interest only. However, since denitrifi-cation causes large economic losses to farmers, it would clearly be advantageous to reduce these losses, irrespective of the effect on the ozone layer.

PESTICIDES AND THE ENVIRONMENT

Pesticides greatly reduce pest problems in agriculture. They are, unfor-tunately, also responsible for serious environmental and health problems. Some of these undesirable effects are as follows: poisoning of humans, animals and fish; concentration of pesticide residues in humans, animals and fish; development of biological resistance in pests; destruction of natural pest control such as insect-eating birds and predatory insects.

Pimentel and Pimentel (1979) report that use of pesticides on a world-wide basis has caused an estimated 200,000–300,000 cases of human poisoning annually, of which about 5 per cent or 10,000–15,000 were fatal. Although this is a small number when compared to annual deaths caused by starvation, it is nevertheless an issue that cannot be ignored. Poisoning and concentration of residues in humans, animals and fish are caused by the intake of polluted food, feed, water and air, or may be caused by direct contact with pesticides. Most of the poisoning and residue concentration can be avoided through proper handling and application and the banning of some pesticides. Such action would pro-bably not have serious negative effects on pest control and food production.

Extensive pesticide application promotes a process of natural selection in pest populations. Those possessing some immunity to pesti-cides are the most likely to survive and reproduce. This leads to the appearance and proliferation of new strains for which the particular pesticide may be ineffective or effective only if applied in greater quantities. A great genetic flexibility in developing resistance to insecti-cides has been observed among insects regularly exposed to insecti-cides. As genetic resistance develops in pests, greater quantities of pesticide must be applied and new pesticides or alternative pest control methods must be developed. Furthermore, pesticides may destroy beneficial species along with pest species. Thus, natural enemies of pests may be eliminated and the need for chemical pest control increases.

This vicious circle or treadmill can be broken either by ensuring proper application of chemical pesticides or by means of alternative pest control, e.g. further development of genetic pest resistance in plants and biological pest control. Heavy reliance on chemical pest control in the future will result in increasing costs, decreasing effective-ness and the increasing risk of developing pest strains for which no effective pesticide with acceptable environmental risks can be found.

Referring to increasing pest resistance in modern rice varieties and the development of integrated plant protection systems, Ruthenberg (1979) argues that the trend is not necessarily towards higher quantities and more frequent application of pesticides. High rates of application may be only an intermediate stage in the process of land intensification.

9 *Measures to enhance the research contribution*

Agricultural research should be viewed as an element of an overall development strategy. Its contribution to the achievement of development goals depends on existing public policy and institutions. Thus, coordination of research strategy and public policy and institutional change is important in achieving the greatest possible contribution of the overall effort. This chapter discusses four types of measure to enhance the research contribution. Measures to guide research and specify the desired technology are discussed first. Then follows a brief discussion on research management. The third section deals with measures to enhance the contribution of agricultural research results to agricultural production and economic growth, and the final section discusses policy measures to correct undesired distributional effects and/or compensate groups in society which may suffer unacceptable losses or obtain only limited economic benefits from technological change.

MEASURES TO GUIDE RESEARCH AND SPECIFY DESIRED TECHNOLOGY

It should be unnecessary to point out the need to adapt new agricultural technology to the conditions and environments for which it is to be used. Nevertheless, it is not unusual to find that agricultural technology developed in developing countries or for developing countries does not fit the existing production environments and farming conditions. Failing to adapt research results and technology to existing conditions is one of the most important – and in many cases the most important – reason why the adoption of new technology has been very slow and limited to a relatively small number of farms.

The severe criticism of the agricultural extension service in developing countries that is frequently expressed is to a large extent based on the faulty assumption that the technology and knowledge made available to the service is appropriate and adapted to the existing production environments, and that the refusal of many farmers to adopt the technology is due to lack of efficiency within the extension service.

It is interesting to view the criticism of the agricultural extension service in developing countries in a historic perspective. During the late 1940s and the beginning of the 1950s, poor production and productivity performance in the agricultural sector of developing countries was explained by irrational economic behaviour on the part of farmers, particularly small farmers. The point that was made was that they did not attempt to maximize net economic gains and thus were relatively uninterested in expanding production and improving productivity. Results from a series of economic and sociological studies in developing countries later showed that farmers in these countries, irrespective of farm size, were just as economically rational as anybody else in society. Hence, it was no longer possible to explain the lack of adoption of modern productivity-improving technology on the basis of irrationality of the farmers. Instead, the critics turned to the extension service, explaining this lack of adoption as a result of inefficiency on its part. Since then, it became clear that a large part of the technology and knowledge imported from the industrialized countries did not meet the needs and requirements of the agricultural sector in developing countries.

Realizing this, more emphasis has been placed on the development of research capacity within the individual developing countries. However, a large part of the technology and knowledge that has been, and currently is being, developed within the individual developing country is not appropriate for large parts of the agricultural sector of many of these countries. This is not caused by lack of desire on the part of researchers and research administrators to develop technology appropriate for the farming sector. It is rather caused by lack of knowledge about the conditions that form the production environment.

Thus, the general criticism of extension services in developing countries should be aimed at their lack of ability or will to improve communication from the agricultural sector to the agricultural research institutions. It is not unusual to encounter the belief, within both research and extension services in developing countries, that the only purpose of the extension service is to facilitate communication from the research and extension services to the farmers, not in the other direction. Such a belief is probably based on the assumption that sufficient knowledge about the conditions determining whether new technology is appropriate for the farmer already exists within the research and extension services. Unfortunately, this assumption is faulty in many cases. The result is that a large part of the research results made available by national research is not adopted by farmers and consequently has little or no value to society.

But which information is needed and how is such information introduced into the decision-making process regarding research priorities and agricultural policy? Decisions regarding priorities within goal-oriented agricultural research is, generally speaking, focused on a specification of the desired technology and choice of the methods to be used in obtaining such technology. The analysis presented here will be limited to the former, i.e. specification of the desired technology. Choice of scientific methods is outside the scope of this book and can be handled exclusively by the researchers themselves within the different research areas.

Decisions regarding the specification of the desired technology should be taken with due consideration to the general development goals and should contain answers to a number of questions, the first of which is: For which agricultural commodity is new technology sought? It is unlikely that sufficient research resources are available to maintain an efficient research programme for all the agricultural commodities produced or of interest within the individual developing country. Instead of distributing insufficient research resources among all agricultural products, it is important to establish priorities in order to ensure sufficiently large research programmes for selected commodities. Of course, a number of research activities are not commodity specific – research on soil and water conditions is an example. The question of commodity priority would obviously not be relevant for such projects.

The second question to be answered in the process of establishing research priorities is whether the desired technology should facilitate improved efficiency, changed commodity characteristics, reduced production risk or a combination of some or all of these. If improved efficiency is the main objective – and it has always been so for a very large part of agricultural research – it is necessary to specify the resources for which the improved efficiency is desired. Should the new technology be labour saving or labour using? Is the primary purpose of the desired technology to increase production per unit of land, or is it more important to reduce production risk? The various forms of technology may have very different impact on the demand for, and return to, the individual resources. Some forms of mechanical technology may result in severe reductions in labour requirements. Thus, such technology may have a negative effect in societies with large unemployment, while it may be advantageous for those societies where labour shortage is a severe handicap to development. In this regard it is important to distinguish between seasonal and year-round unemployment. Seasonal labour shortages are common in agriculture, even in countries with large 'agricultural labour surpluses'. Technology that requires additional labour input during periods of shortage of labour does not conform to the needs of the agricultural sector and is not likely to be adopted.

Some forms of technology require more capital, while others may be introduced without significant increases in capital requirements. The importance of this issue for farmers with small plots and tenants has already been mentioned. The extent of capital requirement is also of great importance for economic growth outside the agricultural sector in countries where the total capital is very limited. Therefore, the question of choice of technology from a resource point of view is important. Development and diffusion of technology that does not correspond to the relative resource endowment of the individual country may hamper economic development, both with regard to growth and income distribution.

If, instead of improved efficiency, the purpose of developing technology is to change commodity characteristics or reduce production risk, the desired characteristics or risk factors that should be changed must be specified before the research is initiated.

The third principal question related to decision-making on research priorities is: For which production environments is the technology to be developed? Should the technology be appropriate for optimal production environments? This issue is of great importance, not only for the possible increase in efficiency and production but also for the distribution of the economic benefits from the new technology among groups of farmers, primarily in so far as regional distribution is concerned. It is likely that the largest increase in production may be obtained through technology adapted to optimal production environments. However, to the extent that these optimal environments are controlled by high-income farmers, such technology may have a negative impact on income distribution. It is important that these relationships are identified before research priorities and agricultural policy measures are decided.

The fourth principal question to be considered in establishing research priorities has to do with the identification of the yield- and production-limiting factors that new technology should remove. The focus here is on factors that limit yields and production within the individual farm, e.g. plant diseases, availability of water, etc. Knowledge of these factors and their influence on yields and production makes it possible to establish research priorities on the basis of the expected impact of alternative technologies on agricultural production and its efficiency.

The fifth and last principal question is that related to the cost and time requirements of the various lines of research, as well as the probability of success for each of these lines.

AREAS WHERE INFORMATION IS REQUIRED

The information necessary to answer the five questions mentioned above may be divided into six areas. These are as follows:

1. The goals of society.
2. Expected future demand for individual agricultural products and their elasticities.
3. The relative scarcity of each of the resources – land, labour and capital, as well as their expected future prices and price elasticities.
4. Yield- and production-limiting factors for each of the agricultural products and the extent of these limitations.
5. The structure of the agricultural sector with primary emphasis on the distribution of land-ownership and control of the various production environments.
6. Cost and time requirements of each of the research strategies and the associated probabilities of success.

Each of these six areas will be discussed in more detail below.

The goals of society

The overall goal of public investment in agricultural research is to obtain benefits of use to society. The usefulness of research output to society depends partly on the nature of the research results and partly on the goals of society. The measurability of the value to society of a given research output should not be used as a criterion for the allocation of research resources. In fact, the value to society of research output cannot usually be estimated *ex ante* with any great certainty. What is important is that research priorities are established and research resources allocated on the basis of well-defined goals and, utilizing the best possible available information, to attempt to obtain the largest possible contribution to these goals.

Decisions regarding research priorities are relatively uncomplicated in cases where economic growth is the sole objective. However, most societies attempt to meet multiple objectives through public investment and economic policy, and it is not unusual for conflicts of interest to occur. Attempts to accelerate economic growth may have undesirable effects on income distribution. Redistribution of existing incomes may result in decreasing GNPs, e.g. negative economic growth. Likewise, alternative research strategies may have quite different impacts on the achievement of the individual goals. Therefore, it is important to keep the aims of society in mind when establishing research priorities. This does not mean that research priorities must necessarily be established in such a way that the research results meet all the requirements of society. Agricultural research must enter into the overall development strategy and must be aimed at the goals that it is most capable of meeting.

Agricultural research is particularly capable of contributing to economic growth through improved efficiency, increased production of agricultural commodities and the freeing of resources from agriculture for use in promoting economic growth outside the agricultural sector. Therefore, the expected contribution of alternative agricultural research strategies to growth should play an important role in establishing research priorities. The distribution of the benefits associated with economic growth is also of considerable interest within most societies and must also be incorporated into decisions on research priorities.

As mentioned above, agricultural research should be viewed as one of a series of elements which together form the total development strategy. With this in mind, the sole purpose of agricultural research could be interpreted as that of contributing to economic growth, while distributional issues were to be taken care of by other public measures. It could be argued that the purpose of agricultural research is to expand the total GNP as much as possible, irrespective of the distribution of such benefits. If the resulting distribution is unacceptable to society or does not meet distributional aims, this problem should be dealt with by other measures and not by changing research priorities.

If this in fact is the attitude, it is not necessary to know the goals of society to establish research priorities. It is only necessary to know that larger quantities of food and lower costs of production per unit of product are preferable to smaller quantities of food and higher production costs. But if income distribution is one of the objectives, the question is whether other public measures can in fact adjust any undesired distributional effects. This may be the case in some, but certainly not in all situations. In the cases where the undesired distributional effects cannot be corrected by other public measures, the distributional goals must enter into the decisions regarding research priorities. But even if it is possible to change these effects, distributional goals may best be met through the adjustment of research priorities. However, it is important not to place too great an emphasis on distributional goals when establishing research priorities in agriculture, if it implies that most of the potential improvements in efficiency cannot be obtained, and if the problem of distribution can be solved effectively by some other means.

Agricultural research must be viewed first and foremost as an instrument for the promotion of economic growth. Questions of distribution may in many, but not all, cases be dealt with more effectively by alternative measures.

Demand relationships for agricultural products

The expected future demand for each agricultural product, import and export conditions and price elasticities play an important role in determining the degree of benefit to society of agricultural research focused on each agricultural product. Therefore, information regarding these and related conditions must be used to establish priorities among individual commodities. The relationship between socio-economic benefits and their distribution and demand, import, export and price elasticities has been analysed previously, and this section is limited to a discussion of the necessary information and how it may be obtained.

Estimates of the expected future demand for each agricultural product are carried out mainly for other purposes. These estimates should be available for use in establishing research priority without further analysis. On the basis of such estimates alone, research on those commodities for which the largest increase in future demand is expected will take priority. Estimates of price elasticities for the market as a whole are frequently available. However, information on price elasticities for the various consumer groups, e.g. income groups, is very limited. Knowledge of disaggregated elasticities may contribute to a more effective research resource allocation in cases where there is a bias towards distributing research benefits in favour of certain groups, e.g. malnourished or low-income groups.[1] The impact of changes in income distribution on future demand for individual food commodities is another factor which is rarely taken into account in estimations of the future demand for agricultural products. This factor may be of great importance, particularly in countries where the existing income distribution is very skewed and where changes are expected.[2]

Demand conditions for agricultural commodities may have considerable impact on the distribution of research benefits between the agricultural and consumer sectors. It may be expected that the agricultural sector will obtain the largest proportion of the economic benefits from research on export commodities, commodities which at present are mostly imported, and those with high price elasticities. The latter group includes goods where popular demand is dampened down by high prices. This is the case for many animal products in a number of developing countries. Consumers tend to obtain a large proportion of the economic benefits from research on commodities which are totally consumed within the individual country, and which occupy a large proportion of the total food budget. These include most grains, potatoes, cassava and other staple foods in most developing countries.

Changes in the distribution of incomes may, as mentioned above, greatly influence food demand. Generally, a more even income distribution implies an increase in demand. Such increases may be considerable, even though the total national income remains unchanged. However, it is difficult to project the impact of changes in the income distribution on the demand for the individual food commodities without information on the income elasticities for the various income groups. The reaction of the individual income groups to changes in incomes may vary considerably from one country to another.

Relative resource scarcity and resource prices
Information on resource scarcity and relative resource prices is important as a basis for establishing research priorities. Such information is concerned with, for example, expected future employment in society as a whole, expected future capital scarcity and the extent to which the particular country is expected to be dependent on imports to cover increasing demand for the individual factors of production, e.g. fertilizers. To the extent that commitments to other objectives permit, effective research priorities should direct future research along a path that would imply increasing demands for resources in ample supply, as well as those that are currently underutilized. Thus, in societies with high unemployment and with very limited possibilities of expanding the agricultural area, research priorities should attempt to develop technology that is labour using and land saving. Where lack of foreign exchange is a serious problem, agricultural research should be directed towards saving resources that can only be obtained through imports. Examples of such resources might be some forms of energy and fertilizers in a number of developing countries.

The relative resource scarcity is, of course, only one of the conditions, which together form the basis for establishing research priorities. Hence, it is not unusual to find conflict between research priorities dictated by relative resource scarcity, and those dictated by other factors. Relative resource scarcity should not be blindly followed in establishing research priorities. Rather, the trade-off between a number of factors important in establishing research priorities must be considered.[3]

Yield-limiting factors and knowledge of the existing farming system
Effective agricultural research priorities must be based on information on the most important yield-limiting factors within the individual farm,

as well as the impact of each of these factors on yields and production of the commodities on which research is desired.

Yield and production losses caused by one yield-limiting factor are a measure of the improvement in yield and production which could be obtained if this factor were removed, for example through agricultural research. Knowledge of the particular yield-limiting factor and its influence on yields and production may be a very useful guide in establishing research priorities within the given commodity. Removal of factors which cause large production losses will naturally have a greater value than the removal of those causing smaller production losses within any given commodity.

In some cases, the most important yield-limiting factors may be pointed out on the basis of general knowledge of the production environment without further data collection and analysis. This was the case in wheat and rice at the time of initiation of international research on these commodities in CIMMYT and IRRI. It was generally known that lodging very largely prevented yield increases. Furthermore, rust disease was a dominant yield-limiting factor in wheat.

However, in most cases it is not immediately obvious which factors cause the largest loss of yield and production. Lack of information in this area is largely due to insufficient knowledge of the individual farm and its production conditions, as mentioned earlier. A continuing flow of information regarding production problems from the individual farm through the extension agent to researchers must be attempted. If this cannot be realized, it may be possible to obtain the necessary information by means of special projects.

Such projects have been carried out at a number of international agricultural research institutes. The purpose of these projects is partly to obtain the necessary information for use by the international institutes in their research planning, and partly to attempt to introduce such projects in countries where there are no effective means of ensuring a continuing flow of information on production problems.

The approach used in the above-mentioned projects vary among the international institutes. It generally involves the collection and analysis of data from samples or panels of farmers and possibly other rural groups. In some cases, the primary data are obtained from interviews. Other studies rely on a combination of interviews and field observations. Still others combine interviews, field observations and field trials. In some cases, panels of farmers are under study for an extended period, with frequent or almost continuous data collection. In other cases, data are obtained from one or a few visits to each farm (interviews and/or field observations). A few examples are presented below to illustrate the various approaches used.

The first approach is exemplified by work done by IRRI and collaborating institutions in various Asian countries. This work estimates and analyses the gap between potential and actual farm yields. Some of the questions addressed are as follows (De Datta, et al., 1978):

1. What is the gap between yields with current farming practices and the highest yield possible after predetermined production factors are modified?
2. How much of the yield gap can be attributed to each of the predetermined production factors?
3. What are the economic costs and returns associated with the difference between current practices and the maximum yield level of the selected factors?
4. How much of the yield gap can be profitably recovered?
5. If the inputs that are most profitable differ from the actual inputs used by farmers, what personal, social, institutional or political factors prevent them from using the most profitable levels?

The approach consists of on-farm trials and farm surveys. Major emphasis is on the former, while the latter plays a supporting role only. On-farm trials are designed to provide information on the yield effect of each of a series of selected changes in the production system. Furthermore, the impact of such changes on costs and net returns is estimated. Using this approach, it is possible to estimate the contribution of each of the yield constraints to the total yield gap. It is also possible to estimate which changes in the production system would lead to higher net returns to the farmer. Thus, this approach serves as a guide for adaptation of available technology and design of new technology, and provides a means for improving the relevance of agricultural research and technology to current problems.

The concept of yield gaps is illustrated in Fig. 9.1. Yield gap I refers to the difference between experimental station yields and potential farm yields caused by differences in climatic, soil and other physical-environmental factors that cannot be changed. Yield gap II reflects a series of biological and socio-economic constraints. It is on this latter yield gap that the research is focused.

The approach has been used since 1974 in a number of Asian countries. The work has been coordinated by IRRI through the International Rice Agro-economic Network (IRAEN). The project is interdisciplinary in nature with the participation of agronomists, agricultural economists, statisticians and others.[4]

Another approach is exemplified by the ICRISAT village level

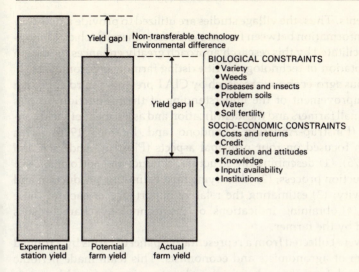

Fig. 9.1. The concept of yield gaps (Gomez, 1977).

studies. These are based on frequent collection of data over a relatively long period. They were initiated in 1975 in six villages. Two villages were selected in each of three agro-climatical regions of semi-arid tropical India. (Binswanger and Ryan, 1979; Jodha, Asokan and Ryan, 1977). Within each village a sample of 30 farmers in three size classes and 10 landless labourers were randomly selected as a panel to be monitored over a number of years. An investigator was stationed in each village to interview the panel households every three to four weeks and to undertake a number of agro-biological investigations. He was also to act informally as a participant observer. Data are collected on agricultural operations on a plot basis. They include labour inputs and time allocation of each household member, economic transactions, farm structure, capital endowment and a series of anthropological data. Data on nutrition and health were collected by a special team. The primary objectives of the activities mentioned above are (a) observation and documentation of existing practices to help in the assessment of research priorities and potential technology, and (b) generation of a data bank for a broad range of socio-economic inquiries (Binswanger and Ryan, 1979).

In addition, the villages are being used for testing and adapting new technology and farming systems components. Examples of such activities are field trials on potential yield effects of herbicides, studies of traditional tank irrigation systems and a series of land-management experiments. Thus, the village studies are utilized to provide a two-way flow of information between farmers and researchers. Such close interaction facilitated by this research approach greatly enhances the design and adaptation of technology to fit existing farming environments.

Previous agro-economic research by CIAT presents a third approach to the improvement of the understanding of the production process among small farmers and the identification and assessment of yield constraints (Pinstrup-Andersen, Londono and Infante, 1976). This approach focused on four principal aspects (Pinstrup-Andersen and Diaz, 1975): (1) describing the structure, conduct and performance of the production process; (2) identifying factors limiting production and productivity; (3) estimating the relative importance of each of these factors; (4) obtaining indications of the technology characteristics preferred by the farmer.

Data were collected from a representative panel of farms by a trained field team of agronomists and economists. This team made periodic visits to each farm throughout a complete growing season. Most data were obtained from direct observation and measurement in the fields, supplemented by subsequent laboratory analyses of soil samples and plant or insect samples for which no immediate diagnosis could be established in the field. Field observations were further supplement by interviews with farmers on issues not identifiable in the field, such as input use.

Data were collected on the occurrence and severity of each of the factors expected to limit yields in the crop for which the analysis was carried out. These factors vary according to crop and region. In general, they included crop diseases, insects, weeds, soil characteristics and fertility, cultural practices, rainfall and water management, plant type, cropping system and use of fertilizers, seed, insecticides, labour and other inputs.

Yield losses were estimated on the basis of a production function analysis, in which observed yields were regressed on the factors expected to influence yields. No on-farm trials were performed. The area affected by each of the factors was estimated directly from the sample data, and production losses were then estimated as average yield losses multiplied by the area affected.

In order to estimate the market value of the losses caused by each yield-limiting factor, an estimate was made of the expected price change due to the production increase which would occur if the factor were removed. This price change was estimated on the basis of existing price elasticities of demand and supply for the particular crop.

This approach was used for cassava and beans in a number of regions of Colombia. Figure 9.2 illustrates the result (average yield losses) obtained from one such analysis. The estimated value of losses caused by each of the identified yield constraints provide guidelines for the benefits from research and technology capable of alleviating the particular constraint, and thus assists in establishing research priorities.

The work of CIMMYT in a number of developing countries may be mentioned as a fourth example of the kind of research discussed here. The CIMMYT work uses farm surveys as a first step to the planning and execution of adaptive agricultural research. Following the surveys, on-farm trials are being carried out. An overview of CIMMYT work is provided in Fig. 9.3.[5]

All the above activities are carried out either by multidisciplinary teams, including social and natural scientists, or by agricultural economists in close collaboration with biological scientists.

The agricultural structure
The structure of the agricultural sector may greatly influence the rate of adoption of new technology and the associated distribution of economic benefits. Information regarding the geographic distribution of the various production environments and the relationship between land-ownership, farm size and infrastructure on the one hand, and production environment on the other, is of particular importance for establishing research priorities. Are the optimal production environments controlled by the better-off-farmers? How will the adoption of the technology be distributed among the various groups of farmers? The relationship between farm size and access to the markets for production factors and agricultural products is also a topic on which information is required. The importance of the structure of the agricultural sector for the introduction of modern technology is further discussed in Chapters 2 and 5.

Costs, time requirements and probabilities
Information on costs and time requirements associated with the individual research programme, as well as the probability of obtaining the desired technology, are natural elements of decision-making on research priorities. This is an area where exact quantitative estimates may be very difficult or impossible to obtain. In most cases the best information regarding these topics is obtained through personal estimates made by individual researchers and research groups. While the annual costs can be estimated, it is frequently very difficult or impossible to estimate time requirements and the probability of success because of the nature of the research. However, active researchers are

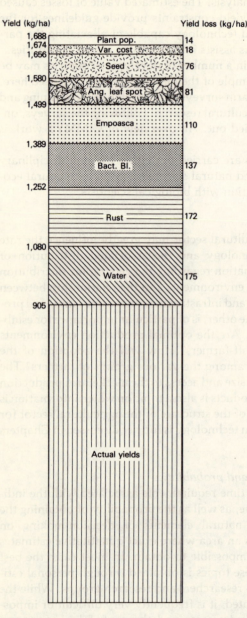

Yield (kg/ha)   Yield loss (kg/ha)

1,688	
1,674	Plant pop. — 14
1,656	Var. cost — 18
	Seed — 76
1,580	
	Ang. leaf spot — 81
1,499	
	Empoasca — 110
1,389	
	Bact. Bl. — 137
1,252	
	Rust — 172
1,080	
	Water — 175
905	
	Actual yields

Fig. 9.2.   Loss estimates in bean production in Cauca Valley, October 1974–January 1975 (Pinstrup-Anderson, Londono and Infante, 1976).

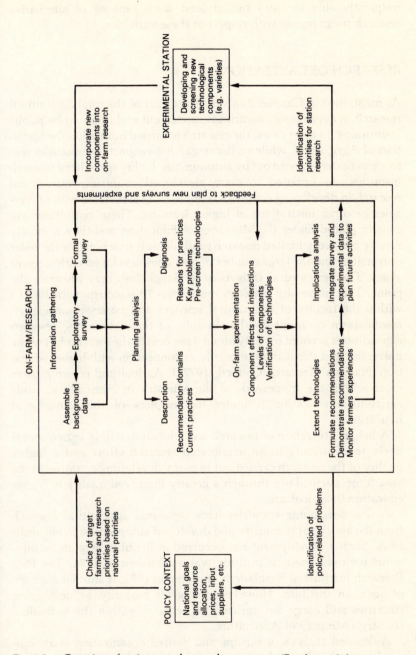

Fig. 9.3. Overview of an integrated research programme (Byerlee et al., 1979).

frequently able to carry out at least some ranking of alternative research programmes with respect to these variables.

RESEARCH ORGANIZATION

As mentioned in Chapter 3, a very large part of the total agricultural research in developing countries is carried out and financed by public institutions. In most cases, the research is carried out within the Ministries of Agriculture, while earlier research on export commodities was to a great extent carried out by autonomous, highly specialized research institutes. As opposed to many developed countries, agricultural research in developing countries is not usually associated with universities or other institutions of higher learning. These institutions are usually placed under the Ministries of Education and they normally receive only very limited research funds. This is true both for the older universities and the large number of new ones developed within recent years. The agricultural University in Bangladesh may illustrate the point. This university employs more than 70 scientists with Ph.D.s within the faculty of agricultural sciences and possesses an experimental farm of about 250 ha. In spite of these resources, research expenditures account for only about 5 per cent of the total budget of the university and this is used primarily in connection with higher education (National Research Council, 1977a). Agricultural research takes place within the framework of the Ministry of Agriculture, while agricultural education is under the auspices of the Ministry of Education.

A better integration of research and education within agriculture is likely to contribute to an accelerated research effort and a higher quality of the research carried out in many developing countries in the long term, particularly through a greatly improved quality of higher education in agriculture.

A few developing countries have separated agricultural research from the agricultural ministry and developed autonomous public institutes. Such a development has occurred in Brazil, where an autonomous national research institute was established in 1974. The Rice Research Institute in Bangladesh, initiated in 1973, is another example of such an institute. However, the great majority of developing countries still carry out agricultural research within the individual country's Ministry of Agriculture.

A detailed analysis of existing and desired organization of agricultural research is beyond the scope of this book (Arnon, 1968). Only a few of the organizational issues believed to be of great importance in ensuring an effective research effort and a large social value of the resulting technology will be discussed here.

The research efforts must be organized in such a way that they are goal oriented. The individual research activities must be coordinated in order that they provide a single focus and not a series of more or less unrelated projects. The research organization must ensure a close and efficient working relationship between national researchers and researchers working at regional and international institutes. Likewise, it is important that the organizational structure facilitates effective contact between researchers and the agricultural sector, directly, through the extension service or perferably both. As mentioned in Chapter 2, such contact is extremely important to ensure that research efforts are focused on those problems that are most important for the agricultural sector. Unfortunately, effective contact between research institutions and farmers is not often found in developing countries. Awareness of this problem might influence the future research organization in such a way as to improve this contact. In addition to consideration of the needs within the agricultural sector, it is important that planning and priority setting within agricultural research is carried out on the basis of the overall development strategy and objectives within the individual country, the relative resource endowment, and related issues. Agricultural research must be viewed as an integral part of the total development strategy and not as an isolated activity.

Although the individual research activities must be coordinated, it is important that each scientist is given sufficient flexibility in his daily work and protection against unnecessary control and other bureaucratic obstructions. Success in research depends to a very large extent on the abilities and motivation of the individual scientist, as well as the opportunities afforded him for carrying out his work within a favourable environment. The need for an organizational structure and administration that facilitate research instead of controlling it, is not well understood in many developing countries. This lack of understanding is primarily due to the fact that no difference is made between organization and administration of research and organization and administration of other more routine-type activities. The carrying out of research within independent institutes may facilitate the right research environment to a greater extent than would be the case within a country's Ministry of Agriculture.

However, irrespective of where in the government sector the research institution is placed, a flexible and decentralized organization and administration of research place large demands on the individual researcher. An insufficient number of well-qualified and highly moti-vated agricultural researchers is one of the most important obstacles to an accelerated and improved agricultural research sector in many developing countries. This situation is closely connected with the fact that a relatively small number of people from these countries have obtained a sufficiently good research training. Furthermore, a rela-tively large number of these work elsewhere, i.e. outside the area of research or in research in developed countries or international institu-tions. The poor ability of research institutions in developing countries to compete with private enterprise and with research institutions in developed countries, in so far as salaries and working conditions are concerned, together with poor financial support for agricultural research, are probably the most important reasons why many of the highly qualified and highly trained agricultural researchers in develop-ing countries do not work in their own countries. Thus, there is a great need to improve working conditions, salaries and other related matters, and at the same time to ensure that a larger number of researchers are given adequate training.

MEASURES TO PROMOTE ADOPTION AND GROWTH

Measures aimed at a better adaptation of new technology to existing conditions, – i.e. planning of research and technology development in such a way that the desired technology would be specified prior to its development – were discussed in the previous section. Such measures contribute, of course, to an accelerated introduction and use of new technology. In this section, the point of departure is a situation where a given technology is already available. The focus is on measures which may accelerate the diffusion and adoption of such technology. Of course, the need for such measures would depend on the extent to which it was possible to adapt the technology to the needs of agriculture and the existing production environment.

Two requirements must be met before the individual farmer will adopt new technology. First, he must be aware of the existence of the technology and its characteristics. Secondly, he must be convinced that the adoption and use of the technology will contribute to increased earnings, reduced production risk, reduced labour requirements or in some other way meet his personal aims. If these two requirements are met, adoption of the technology would depend on the presence or absence of adoption-limiting factors, and whether such factors are removed. Measures that may be available to ensure that both the above-mentioned requirements are met and to assist in removing existing adoption-limiting factors, are discussed below.

KNOWLEDGE OF NEW TECHNOLOGY

In order to ensure that the farmers become familiar with new technology and its characteristics, there is a need for an extension service or some similar activity capable of disseminating the necessary information effectively. Local testing and demonstration are a very important part of such dissemination. It is important that both testing and demonstration in the last instance take place on actual farms and not on experimental stations. The reason why this is so important is that the testing must take place in a production environment and under typical local production conditions (apart from those that the new technology is supposed to change) in order to ensure that the test results will, in fact, be applicable locally. It is also important because farmers, for obvious reasons, have greater confidence in results from tests and demonstrations carried out under conditions with which they are familiar. It follows that the primary purpose of local testing and demonstration is to ensure that the technology in fact produces advantages under existing production conditions, as well as to convince the farmer that he can obtain these same advantages.

The possible difference between the real and perceived advantages of new technology should be pointed out here. Decisions regarding the adoption and use of new technology on the individual farm are based on the individual farmer's perception of the benefits he may obtain and not on those that he would actually obtain. On the other hand, the continued use of an adopted technology is determined by the benefits that the farmer actually obtained on the basis of prior use. Attempts must be made by the extension service, and by local testing and demonstration, to ensure that the benefits perceived by the farmers are, in fact, real. Unfortunately, in many cases the information given to farmers regarding new technology and other changes in the production system promise considerably more than could be delivered under the existing production environment. This, of course, is not due to any desire on the part of the extension service to harm the farmers. It is rather due to lack of knowledge regarding the existing production environment and the production constraints within which the farmer operates. Closely related to this is the problem of lack of local testing before new technology and recommendations are released. Recommended fertilizer practices are a case in point. Such recommendations are frequently made on the basis of very little or no local testing.

Deviation between what the farmer is told he will gain if he adopts a certain new practice, and what he actually gains contributes to a lack of confidence in the extension service. Such lack of confidence, in turn, makes it very difficult for the service to convince the farmers to adopt new technology that in fact may deliver what it promises. Close inter-action between the development and diffusion of new technology, the knowledge of extension agents, the experience gained by farmers and existing production environments and constraints must exist to make the recommendations to farmers as realistic as possible and thus avoid a communication gap. Such interaction implies two-way communi-cation, i.e. from the extension service to farmers as well as in the reverse direction. Unfortunately the latter is often missing. Integrated rural development programmes in a number of developing countries are now trying to introduce such interaction. Unfortunately, the great majority of developing countries still maintain a traditional extension service where the majority, or all, communication takes place only in one direction, i.e from the extension service to farmers.

INCREASED EARNINGS

As mentioned above, farmers are unlikely to adopt new technology unless they expect that such adoption will contribute to the achieve-ment of their personal objectives. The nature of these objectives may vary among indivdual farmers. However, some of the more common are increased earnings, reduced production risk, reduced requirements for family labour and the assurance of a certain minimum standard of living for the family. The extent of the economic gains for the individual farmer associated with the introduction of new technology depends on changes in the value of production and in costs. Thus, the economic gains may be increased by means of higher product prices, lower input prices or a more effective utilization of the inputs.

Government intervention in the price fixing of agricultural products is very common in developing countries, either directly or through trade policies. In some cases, such intervention may be focused on maintaining a sufficiently high product price to ensure a reasonable income to the farm family. Such price-support schemes may also be maintained to promote the introduction of new technology. But government intervention in price fixing of agricultural products may also be disadvantageous to the agricultural sector. Therefore, govern-ment policy to keep food prices at low levels in order to achieve goals related to nutrition, income distribution and political stability are not unusual. It may be argued that such price policy promotes the introduction of new technology because a greater efficiency in production is simply essential under lower prices. However, price policies aimed at maintaining low food prices have severe negative effects on investment in the agricultural sector and will lead to lower production.

Input subsidies may contribute to increasing the economic gains associated with the adoption of new technology. A case in point is the widespread subsidies on fertilizers (see Ch. 7). Public investment in irrigation facilities and other infrastructure may likewise promote the introduction of new technology. Large-scale investments of this nature are currently being made in many rice-producing countries for the purpose of increasing the economic gains associated with the use of new rice technology.

PRODUCTION RISK

New technology expected to increase net earnings by farmers may not be introduced because it also increases production risk. Measures to avoid this for the individual farmer would therefore be effective in promoting the adoption of such technology. These measures may be based either on a collective insurance principle, where the risk is distributed among a group of farmers, or the risk may be assumed by private insurance companies or by the government or a government agency. The government may assume production risks, through such measures as government loans for purchase of fertilizer and other inputs, in such a way that the loan payment may be deferred or eliminated in cases of poor harvest. A great variety of public and private measures to remove or reduce the adverse economic results of production risk for the individual farmer has been tried.

However, it is common for most of these measures that reliable information regarding yield levels and other indicators needed to estimate the consequences of risk is very difficult to obtain. This is a particular problem in crops which may be harvested over a longer period, because it is very difficult to verify and control the actual yields obtained. Measures based on a collective insurance principle among farmers suffer from the problem that adverse climatic conditions, e.g. draughts, which are very significant in causing production risk, frequently affect large areas. This may imply that all or a very large part of the farmers participating in the scheme may suffer from production losses at the same time. The collective insurance principle thus has little to offer.

In general, it may be concluded that a very large part of the measures aimed at reducing or eliminating production risk or its consequences for the individual farmer has not been very effective. Thus, the problems associated with production risk must necessarily be taken into account in decision-making regarding research priorities and technology specification. Risk problems associated with new technology must to a very large extent be solved by specifying the technology in the proper way rather than by additional public measures.

OTHER FACTORS LIMITING ADOPTION

In addition to the above, a number of other factors may limit the adoption and use of new agricultural technology. The occurrence of each of these factors and their relative importance vary from one place to another. Four factors seem to be very common. First, lack of capital and credit for purchase of inputs necessary to obtain the full economic gains of modern technology is a very widespread phenomenon. This implies that farmers may be unable to obtain such inputs as fertilizers, irrigation equipment and the like. Secondly, lack of the required inputs at the place and time needed is also a common problem in many developing areas. Thirdly, land tenure issues may hamper the adoption and use of new technology. Fourthly, seasonal labour shortages appear to be an important factor in many localities. Government policies to remove these limiting factors must concentrate on extended credit to agriculture, improved distribution of inputs, larger investment in irrigation facilities and other infrastructure, increased mobility of labour and changes in land tenure legislation.

One obvious problem which many developing countries have been unable to solve satisfactorily is the lack of access to the desired production inputs, and credit at the right time and in the right place. In cases where the public sector is responsible for the distribution of fertilizers and other inputs the timing problem seems to be very widespread, i.e. the inputs do not arrive at the time they are needed by the farmers. On the other hand, where distribution is handled by the private sector the major problem seems to be that the agricultural regions are not sufficiently well covered, i.e. a large number of farmers have absolutely no access to these inputs. This latter is because of the desire on the part of the private sector to limit the distribution to regions with great demand and favourable transportation facilities. Farmers in less populated regions and regions with relatively poor transportation facilities may have no access to these production inputs within a reasonable distance. This, of course, is the policy of the private distribution companies – to concentrate sales where the largest profits can be obtained.

Thus, economic support in some form to private distribution firms and/or improvements in transportation facilities may be necessary to expand input distribution to regions where it is currently insufficient. Solving the problem of correct timing requires improvement of efficiency within the public sector responsible for input distribution. Increased efficiency and reduced bureaucracy are also required in the administration of government credit to agriculture. Existing regulations and requirements frequently make it impossible for the individual farmer – or discourages him from trying – to obtain credit altogether or to obtain it at the right time.

Details of the most effective public measures for a given region must be adapted to existing conditions. Only conditions of a more general nature can be treated here. Attempts to describe specific public policy measures for the individual regions without satisfactory knowledge of the relevant conditions in each region would be just as mistaken as attempting to develop technology for a region without detailed knowledge of the relevant conditions existing in that region.

MEASURES TO INFLUENCE DISTRIBUTION

Equity goals should direct agricultural research priorities only within certain limits. In most cases, agricultural research is more capable of achieving growth than equity objectives. In cases where it is necessary to forgo large production increases and/or efficiency improvements in order to meet equity goals *directly* through new agricultural technology, it may be advisable to try to meet these objectives in some other way. However, there are many cases where they can be taken into account at the time of research planning without significant reductions in the expected impact on economic growth. There are other cases where new agricultural technology may have considerable negative impact on income distribution and where such impact cannot be effectively corrected by other measures. In such cases it is important that equity goals are fully considered as part of research planning. These issues were discussed in more detail in Chapter 2. The purpose of this section is to take a closer look at policy measures that might be available to either correct undesirable income distribution effects or to compensate groups in society that either lose from new agricultural technology or gain less than is socially desirable.

Theoretically, income distribution objectives could be met solely by redistribution of the incomes obtained through taxes, subsidies and other similar measures. However, in practice this is not possible in the great majority of developing countries, partly because it would be impossible to gain the necessary control over individual incomes without unacceptable secondary effects, and partly because the administrative requirements would be greater than could possibly be met. However, measures such as taxes and subsidies do offer some possibilities for the redistribution of the economic gains of agricultural technology. There are a number of other ways in which the desired income distribution may be brought about. A few of these will be discussed below.

The basic relationships between agricultural technology and income distribution were analysed in Chapters 2 and 6 and will be discussed in this section only to the extent necessary to deal with policy measures aimed at changing the income effects. The distribution between the agricultural sector and consumers will be treated first. The distribution pattern without political intervention and its importance for determining research priorities for the individual products have already been analysed. Changes in the distribution patterns may be promoted through price policies, policies regarding exchange rates and policies on export and import of the individual commodities. Price subsidy programmes, export subsidies and policies facilitating import substitution for the commodity for which new technology is being developed contribute to increasing earnings in agriculture, while domestic consumers will obtain a smaller proportion of the total economic gains of such technology. Savings of foreign exchange may, of course, also influence the final income distribution.

Foreign food aid may play an important role in the distribution of economic benefits associated with new technology. External food aid contributes to a larger food supply on the domestic market which, in turn, may lead to downward pressures on prices obtained by domestic farmers. Importation of large quantities of food through aid programmes and the pursuit of low food price policies have contributed to a slow increase in food production in a number of developing countries. On the other hand, food aid has been of great importance for consumers, particularly those with low incomes, in many receiving countries. However, efforts to increase domestic food production through new technology or in some other way, must be accompanied by some measures to protect the domestic farmers from severe negative price effects caused by food aid and adverse price policies. Such protection may be accomplished, or at least attempted, by distribution of the necessary food aid only to those population groups with very limited purchasing power through price discrimination. However, such measures are very difficult to enforce and a negative effect on domestic farm prices probably cannot be entirely avoided, although it might be significantly reduced. Measures resulting in a reduction of domestic production costs, e.g. fertilizer subsidies, transport subsidies for agricultural products or similar measures, may be very useful in protecting domestic farmers from the negative effects of external food aid on their net returns.

To the extent that they have a greater effect on certain groups of farmers, the above-mentioned measures may also be important for the distribution of benefits within the agricultural sector. Policy measures regarding access to credit, water, irrigation facilities, fertilizers, extension services, etc. may be developed and executed in such a way that they carry greater benefits to certain groups of farmers, e.g. farmers with small landholdings. Measures regarding land tenure may likewise influence the distribution of economic benefits from new technology among farm groups. Such measures may also be used to facilitate the necessary adjustments in the agricultural sector. Such adjustment will by itself imply certain changes in the distribution of incomes, and it may be necessary to compensate the losing groups by measures on incomes and employment. A large part of the economic benefits associated with new technology may be taken up by rapidly increasing land prices. This is a topic on which government attention is likely to be urgently needed. Significant changes in the distribution of wealth may occur, partly as a result of the increasing wealth of landowners relative to others in society, and partly because of increasing farm size. Even though such a development may conflict with equity goals in some countries it should be noted that increasing land values imply increasing capital accumulation in agriculture. Such additional capital accumulation makes it easier for the agricultural sector to obtain the necessary credit for the introduction and use of new technology, as well as other production- and productivity-promoting activities. Whether any measures should be introduced to alter the resulting distribution of wealth would, of course, depend on the aims of the individual country.

Finally, with respect to the economic benefits obtained by landless labour, measures to increase the mobility of the labour force should be implemented to the extent possible without undesirable secondary effects on the individual worker and his family. Extensive introduction of biological and chemical technology in some regions has resulted in considerable increases in the demand for labour. In cases where such increases have not been met by a sufficiently large increase in supply, there has been a tendency to introduce labour-saving technology, even though the country as a whole may be experiencing considerable unemployment. Such was the case in the Punjab region of India, as well as a number of other regions particularly well suited to new agricultural technology in a number of developing countries. Lack of geographical labour mobility may thus imply that the possibilities offered by biological and chemical technology for reducing unemployment are not fully utilized. In fact, it is important that government policy aimed at employment within agriculture be carried out with due attention to the employment situation outside the agricultural sector. In this connection it should be noted that rapid technological change in the agricultural sector may have a very significant impact on employment outside the farm in such activities as processing, input and output marketing, construction, input manufacturing, etc. As the effects of technological change penetrate deeper into the economy the employment effect will spread further through input and consumption linkages.[6]

NOTES

1. A method for estimating price elasticities of demand for each of a number of consumer groups and the application of such estimates for research planning is presented by Pinstrup-Andersen, Londono and Hoover (1976) and Pinstrup-Andersen (1977).

2. The importance of changes in the distribution of incomes for the demand for food commodities is illustrated by Pinstrup-Andersen and Caicedo (1978).

3. A method for establishing research priorities on the basis of relative resource endowment, resource prices and output demand is developed by Ramalho de Castro and Schuh (1977). Further discussion of these and related issues is presented by Binswanger and Ruttan (1978).

4. See Herdt and Wickham (1975) and Herdt and Bernsten (1975) for additional details on the IRRI approach.

5. See also Winkelmann and Moscardi (1979), Biggs (1980), and Byerlee and Collinson et al (1980), for interesting presentations of CIMMYT work in this area.

6. See Mellor (1976) for further discussion of the linkage effects.

10   *The need for external assistance*

As discussed in the preceding chapters, agricultural research and the resulting technology may be very effective in increasing food production and improving standards of living in developing countries. However, in spite of large increases during recent years, the extent of agricultural research projects in developing countries is very limited and apparently far below the optimal level from a socio-economic point of view. Furthermore, there are reasons to believe that a large part of the potential socio-economic benefits from current investment in agricultural research in developing countries is not being obtained. This is caused by a number of factors including suboptimal research priorities, reduced research quality and lack of public policy and institutions to facilitate the best possible utilization of the research results.

The possibilities of accelerating economic development and improving living standards in developing countries by means of modern technology are primarily to be realized through expanded research activity, improvements in the quality of the research, improvements in the establishment of research priorities and planning and development of the necessary measures to ensure the best possible utilization of research results.

How may the industrialized countries assist developing countries in their efforts better to utilize the advantages offered by agricultural research and technology? Is there in fact a need for such assistance? If such a need exists, in which areas is it most urgent? How can the greatest effect be obtained per dollar spent in such assistance? These and related questions will be discussed in the present chapter. But first, the degree of past and current external assistance will be briefly discussed.

MAGNITUDE OF EXTERNAL ASSISTANCE

External assistance for agricultural research takes many forms and is frequently closely integrated with that for other agricultural development activities. Furthermore, in some external aid, a clear distinction between research and other activities may not be relevant. Thus, external assistance for agricultural research does not represent a clear, well-defined and delimited area of aid, and only rough approximations of its extent can be provided.

The most reliable app oximation is probably that provided by a CGIAR task force in 1978 (CGIAR, 1978). According to the task force, 'financial commitments by all donors are probably about $200 million a year, perhaps double the level in 1970' (CGIAR 1978: 13). Adjusting for inflation, the real increase was somewhat less than half, i.e. less than 50 per cent over the 1970 level. This figure does not include support of the international agricultural research institutes discussed in Chapter 4.

A large part of external aid for agricultural research consists of investment in research facilities in developing countries and payment of external technical assistance. In addition, financial assistance for graduate training in agricultural sciences outside the developing countries is considerable.

The World Bank and the United States Agency for International Development are the largest contributors of external aid for agricultural research. The World Bank support for national agricultural research is provided in three ways (CGIAR, 1978):

1. For research components within agricultural development projects.
2. For projects solely in support of national research and extension.
3. For research activities of agricultural universities through educational projects.

A summary of World Bank support in each of the three categories for the fiscal years 1970–78 is provided in Table 10.1. While support of agricultural research activities received low priority in World Bank lending until the mid-1970s, it has been the fastest-growing component of the lending programme of agricultural and rural development during recent years, and accounted for 8.6 per cent of total lending in this programme during the 1978 fiscal year (World Bank, 1979).

Support for agricultural research and related activities has also gained increasing recognition within the US Agency for International Development (AID) during recent years. Thus, AID support of agricultural research during the period 1962–68 was estimated at $19.6 million, with an additional $3.5 million spent in 1969. By 1976, support in this area had increased to about $50 million per year (National Research Council, 1977a), and estimates for the 1978 fiscal year are about $75 million (CGIAR, 1978).

Regional development banks provide another significant source of financial support for agricultural research. The Inter-American Development Bank provided loans for agricultural research and agri-

Table 10.1 Summary of World Bank support for agricultural research and extension activities: 1970–78.*

Type of activity	Number of projects	Number of countries	Loan/Credit amount (US$ m.)
Research components in agriculture and rural development projects†	225	71	161.5
Research and extension projects‡	19	10	455.2
Research components in education projects (agricultural universities)§	18	12	50.9

* Excluding support of the CGIAR system.
† Excludes research components in agricultural and rural development projects approved prior to 1970.
‡ Six additional projects, with loans and credits of $122 million, received Board approval in 1979 and raise the total number of countries to 13.
§ Four of these projects were approved prior to 1970.

Source: World Bank (1979).

cultural research and extension projects to the amount of $116 million during 1968–77 (CGIAR, 1978). In addition, the Inter-American Development Bank provided support for other research-related activities and agricultural development projects with research components.

FAO provides very extensive technical support to developing countries in their efforts to create or improve agricultural research institutions and activities. Furthermore, FAO support in other areas of agricultural development, including extension, is of great significance for the utilization of research results and technology. The United Nations Development Programme (UNDP) is the major source of donor funding for FAO research projects, and thus contributes greatly to the overall research support.

In addition to AID, a large number of bilateral donors provide substantial financial and technical support to developing countries in the area of agricultural research. Only a few will be mentioned here.

France maintains extensive collaboration in agricultural research with a number of developing countries through contractual, bilateral arrangements with each country. Under the auspices of two institutions – GERDAT and ORSTOM[1] – agricultural research is carried out in France and many developing countries – primarily former French colonies in Africa. Thus, GERDAT, through its nine research institutes, undertakes research on selected tropical commodities and related issues within a network of about 50 research stations in developing countries and at its headquarters in France (National Research Council, 1977a).[2]

The United Kingdom, Holland, Canada and Japan provide other

examples of extensive bilateral support of agricultural research in developing countries. In addition to financial and technical support in developing countries – either bilaterally or multilaterally – the countries mentioned above provide financial support for research on developing country problems, but which are undertaken in the donor countries themselves. Examples of such activities are institutes or departments of tropical agriculture.

In the area of technical assistance for agricultural research in developing countries, two recently created institutions are of particular interest: IADS and ISNAR. IADS was established in 1975 by the Rockefeller Foundation to assist developing countries in their efforts to strengthen and improve the productivity of agricultural research and development programmes. ISNAR was created in 1979 and has the somewhat narrower focus of assistance for agricultural research. Both institutes work in areas where additional technical assistance is likely to have high returns in terms of expanded food production, improved resource utilization and higher standards of living in low-income countries. However, as in the case of other support to agricultural research, the benefits may not be immediate, and one of the critical issues is whether donors will have the patience to wait for the longer-term results while continuing the financial support. The search for short-term, highly visible results from external assistance is only useful if it does not result in the forgoing of large potential gains in the longer term.

CURRENT AND FUTURE NEEDS FOR EXTERNAL ASSISTANCE

Do developing countries have a need for additional external assistance within the area of agricultural research? The answer is clearly affirmative. Effective planning and execution of agricultural research and the best possible utilization of research results require human resources which, in spite of great progress during recent years, are still very limited in most developing countries. The need for assistance is particularly focused on the expertise developed in the industrial countries over a long period within agricultural research, higher agricultural education and related areas. This does not imply that such expertise may be directly transferable to developing countries. There is also, of course, in this case a need for adaptation to fit local environments and problems.

In addition to the need for human resources, there is a great need for financial assistance in a number of areas. Such financial assistance is needed to cover the cost associated with the utilization of the above-mentioned human resources, as well as importation of materials of various types – whether these are to be used in the actual research or in measures necessary to make research results relevant for the existing conditions and utilize them in the best possible way.

A precise estimate of future needs for financial support for agricultural research cannot be provided. According to estimates by the World Food Conference, expenditure on national agricultural research in developing countries would need to be increased by three and a half times to achieve an annual growth rate in food production of 4 per cent (CGAIR, 1978). Furthermore, the conference estimated that external financial support for such research should be doubled. This would mean about $1.4 billion (in 1977 prices) annually from domestic sources and about $400 million from external sources by 1985 (CGIAR, 1978).

Oram (1978) and Oram et al. (1979) provide additional evidence of the need for accelerated external assistance. According to estimates by these sources, annual research expenditure for 36 low-income countries should increase from $206 million in 1975 to $935 million (in 1975 prices) by 1990. Furthermore, the cumulative capital costs of improvements of research establishments related to food crops in these countries by 1990 was postulated to be $1.58 billion (Oram et al., 1979). Additional investments would be needed for research on other commodities. Expenditure on agricultural extension is estimated to increase from $386 million in 1975 to $1.0 billion by 1990, assuming a standard extension system, and to $1.3 billion if an improved extension system is introduced.

The needs for financial support are not of equal urgency in all developing countries. As shown in Chapter 3, the needs for assistance to promote effective agricultural research are greatest in the poorest countries. But even among some of the relatively better-off developing countries there is a great need for external assistance within agricultural research. The type of assistance mostly needed – as well as the areas within which the assistance is required – may vary considerably from one developing country to another. Some developing countries have a relatively large number of well-trained agricultural researchers. However, in certain of these countries, there may be a need for assistance better to aim research planning and priorities towards the needs of agriculture and society as a whole. Other countries have a very limited number of well-trained researchers. But these countries may perhaps have a well-developed extension service. A number of other examples could be given to illustrate the variation in needs for external assistance among the various countries, with regard both to the extent and type of assistance, and the areas where aid is most urgent. Finally, it should be mentioned that there is reason to believe that external assistance of the above-mentioned types may have very high economic returns. This argument is supported by the information presented in Chapters 5 and 6. However, the magnitude of the benefits will depend on the extent to which the assistance is relevant to the existing and expected future research-related problems in particular developing countries.

As implied in the above discussion, external assistance and collaboration must be tailored to the needs of each country. In general, however, there seems to be an urgent need for external assistance and collaboration in five areas. These are:

1. Training of agricultural researchers.
2. Establishing priorities in research and research planning and execution in the particular developing country.
3. Planning, development and administration of research and testing facilities and institutions in the particular developing country.
4. Execution of research with large external factors or with very specific resource requirements (international or regional research), certain types of basic research (possibly in the industrialized countries) and general international research collaboration and technology transfer.
5. Planning, development and execution of measures to promote the best possible utilization of research results.

Each of these areas will be briefly discussed in the following.

TRAINING OF RESEARCHERS

An increase in the number of qualified agricultural researchers in developing countries is of very great importance for future agricultural development and food production in these countries.

Oram et al. (1979) estimate that the need for agricultural research scientists in 36 low-income countries will increase from about 13,000 in 1975 to more than 76,000 by 1990 or roughly a six-fold increase during a 15-year period. Furthermore, they estimate that the number of extension workers will need to increase from 222,000 in 1975 to about 578,000 by 1990. Clearly, such increases in well-trained manpower will only be possible if supported by extensive training outside the individual developing country, because the necessary training capacity is not yet available within many of these countries.

It has been estimated, that during the next 10 years, there will be a need to provide external agricultural research training for 5,000–6,000 people from developing countries annually. (CGIAR, 1978). Currently, a little more than 3,000 persons from developing countries annually receive such training in the industrialized countries. This training is to a large extent meant to improve the actual research capacity in the various countries. However, an equally or perhaps even more important purpose of this training is to prepare the trainees to contribute to the development of training capacity in their own countries. The best long-term solution must necessarily be to develop the required training capacity within each developing country or, in the case of very small countries and to the extent permitted by national sovereignties, on a regional basis.

The large and increasing need for external research training requires considerable resources and assistance from the industrialized countries, both financial and technical. In particular, institutions of higher agricultural education in these countries will be expected to make a major contribution.

The training offered by the industrialized countries to agricultural researchers from developing countries must be adapted to the specific needs of these countries. Although the need for such adaptation may appear obvious, it should be pointed out that a considerable part of such training has been only of little relevance for their future work. One of the problems has been a strong emphasis on training within basic research, in particular the type of basic research requiring highly specialized technical equipment and high capital investment per researcher. It is very likely that such research will not, or should not, take high priority in the researcher's own country. Furthermore, it is very likely that the kind of specialized technical equipment required to make such research successful will not be available in these countries for many years to come. The research training is frequently very narrow and does not provide the necessary foundation for a broader research effort aimed at the solution of the most pressing research problems in the particular developing country. In addition, research training in industrialized countries frequently does not motivate researchers from developing countries to focus their future research on these problems.

The next issue to be treated is assistance to the development of training capacity in agricultural research within the individual developing country, i.e. the longer-term solution. Such capacity must necessarily be developed in close collaboration with existing agricultural education and agricultural research. It is important that higher education within agriculture, and in particular the section dealing with training of researchers, takes place in very close collaboration with the actual agricultural research. The interaction between active research and research training is extremely important in obtaining the best possible training, and thus the best possible future research staff. Interaction between research training and research activities should not be limited to the minimum required as a part of the actual training, i.e. research forming the basis of theses and dissertations, but should also include actual independent research projects.

Effective interaction between higher education in agriculture and the actual agricultural research is lacking in a number of developing countries. There has been a tendency to separate the two, with the result that research activities by the educational institutions tend to be limited to those required as bases for theses and dissertations. The remainder of the agricultural research is frequently carried out in other institutions and the collaboration between training and research institutions may be very poor indeed.

External aid to develop the educational capacity within agricultural research or to improve the existing capacity in developing countries must be viewed as an element of the overall assistance for agricultural research. Development of institutions that ensure a close collaboration between training and research must be attempted. A number of international assistance projects during recent years have in fact promoted separation of the two activities. While this may facilitate short-term gains in research efficiency, it is likely to have negative effects on research training and future research capacity. Decisions regarding the structure of national training and research are, of course, made by national agencies. However, advice and assistance from industrialized countries have had and still have a significant influence on these decisions. Thus, external assistance must bear a considerable part of the responsibility of ensuring an optimal structure.

The need for assistance in the development or expansion of training capacities in agricultural research in developing countries includes financial and technical assistance with the planning, construction and administration of training facilities and programmes, as well as expatriate teachers. The latter should be viewed as a temporary measure to be discontinued as soon as a sufficient number of nationals have been trained. The long-term solution must be that the individual developing country should become self-sufficient in this respect. The quality requirements used to select expatriate teachers for these positions must be as high, or higher than, those used for filling similar positions in the expatriates' home countries. Unfortunately, such quality requirements have not always been enforced. The importance of the professional and human qualifications of the teacher in a country where the foundation for future research training is being established is difficult to overemphasize. Precisely because most developing countries do not have a long training tradition within agricultural research to fall back upon, the individual teacher has a much greater responsibility and opportunity to influence the future philosophy, quality and priority setting within agricultural research in these countries. It is precisely for these reasons that we must ensure that only persons with very high qualifications in the relevant areas, including a thorough understanding of the situation within which the research problems appear and a deep sense of commitment to development, are selected for the above-mentioned positions in developing countries.

PRIORITY SETTING, PLANNING AND EXECUTION OF RESEARCH

A considerable proportion of agricultural research in developing countries is carried out in isolation. In some cases research is carried out exclusively for its own sake. The importance of integration between research and higher agricultural education has already been mentioned. It is even more important that the priority setting, planning and execution of research is carried out in close collaboration with the total development strategy of the country. Agricultural research must be as relevant as possible for the goals and existing problems in the particular country, whether these problems are found in agriculture, in human nutrition or elsewhere. The establishment of research priorities must be attempted in such a way that the research results – together with other elements of the development strategy – would be expected to make the largest possible contribution to the achievement of the aims of society.

However, many developing countries do not have the necessary expertise to ensure that the research resources are utilized in the best possible way. This situation, together with the possibility of a considerable increase in public funds for agricultural research and the need to ensure the best possible use of these additional funds, means that there is an urgent need for external technical assistance in the area of priority setting and planning of agricultural research. The benefit to society of increasing investment in agricultural research is likely to be very limited in a number of developing countries unless a simultaneous improvement in the expertise related to priority setting and planning is assured. Expanding research investment does not by itself ensure high returns.

Furthermore, in a number of developing countries there is an urgent need for assistance in carrying out the research. This is the case in countries where the number of trained natural researchers is insufficient. In such cases there may be a need to hire expatriate researchers for a shorter or longer period. Such hiring is quite frequent in a number of countries today. However, it is important to point out that the long-term goal must be that the individual developing country becomes self-sufficient in highly qualified agricultural researchers. This does not mean, of course, that researchers from the various countries should not continue to interact, even through stays of longer duration in other countries. It does mean, however, that such interaction in the long term should preferably be a balanced one between equal partners.

RESEARCH AND TESTING FACILITIES

The planning and construction of research and testing facilities require a considerable amount of external assistance in a number of developing countries. Such assistance may be needed both in the physical planning and construction of these facilities and in institutional development. Except for a few developing countries, there is likely to be a need for both technical and financial assistance in this area for a long time to come. The extent of investment requirements in this area was discussed previously. The institutional development is, of course, closely connected with research planning, and the two activities must necessarily be carried out in close collaboration. In addition to the above, some developing countries may have a need for technical assistance for the administration of research and testing facilities. Such assistance may be in the form of stationing expatriate experts for a time, or it may take an advisory form through periodic short visits. However, the goal must be to gain sufficient national capacity within the individual country as soon as possible. Thus, external assistance for administration of research testing facilities, to the extent that it is in fact needed, should be viewed as a temporary solution.

RESEARCH COLLABORATION AND TECHNOLOGY TRANSFER

International transfer of agricultural technology may be divided into three phases (Agrawal, 1979): (1) material transfer; (2) design transfer; (3) capacity transfer.

As mentioned in Chapter 3 international transfer of materials, e.g. seed, machines and equipment, may not produce the desired results in developing countries because the material was developed for production environments and relative resource endowments quite different from those existing in the recipient countries. The problem is particularly obvious in the case of biological technology suited only for certain agro-ecological conditions or mechanical technology developed for certain relative resource endowments and prices. Transfer of material from industrialized to developing countries would tend to be less likely to be successful than transfers among developing countries. This is because the differences in agro-ecological conditions and resource endowments are generally much more pronounced between the former than among the latter. International agricultural research institutes located in developing countries have successfully developed materials, i.e. seed, with transferability to certain well-defined agro-ecological zones in many developing countries. Successful transfer of materials among national agricultural research institutions in developing countries has been more limited, although it appears to offer considerable potential. As research testing networks are developing, this potential is being exploited to a somewhat greater extent.

However, although considerable success has been encountered in the transfer of seed from international agricultural research institutes to various developing countries, transfer of design, e.g. improved lines of plant materials and information, offers much greater opportunities. However, certain national capacities are needed to utilize fully such design. Thus, a combined effort is needed to improve national research, testing and extension capacities, together with a continuation of the development of design which can be successfully transferred to or among developing countries. The need for external assistance on the former was discussed earlier in this chapter. With respect to the latter, it is essential that external assistance to the international agricultural research institutes be continued and expanded as appropriate. Furthermore, some of the research needs of developing countries may be met through research in the industrialized countries. However, the great majority must be carried out in the developing countries themselves.

While external assistance – both financial and technical – for agricultural research will be needed in many developing countries for a long time to come, the ultimate goals must be research collaboration among equal partners. It is particularly important that the collaboration among researchers and research institutions in the various developing countries be strengthened. Common characteristics among many of these countries and great differences in research capacity contribute to a potentially useful interchange of ideas, information, knowledge and materials. Unfortunately, however, for historical, political and possibly other reasons, communication and linkages in the area of agricultural research are much stronger between developing and industrialized countries than among developing countries. The recent development of international research and testing networks is contributing to a somewhat better interaction among developing countries.

EXTERNAL ASSISTANCE FOR TECHNOLOGY UTILIZATION

The importance of a series of measures to facilitate the best possible utilization of research results and technology was discussed in detail in Chapter 9. These measures include such items as extension service, public policy measures, rural development projects and a series of related activities. In reality, agricultural research and technology should be viewed as an integral part of the total agricultural development strategy because the return from research and technology would depend on interactions with other elements of such a strategy. A discussion on the need for external aid for agricultural development as such is beyond the scope of this book. It should be pointed out, however, that there is an urgent need for technical assistance in a number of areas, and that the magnitude of the benefit to society from agricultural research and technology depends to a very large extent on whether such assistance is forthcoming. The specific needs, of course, vary from one country to another and must be specified in each individual case.

NOTES

1. GERDAT is 'groupement d'Etudes et de Recherches pour le Developpement de l'Agronomic Tropicale,' and ORSTROM is 'l'Office de la Recherche Scientifique et Techniques l'Outre-Mer'.
2. See International Agricultural Development Service (1979a) for further details on these institutions.

Conclusion

Food scarcity, malnutrition and absolute poverty are widespread in many developing countries, both within and outside the agricultural sector. Continuation of past growth trends in population, incomes and food production will lead to further deterioration of the current food and nutritional situation. Prevailing hunger, malnutrition and absolute poverty and the prospects of further deterioration are unacceptable on humanitarian, economic and political grounds.

The symptoms of extreme poverty such as hunger and malnutrition, may be treated through public transfers of the goods and services required, e.g. food, to the poor. However, sustained alleviation of extreme poverty requires complex political, institutional and economic changes, including increased participation by the poor in the political process and a higher degree of control over productive resources, increased purchasing power and improved supplies of goods and services needed to fulfil basic human needs.

This book deals with one of the elements of such change: research and technological change in food production. By itself, this will not solve the poverty problem, nor will it end hunger and malnutrition. However, most developing countries will be unable to solve these problems without it: though not sufficient, it is essential.

Successful research and technological change in food production facilitate increased food production at lower unit costs and, thus, generate an economic surplus which may be gained by the poor. The extent to which the surplus is in fact acquired depends on the existing political and economic environment. Increased food production and reduced unit costs may result in lower food prices. Lower food prices, in turn, increase the purchasing power of consumers. Consumers spending a large proportion of their total income on food, i.e. the poor, would be those mostly affected by such expansion in purchasing power. Expanded food production and reduced unit costs may also increase net incomes of food producers and agricultural workers.

Technological change in agriculture provides a vehicle for development that reaches far beyond the more immediate goals of satisfying food and nutritional needs. But the full potential of agricultural research and technology to assist in the achievement of growth and equity goals will be exploited only if they are properly conceived within the overall development strategy and supported by the proper public policy and institutional change. Thus, it is essential to perceive and employ agricultural research and technological change as integral elements of a broader development strategy.

Food production may be increased through expansion of the area used for food crops or through increased yield. New agricultural areas are likely to play a significant role in efforts to expand food production in parts of Africa and Latin America. However, such area expansions frequently require large investments in physical infrastructure and soil-improvement measures. Furthermore, expanding agriculture into marginal lands may cause severe land degradation leading to irreversible damage to the natural environment. Substitution of food for non-food crops on current agricultural land is another possibility of considerable magnitude in some countries. The extent to which this will occur depends on a series of economic and political factors such as relative prices and the dependence of a given country on foreign exchange generated by non-food export crops. Recent emphasis on security of energy supply may lead to extensive use of agricultural land for energy cropping, i.e. production of agricultural commodities for the purpose of making gasohol. Such expansions may reduce the area available for future food production. (Pinstrup-Andersen, 1981).

It follows that while expansion of the area used for food production offer some – however limited – possibilities for expanded food production, they offer little opportunity for reducing unit costs, and we must look to increases in yield as the primary source of increased food production and reductions in unit costs for the future. Agricultural research and technology play a key role in efforts to increase crop yields and reduce unit costs. However, the impact of agricultural research and technology on future food production and on the poor depends very much on the character of the research and technology and the economic, political and institutional context within which technological change occurs.

What are some of the lessons to be learned from past achievements of research and technological change in food production of developing countries? First of all, public investment in agricultural research may be a very profitable undertaking. Internal rates of return in the order of 50 per cent and above are not uncommon, and research and technology are responsible for large increases in the production of certain food commodities in developing as well as developed countries. Thus, it is estimated that about one-third of the 1976/77 wheat production in the

Far East resulted from modern technology. For developing countries as a whole, modern technology was responsible for more than one-fifth of the wheat production. The impact on the production of other crops is less spectacular but highly significant for such crops as rice and sugarcane. While the current food and nutritional situation is bad, it is clear that research and technological change in food production have made a great contribution towards avoiding a much worse situation. Therefore, research and technological change has made food consumers considerably better off than they would have been in its absence. Poor consumers obtained the largest relative gains in purchasing power because they spend a larger proportion of total income on food, and thus are more seriously affected by food price increases than the more affluent consumers.

Technological change in food production – except for certain mechanical technology – has generated additional employment both within and outside agriculture. Accordingly, low-income agricultural workers have obtained additional purchasing power through increased employment, higher wages and reduced food prices. However, in many locations, the availability of labour-saving mechanical technology placed severe limitations on wage increases.

Available empirical evidence shows that new agricultural technology has, in general, contributed to a somewhat more unequal distribution of income and wealth in the producer sector. This is particularly clear where income and wealth distributions were very skewed prior to the introduction of new technology. On the other hand, it appears that the distribution of economic benefits obtained by the consumer sector has in many cases improved the existing relative income distribution among consumers. There has been a tendency for the consumer sector to obtain much larger economic gains than the producer sector, where economic losses are quite common. Early adopters of new technology have, in general, obtained large economic gains. These early adopters are primarily larger, better-off farmers controlling optimum growing conditions.

In many cases, these early adopter gains have been used to acquire more land, e.g. the purchase of smaller neighbouring farms on which modern technology had not yet been adopted. The results have been increased concentration of land-ownership and more landless workers in certain areas. Such adverse development is most pronounced where land-ownership was very skewed prior to the introduction of modern technology and where institutional arrangements and factor markets favoured the larger farmers. In many cases, public policy has implicitly or explicitly promoted concentration of land-ownership on the assumption that larger farms would be more efficient. Most of the new technology developed for the agriculture of developing countries has required additional capital, although the degree of increase in capital demand varies greatly among individual geographical regions and types of technology. Since the efforts to develop new agricultural technology for the developing countries have concentrated heavily on increased production per unit of land, it is no surprise that land productivity and demand for land have increased considerably where such technology has been adopted. Thus, in cases where the sector as a whole, or groups of farmers within the sector, have obtained large economic gains, a considerable proportion of such gains has been capitalized into land values.

In general, it appears that the economic gains associated with the development and introduction of new technology are sufficiently large to compensate those who lose from such technology. But such compensation has rarely – if ever – been paid.

A considerable amount of information about the distribution of benefits from new agricultural production technology is based on incomplete analysis and casual observations. As a result, the effect of new technology has been confused with effects of other changes occurring simultaneously, and causal effects are frequently not fully understood. Furthermore, the performance of new agricultural technology has, in many cases, been evaluated on the basis of a set of criteria quite different from those used when efforts to develop the technology (research and development) were initiated. The overall goal of a large part of agricultural research for developing countries, including research leading to the green revolution, was to facilitate the rapid and efficient expansion of food production through yield increases and reductions in per unit costs to reduce existing and expected future food shortages. If the problem was correctly identified, i.e. large current and/or expected food shortages and low crop yields, so was the research focus.

This does not mean, however, that we should accept undesired side effects of such efforts without taking corrective steps. But we should not discourage effective agricultural research and technology development just because it does not contribute equally to all social and economic goals. New agricultural technology should be viewed as one of the components of an overall strategy for achieving these social and economic goals. Although experience has shown that agricultural technology, more or less by itself, can make major contributions, it is only together with a series of other effective measures, whether facilitating, corrective or compensatory, that its full potential is utilized.

While contemporary distribution of benefits and costs among groups is important, the effects on inter-generational distribution should not be overlooked. What has been the impact of recent technological change on the resource base needed by future generations to meet their food and other needs?

A continuation of current trends of agricultural expansion into marginal lands, rapid rates of deforestation and overgrazing in dry areas are likely to have severe adverse environmental consequences. Land and water erosion and loss of organic matter lead to land degradation and desertification, which in turn will make it more difficult for future generations to fulfil their needs for food, fuel wood and other agricultural and forestry products. Existing poverty and unsatisfied food needs, together with opportunities for quick political and economic gains without having to bear associated environmental costs, naturally lead to exploitation of the land base.

Such exploitation and the resulting degradation of the future land base may be avoided through a combination of technological change and public policy without adverse effects on short-run food supplies. New technology facilitates higher yields on existing agricultural land. Thus, expanded development and use of yield-increasing technology reduces the pressures on new lands to meet increasing demands for food and other agricultural products. New technology may also facilitate conservation of current agricultural land, and it may assist in avoiding adverse environmental effects of incorporating new land into production. But technological change may also promote further degradation of land and water resources. Examples are waterlogging and salinization of land and excessive usage of ground-water.

In addition to accelerating the development and use of modern technology, successful efforts to maintain or improve the productive capacity of the land base must include the appropriate public policies and investment. In particular, policy measures are needed to ensure that long-term social costs are reflected in both public and private decision-making. Such policy measures are frequently absent in developing countries.

Application of large quantities of pesticides may affect the ecological system adversely in a variety of ways. However, a continuation of current efforts to include genetic pest resistance in plants, together with greater emphasis on biological pest control and proper pesticide handling and application, may greatly reduce the environmental risks associated with pest control.

Reduction of the genetic diversity in plants is another important environmental risk associated with technological change. As the diversity decreases on farms, effective steps must be taken to ensure that the genetic material is maintained elsewhere. A considerable amount of work is under way in this area.

Environmental risks associated with the use of chemical fertilizers appear to be rather insignificant, although excessive application rates and poor cultural practices may result in some eutrophication of streams and lakes. However, compared to the effects of urban and industrial sewage and wastes, fertilizers used in agriculture play a minor role.

What are some of the measures that may be introduced to enhance the contribution of agricultural research in the future? Agricultural research and the resulting modern technology clearly offer great opportunities for expanding food production, accelerating economic growth and improving the standard of living of the poor. They may also increase environmental risks and worsen the disparity in the distribution of incomes and assets. The end result will be determined by the efficiency of the research process, the characteristics of the technology developed, the economic and institutional frameworks within which the technology is introduced and the political desire and ability to maintain economic policies aimed at the utilization of research and technology for the benefit of particular groups while avoiding adverse side effects.

Five types of measures are critical to enhance the contribution of agricultural research to growth and equity goals. These are:

1. Expanded public investment in research on food production.
2. Effective research and research management.
3. Measures to guide research and specify the most appropriate technology.
4. Measures to accelerate technology adoption.
5. Measures to avoid or correct undesired distributional effects and/or compensate groups in society which may suffer unacceptable losses or not obtain a sufficiently large part of the economic benefits from technological change.

The high rates of return from agricultural research, mentioned earlier, provide a convincing argument for additional investment in that area. However, merely expanding the amount of financial support is not likely to be sufficient. Ineffective research and research management, together with lack of a proper research aim may prevent potential benefits from materializing, whether or not financial support is increased. Thus, an integrated effort is needed to expand the quantity and quality of research, including measures to assist in the design of technology appropriate for existing farm level problems, resource endowments and development goals in general. Furthermore, additional efforts may be needed to identify and alleviate factors limiting the adoption of appropriate technology, and economic gains from such adoption, with primary emphasis on low-income farmers. Such efforts should not be confused with those to remove constraints to the adoption of inappropriate technology – an exercise that, unfortunately, is not uncommon. Correct technology design is critical for subsequent adoption.

If the distributional effects of new technology are unacceptable to society, various corrective or compensatory measures may be applied. The choice of measures would depend on a variety of factors and should be tailored to each individual case. Therefore, no attempt is made here to suggest specific measures. It may be useful, however, to mention some of the types of measures available to government. These may be preventive, curative or a combination of the two. Preventive measures aim at avoiding undesired distributional effects before they appear or, in a positive sense, to attempt to obtain the desired distributional effects. Such measures may conveniently be divided into two types: (1) those that attempt to influence the technology design; (2) those that attempt to change the socio-economic environment where modern technology is expected to be introduced.

Specification of the desired technology and the establishment of research priorities aimed at obtaining such technology may be an effective way of reducing or avoiding undesired distributional effects. Research to develop technology particularly well suited for low-income farmers and priority on basic food staples are examples of research priorities expected to result in a more equal distribution of benefits. However, the comparative advantage of most new technology is its ability to increase efficiency and production rather than improve income distribution. Looking towards new agricultural technology *per se* as a means to improve significantly the very skewed income distribution currently found in many developing countries would be a mistake. However, together with other measures, new technology may make a major contribution to achieving equity as well as efficiency goals, and has in fact done so in many cases.

These other measures must focus on the roots of the existing skewed income distribution, i.e. uneven distribution of the ownership of productive resources, particularly land, the existing power structure and differential access to factor and product markets. Such measures might include land reform, development of infrastructure and irrigation facilities, subsidized credit programmes for low-income farmers and a series of other government intervention schemes aimed at changing the socio-economic environment. Without such measures it is unlikely that modern technology will be capable of greatly increasing production efficiency, as well as improving income distribution, in situations where the existing income distribution is very skewed.

If preventive measures are not introduced or not sufficiently effective, the distributional effects may be changed through curative measures such as price policies or direct transfers. The above measures, i.e. land reforms, credit programmes, etc. may, of course, also be introduced as curative rather than preventive measures. In particular, curative measures may be needed to correct undesired changes in the socio-economic environment brought about by modern technology.

Severe criticism of modern technology from an equity point of view is likely to have an adverse effect on future investment in technology-generating research and thus on future food supply and standards of living of the poor. Such an outcome can be justified only if modern technology is in fact guilty as accused. Certain things can – and should – be done to improve the design of new technology better to meet equity goals. Thus, some of the criticism is well aimed, although the answer is to change the technology design rather than reduce the research investment. However, the basic issue is one of attacking the root causes of the existing inequality, and modern technology is not one of those. Therefore, the major portion of the above-mentioned criticism should be redirected away from modern technology towards the political inertia regarding the attack on the root causes of existing inequality.

It would be very unfortunate if the large potential social benefits from effective agricultural research and technology were not fully exploited because the absence of facilitating, corrective and compensatory measures made the distributional effects unacceptable to society.

There is an urgent need for external assistance and collaboration within the area of agricultural research and associated activities. The specific content and direction of such assistance and collaboration is likely to vary among countries and should be determined in each case on the basis of needs and expected benefits. In general, external assistance and collaboration are needed for:

1. Training of agricultural researchers including the expansion of training capacities in the various countries.
2. Establishing priorities in research within the individual country and research institution.

3. Research implementation within the individual country as well as internationally.
4. Planning, development and administration of research and testing facilities and institutions within the individual country.
5. A series of measures to promote the best possible utilization of research results including effective extension systems and public policy.

In addition, current international agricultural research must be continued and expanded to meet future needs. The international agricultural research institutes have played a very significant role during the last 15 years. Although the activities and priorities of these institutes may change over time they will continue to be an important element of the overall research effort. Extreme care should be taken to maintain the efficiency of the institute system. As the system expands there is a real danger that it may begin to suffer from unnecessary bureaucratic structures. Furthermore, narrow political interests of the donors may gain ground within the CGIAR. Such developments might seriously reduce the effectiveness of the total research effort with negative effects on future growth in food production. The future funding levels of the system and the individual institutes within the system must necessarily be based on expected returns, both within and outside the system. Donors and institute boards are faced with difficult choices and trade-offs regarding relative levels of funding for international research versus other activities such as national research, extension and rural development projects. Given the long-term nature of most agricultural research and considering past performance and future needs, it is clear that international agricultural research should continue to receive high priority in international economic aid for food and agriculture. Provided that past and current effectiveness of the CGIAR system can be maintained, funding for this system should reflect such priority. Attempts to reduce economic assistance to the system on the grounds that the need for international agricultural research is diminishing cannot be justified for a long time to come.

Increased agricultural research, whether national or international, is critical to improve or avoid a worsening of the current food and nutritional situation. Agricultural research provides a vehicle for economic growth and improving the living standards of the poor. But the contribution made by research is long term. Thus, the adverse effects of failure to invest in research today may be most severely felt 10–20 years into the future. Or, conversely, we are currently benefiting from the foresight of certain people 10–20 years ago in expanding investment in research in food production in developing countries.

Without it, many more people would have suffered from starvation and nutrition-related death, and the income and living standards of many others would have been considerably lower than they now are. Hopefully such foresight will prevail into the future.

References and bibliography

Agble, W. K. (1980) Agricultural research in Ghana. In *Strengthening National Agricultural Research*, Bo Bengtsson and Getachew Tedla (eds). SAREC Report R1-1980, Stockholm: 36–43.

Agrawal, R. C. (1979) Future international cooperation in science and technology for the development of agriculture. In *Science and Technology and the Future*, Hans Buchholz and Wolfgang Gmelin (eds). K. G. Saur, New York, London.

Akino, M. and Hayami, Y. (1975) Efficiency and equity in public research: rice breeding in Japan's economic development, *American Journal of Agricultural Economics* 57, No. 1 (Feb.): 1–10.

Alix, Jesus C. (1978) *The Impact of the MASAGANA 99 Program on Small Farmer Production and Income in the Philippines*. Research Report No. 11. Ministry of Agriculture, The Philippines, Quezon City.

Andersen, Kym (1979) Public agricultural research investment in developing countries: a politico-economic theory. Paper presented at the 17th International Conference of Agricultural Economists. Sept. 3–12, Banff, Canada.

Anthony, Kennedy, R. M. et al. (1979) *Agricultural Change in Tropical Africa*. Cornell University Press, Ithaca.

Ardito Barletta, N. (1970) Costs and social benefits of agricultural research in Mexico, Ph.D. dissertation. Chicago: University of Chicago.

Arndt, T. M., Dalrymple, D. G. and Ruttan, V. W. (eds) (1977) *Resource Allocation and Productivity in National and International Agricultural Research*. University of Minnesota Press, Minneapolis.

Arnon, I. (1968) *Organization and Administration of Agricultural Research*. Elsevier Publication Co., Amsterdam.

Arnon, I. (1975) *The Planning and Programming of Agricultural Research*. Food and Agricultural Organization of the United Nations, Rome.

Asian Development Bank (1977) *Asian Agricultural Survey 1976: Rural Asia Challenge and Opportunity*. Manila, Philippines, April.

Atkinson, L. J. and Kunkel, D. E. (1976) *High Yielding Varieties of Rice in the Philippines: Progress of the Seed-Fertilizer Revolution*. USDA, ERS, Foreign Agricultural Economics Report, No. 113, Washington, DC.

Ayer, H. (1970) The costs, returns and effects of agricultural research in a developing country: the case of cotton seed research in Sao Paulo, Brazil. Ph.D. dissertation. Lafayette: Purdue University.

Ayer, H. W. and Schuh, G. E. (1972) Social rates of return and other aspects of agricultural research: the case of cotton research in Sao Paulo, Brazil, *American Journal of Agricultural Economics* 54, No. 4 (Nov., Part 1):557–69.

Bal, H. K. and Kahlon, A. S. (1977) Methodological issues on measurement of returns to investment in agricultural research, *Indian Journal of Agricultural Economics* 32 (3) July–Sept.: 181–92.

Barker, Randolph (1977) Socio-economic constraints to the production of photoperiod sensitive transplanted rice in eastern India. Paper presented at International Seminar on Photoperiod Sensitive Transplanted Rice of South and Southeast Asia. (Oct.) Dacca, Bangladesh.

Barker, Randolph (1979) Establishing priorities for allocating funds to rice research. Paper presented at the 17th International Conference of Agricultural Economists. Sept. 3–12, Banff, Canada.

Barker, Randolph et al. (1975) *Production Constraints and Priorities for Research*. International Rice Research Conference, IRRI, Los Banos, Philippines.

Barker, R. and Anden, T. (1975) Factors influencing the use of modern rice technology in the study areas. In *Changes in Rice Farming in Selected Areas of Asia*, IRRI, Los Banos, Philippines.

Barker, Randolph and Herdt, Robert (1977) *Trends and Cyclical Fluctuations in World Rice Production*. IRRI, Los Banos, Philippines.

Barker, R., Meyers, M., Crisostomo, M. and Duff, B. (1972) Employment and technological change in Philippine agriculture, *International Labour Review* 106, No. 2–3 (Aug.).

Barney, Gerald O. et al. (1980) *Entering the 21st Century: Report of the Global 2000 Study to the President*, Technical Volume. US Government Printing Office.

Bell, Clive and Hazell, Peter (1980) Measuring the indirect effects of an agricultural investment project on its surrounding regions, *American Journal of Agricultural Economics* 62 (Feb.): 75–86.

Bengtsson, Bo (1977) *Past, Present and Future Swedish Support to International Agricultural Research*. SAREC Report 1, No. R2, Stockholm.

Bengtsson, Bo (1980) *Strengthening National Agricultural Research*. SAREC Report R2–1980, Stockholm.

Bengtsson, Bo and Getachew Tedla (eds) (1980) *Strengthening National Agricultural Research*, SAREC Report R1–1980, Stockholm.

Bente, P. E., Jr (1977) *The Food-People Problem: Can the Land's Capacity to Produce Food be Sustained*. Council on Environ. Qual., Exec. Office of the President, Washington, DC.

Bentley, C. F. et al. (1979) *Soils*. Report prepared for the Conference Agricultural Production: Research and Development Strategies for the 1980's, Bonn, Oct. 8–12.

Berry, R. Albert and Cline, William R. (1979) *Agrarian Structure and Productivity in Developing Countries*. Johns Hopkins University Press, Baltimore.

Bhalla, Surjit (1979) Farm size, productivity and technical change in Indian agriculture. In *Agrarian Structure and Productivity in Developing Countries.* R. Albert Berry and William R. Cline (eds). Johns Hopkins University Press, Baltimore.

Bieri, J., de Janvry, A. and Schmitz, A. (1972) Agricultural technology and the distribution of welfare gains, *American Journal of Agricultural Economics* 54, No. 5 (Dec.): 801–8.

Biggs, Stephen D. (1980) On-farm research in an integrated agricultural technology development system: case study of triticale for the Himalayan Hills, *Agricultural Administration* 7, No. 2 (April–June): 133–45.

Binswanger, Hans P. (1978) *The Economics of Tractors in South Asia.* Agricultural Development Council, New York.

Binswanger, Hans P. (1980) Attitudes towards risk; experimental measurement in rural India, *American Journal of Agricultural Economics* 62, No. 3 (Aug.): 395–407.

Binswanger, H. P. and Ruttan, V. W. (eds) (1978) *Induced Innovation: Technology, Institutions and Development.* Johns Hopkins University Press.

Binswanger, H. P. and Ryan, J. G. (1977) Efficiency and equity issues in ex ante allocation of research resources, *Indian Journal of Agricultural Economics* 32, No. 3 (July–Sept.): 217–31.

Binswanger, Hans P. and Ryan, James G. (1979) *Village Level Studies as a Locus for Research and Technology Adaption.* International Symposium on Development and Transfer of Technology and Rainfed Agriculture and the SAT Farmer, ICRISAT, Hyderabad, India; Aug.

Biswas, Margaret R. and Biswas, Asit K. (eds) (1979) *Food, Climate, and Man.* Wiley, New York.

Borlaug, N. E. (1968) Wheat breeding and its impact on world food supply, *Proceedings of Third International Wheat Genetics Symposium.* Canberra.

Borlaug, Norman E. and Aresvik, Oddvar H. (1973) The green revolution – an approach to agricultural development and some of its economics implications, *International Journal of Agrarian Affairs,* Vol. V., No. 6.

Bowler, Ian. (1979) *Government and Agriculture – A Spatial Perspective.* Longman, London.

Boyce, K. and Evenson, R. E. (1975) *National and International Agricultural Research and Extension Programs.* Agricultural Development Council, New York.

Bredahl, Maury, E., Bryant, W. Keith, and Ruttan, Vernon W. (1980) Behaviour and Productivity implications of institutional and project funding of research, *American Journal of Agricultural Economics* 62, No. 3 (Aug.): 371–83.

Bredahl, M. and Peterson, W. (1976) The productivity and allocation of research: US agricultural experiment stations, *American Journal of Agricultural Economics* 58, No. 4 (Nov. Part I): 684–92.

Brown, A. W. A. et al (1975) *Crop Productivity – Research Imperative.*

Charles F. Kettering Foundation, Yellow Springs, Ohio.

Brown, L. R. (1978) *The Worldwide Loss of Cropland*. Worldwatch Paper 24. Worldwatch Inst., Washington, DC.

Buchholz, Hans and Gmelin Wolfgang (eds) (1979) Science and technology and the future, *Proceedings and Joint Report of World Future Studies Conference and DSE-Preconference*, Berlin, May 4–10, K. G. Saur, Munich, New York, London.

Bunting, A. H. (1979) *Science and Technology for Human Needs, Rural Development, and the Relief of Poverty*, IADS occasional paper. International Agricultural Development Service, New York.

Burke, Robert V. (1979) Green revolution technologies and farm class in Mexico, *Economic Development and Cultural Change* 28, No. 1 (Oct.): 135–54.

Byerlee, Derek, et al. (1979) On-farm research to develop technologies appropriate to farmers. Paper presented at the 17th International Conference of Agricultural Economists. Sept. 3–12, Banff, Canada.

Byerlee, Derek and Collinson, Michael et al. (1980) *Planning technologies Appropriate to Farmers – Concepts and Procedures*. CIMMYT, Mexico.

CGIAR (1977a) *Statistics on Expenditure by International Agricultural Research Center 1960–80*. CGIAR Secretariat, Washington, DC.

CGIAR (1977b) *Report of the Review Committee*. CGIAR Secretariat, Washington, DC.

CGIAR (1978) *Report of the Task Force on International Assistance for Strengthening National Agricultural Research*. CGIAR Secretariat, Washington, DC.

CGIAR (1979) *Report on the Consultative Group and the International Agricultural Research System, An Integrative Report*. CGIAR Secretariat, Washington, DC.

Chesney, H. A. D. (1980) Agricultural research in Guyana. In *Strengthening National Agricultural Research*. Bo Bengtsson and Getachew Tedla (eds). SAREC Report R1-1980. Stockholm: 167–74.

Christensen, Raymond et al. (1964) *How the United States Improved its Agriculture*. USDA: ERS Foreign No. 76, Washington, DC.

CIMMYT Review (1978) CIMMYT, Mexico City.

Colmenares, J. H. (1975) Adoption on hybrid seeds and fertilizer among Colombian corn growers, *Centro Internacional de Mejoramiento de Maiz y Trigo, El Batan*, Mexico.

Commission on Fertilizers (1979). Report from the fifth session, 22–25 January, Rome (FERT/79/3).

Council for Agricultural Science and Technology (1974) *The U.S. Fertilizer Situation and Outlook*. Ames, Iowa.

Crawford, J. G., Development of the international agricultural research system. In Arndt, Dalrymple and Ruttan (1977).

Crosson, Pierre (1979) *Resource, Technology and Environment in Agricultural Development*. International Institute for Applied Systems Analysis, Working Paper, No. 79–103. Vienna.

Dalrymple, Dana G. (1969) *New Cereal Varieties: Wheat and Corn in Mexico*. ID/FAS/USDA, Spring Review, Washington, DC.

Dalrymple, Dana G. (1975a) *Evaluating Fertilizer Subsidies in Developing Countries*, AID Washington, DC.

Dalrymple, Dana G. (1975b) *Measuring the Green Revolution: The Impact of Research on Wheat and Rice Production*. US Department of Agriculture, FAER No. 106, Washington, DC.

Dalrymple, Dana G. (1976) *Development and Spread of High-yielding Varieties of Wheat and Rice in Less Developed Nations*. US Department of Agriculture, FAER. No. 95, Washington, DC.

Dalrymple, Dana G. (1977) *Evaluating the Impact of International Research on Wheat and Rice Production in the Developing Nations*. In Arndt, Dalrymple and Ruttan (1977).

Dalrymple, Dana G. (1978) *Development and Spread of High Yielding Varieties of Wheat and Rice in Less Developed Nations*. US Department of Agriculture, FAER, No. 95, Washington, D.C.

Dalrymple, Dana G. (1979) The adoption of high-yielding grain varieties in developing nations, *Agricultural History* 53, No. 4 (Oct.): 704–26.

Dalrymple, Dana G. (1980) The demand for agricultural research: a Colombian illustration: comment, *American Journal of Agricultural Economics* 62, No. 3 (Aug.): 594–6.

Day, R. H. and Singh, I. (1977) *Economic Development as an Adaptive Process. The Green Revolution in the Indian Punjab*. Cambridge University Press, New York.

De Datta, S. K., Gomez, K. A., Herdt, R. W., and Barker, R. (1978) *A Handbook on the Methodology for an Integrated Experiment-Survey on Rice Yield Constraints*. International Rice Research Institute, Los Banos, Laguna, Philippines.

De Hoogh, J. et al. (1978) Food for a growing world population: some of the main findings of a study on the long-term prospects of the world food situation, *European Review of Agricultural Economics* 3, No. 4: 459–99.

De Janvry, A. (1977) Inducement of technological and institutional innovations: an interpretative framework. In Arndt, Dalrymple and Ruttan.

Dillon, J. L., Plucknett, D. L. and Vallaeys, G. (1978) *Farming Systems Research at the International Agricultural Research Centers*. Technical Advisory Committee on the Consultative Group on International Agricultural Research, FAO, Rome.

Duckham, A. N. and Pearce, John (1979) The changing functions of research management: technology assessment and the challenges to contemporary agricultural research organization, *Agricultural Administration* 6: 123–39.

Duncan, R. C. (1972) Evaluating returns to research in pasture improvement, *Australian Journal of Agricultural Economics* 16, No. 3 (Dec.): 153–68.

Eckholm, Erik P. (1975) *The Other Energy Crisis: Firewood*. Worldwatch Paper 1. Worldwatch Institute, Washington, DC.

Eckholm, Erik P. (1976) *Losing Ground*. W. W. Norton, New York.

Eckholm E. (1979) *Planting for the Future: Forestry for Human Needs*, Worldwatch Paper 26. Worldwatch Institute, Washington, DC.

Eckholm, E. and Brown, L. R. (1977) *Spreading Deserts – The Hand of Man*, Worldwatch Paper 13. Worldwatch Institute, Washington, DC.

Evenson, R. E. (1967) The contribution of agricultural Research to production. *Journal of Farm Economics* 49 (Dec.): 1415–25.

Evenson, R. E. (1968) The contribution of agricultural research to agricultural Production, Ph.D. thesis. Chicago, University of Chicago.

Evenson, R. E. (1969) International transmission of technology in sugarcane production (Mimeographed). Yale University, New Haven.

Evenson, R. E. (1974) The Green Revolution in recent development experience, *American Journal of Agricultural Economics* 56, No. 2 (May): 387–94.

Evenson, R. E. (1977) Comparative evidence on returns to investment in national and international research institutions. In Arndt, Dalrymple and Ruttan.

Evenson, R. E. (1978) The organization of research to improve crops and animals in low-income countries. In *Distortions of Agricultural Incentives*. Theodore W. Schultz (ed.). Indiana University Press, Bloomington and London: 223–45.

Evenson, R. E. and Flores, P. M. (1978) Social returns to rice research. In *Economic Consequences of the New Rice Technology*. IRRI, Los Banos, Philippines.

Evenson, R. E., Flores, P. M. and Hayami, Y. (1978) Costs and returns rice research. In *Economic Consequences of New Rice Technology*. IRRI, Los Banos, Philippines.

Evenson, R. E. and Jha, D. (1973) The contribution of the agricultural research system to agricultural production in India, *Indian Journal of Agricultural Economics* 28, No. 4 (Oct.–Dec.).

Evenson, R. E. and Kislev, Y. (1973) Research and productivity in wheat and maize, *Journal of Political Economy* 81, No. 5 (Nov.–Dec.): 1309–1129.

Evenson, R. E. and Kislev, Y. (1975a) *Agricultural Research and Productivity*, Yale University Press, New Haven.

Evenson, R. E. and Kislev, Y. (1975b) Investment in agricultural research and extension: a survey of international data, *Economic Development and Cultural Change* 23, No. 2 (April): 507–21.

Evenson, R. E., Waggoner, Paul E. and Ruttan, Vernon W. (1979) Economic benefits from research: an example from agriculture, *Science*. 205, (Sept.): 1101–7.

Falcon, W. P. (1970) The Green Revolution: generation of problems, *American Journal of Agricultural Economics* 52: 698–710.

Farmer, B. H. (ed.) (1977) *Green Revolution?: Technology and Change in Rice Growing Areas of Tamil Nadu and Sri Lanka*. Westview Press, Boulder, Colorado.

Fishel, W. L. (ed.) (1971) *Resource Allocation in Agricultural Research.* University of Minnesota Press, Minneapolis.

Flores-Moya, P., Evenson, R. E., and Hayami, Y. (1978) Social returns to rice research in the Philippines: domestic benefits and foreign spillover, *Economic Development and Cultural Change* 26, No. 3 (April): 591–607.

Food and Agriculture Organization (1965) *World Census of Agriculture 1960.* Rome, Italy.

Food and Agriculture Organization (1970) *Provisional Indicative World Plan for Agricultural Development*, Vol. 1, Rome, Italy.

Food and Agriculture Organization (1978a) *Current Situation and Outlook.* Commission on Fertilizer, Fifth Session, January 1979, FERT/79/3.

Food and Agriculture Organization (1978b) *Land Resources for Agriculture Development.* Land and Water Development Division, Rome, Italy.

Food and Agriculture Organization (1979) *Agriculture: Toward 2000.* Rome, Italy.

Food and Agriculture Organization. *Annual Fertilizer Review*, several years, Rome, Italy.

Food and Agriculture Organization. *Monthly Bulletin of Agricultural Economics and Statistics*, several issues, Rome, Italy.

Food and Agriculture Organization. *Production Yearbook*, several volumes, Rome, Italy.

Food and Agriculture Organization and FIAC (1972) *Case Studies on Fertilizer Marketing and Credit.* Rome, Italy: (Nov.).

Food and Agriculture Organization and FIAC (1976). *Fertilizer Subsidies, Alternative Policies*, Rome, Italy (1976).

Food and Agriculture Organization (1977) Recent developments in the world food and agricultural situations, *Monthly Bulletin of Agricultural Economics and Statistics* 26 Rome, Italy, No. 7/8: 1–27.

Frankel, F. R. (1976) *India's Green Revolution: Economic Gains and Political Costs.* Princeton University Press, Princeton, New Jersey.

Gafsi, Salem and Roe, Terry (1979) Adoption of unlike high-yielding wheat varieties in Tunisia. *Economic Development and Cultural Change.* 28, No. 1 (Oct.): 119–33.

Galt, D. L. and Stanton, B. F. (1979) Yield losses as economic weights in plant breeding decisions on tropical maize. Department of Agricultural Economics, Cornell University, Mimeograph 65, April.

Gesslein, Sven (1976) *Report on the Nordic Fertilizer Program Consultancy*, FAO, Rome, Aug.

Golubev, G. N., Shvytov, I. A. and Vasiliev, O. F. (1978) Environmental problems of Agriculture. In *Water Related Environmental Impacts of Agriculture at the Field Level.* International Institute for Applied Systems Analysis, Research Memorandum R.M. 78–32, Laxenburg, Austria.

Gomez, Kwanchai A. (1977) On-farm assessment of yield constraints: methodological problems. In *Constraints to High Yields on Asian Rice Farms: An Interim Report.* IRRI. Los Banos, Philippines.

Goodman, Gordon et al. (1979) *Report of the Energy Resources Working*

Group. International Conference on Agricultural Production: Research and Development Strategies for the 1980s. Bonn, Germany, Oct.

Gotsch, C. H. (1972) Technical change and the distribution of incomes in rural areas, *American Journal of Agricultural Economic* 54, No. 2 (May): 326–41.

Gotsch, C. H. and Falcon, W. P. (1975) The Green Revolution and the economics of Punjab agriculture, *Food Research Institute Studies* 14, No. 1: 27–46.

Griffin, Keith (1972) *The Green Revolution: An Economic Analysis*. UNRISD, Geneva.

Griffin, Keith (1979) *The Political Economy of Agrarian Change*. Macmillan Press, London.

Griliches, Zvi (1957) Hybrid corn: An exploration in the economics of technological change, *Econometrica*. 25, No. 4 (Oct.): 501–52.

Griliches, Zvi (1958) Research costs and social returns: hybrid corn and related innovations, *Journal of Political Economy*, 66, (Oct.): 419–431.

Griliches, Zvi (1964) Research expenditures, education, and the aggregate agricultural production function, *American Economic Review*, 54, (Dec.): 961–74.

Gruener, N. and Shuval, H. I. (1970) Health aspects of nitrates in drinking water. In *Development in Water Quality Research*, H. I. Shuval (ed). Humphrey Science Publication, Ann Arbor, Michigan: 89–105.

Guttman, Joel M. (1978) Interest groups and the demand for agricultural research. *Journal of Political Economy*, 86. No. 31: 467–84.

Hanson, Haldore (1979) *Biological Resources*. Report prepared for the Conference Agricultural Production: Research and Development Strategies for the 1980's, Bonn. Oct. 8–12.

Hanson, Haldore et al. (1979) *Plant and Animal Resources for Food Production by Developing Countries in the 1980s*. International Conference on Agricultural Production: Research and Development Strategies for the 1980s, Bonn, Germany, Oct.

Hardin, Lowell S. (1979) Emerging roles of agricultural economists working in international research institutions such as IRRI and CIMMYT. Paper presented at the 17th International Conference of Agricultural Economics, Banff, Canada, Sept. 3–12.

Hardin, Lowell S. and Collins, Norman R. (1974) International agricultural research: organizing themes and issues, *Agricultural Administration*, 1, No. 1: 13–22.

Harlan, Jack R. (1975) Our vanishing genetic resources. In *Food: Politics, Economics, Nutrition and Research*, Philip H. Abelson (ed.). American Association for the Advancement of Science, Washington, DC.

Hayami, Yujiro (1978) *Anatomy of a Peasant Economy*. International Rice Research Institute, Los Banos, Philippines.

Hayami, Yujiro (1979) Economic consequences of new rice technology: a view from the barrio. Paper presented at the International Rice Research Conference, IRRI, Los Banos, Philippines, April 16–20.

Hayami, Yujiro and Herdt, Robert (1977) Market price effects of technological change on income distribution in semisubsistance agriculture. *American Journal of Agricultural Economics*, 59, No. 2: 245–56.

Hayami, Y. and Ruttan, V. W. (1971) *Agricultural Development, An International Perspective*. Johns Hopkins Press, Baltimore.

Heady, E. O. (1971) Welfare implications of agricultural research. In *Resource Allocation in Agricultural Research*. W. L. Fishel (ed.), University of Minnesota Press, Minneapolis.

Heady, E. O. et al. (1975) *Roots of the Farm Problem*. Iowa State University Press, Ames, Iowa.

Herdt, Robert W. et al. (1977) *The Prospects of Asian Rice Production*. International Rice Research Conference, IRRI, Los Banos, Philippines.

Herdt, Robert W. and Barker, Randolph (1975) Possible effects of fertilizer shortages on rice production in Asian countries. In *Impact of Fertilizer Shortages, Focus on Asia*. Asian Productivity Organization, Tokyo.

Herdt, Robert W. and Barker, Randolph (1977) Multi-site tests, environments and breeding strategies for new rice technology. IRRI. Research paper series, No. 7.

Herdt, Robert W. and Bernsten, Richard H. (1975) *Methodology for Assessing Rice Yield Constraints*. IRAEN Workshop Bangkok, Thailand, March 11–14.

Herdt, Robert W. and Mandac, A. M. (1979) Overview, findings and implications of constraints research 1975–78. Paper prepared for the IRAEN Constraints Workshop, Kandy, Sri Lanka. April 30–May 3.

Herdt, Robert W. and Ranade, C. G. (1978) The impact of new rice technology on the shares of farm earnings, Laguna and Central Luzon, Philippines. In *Economic Consequences of New Rice Technology*. IRRI, Los Banos, Philippines.

Herdt, Rolbert W. and Wickham, T. H. (1975) Exploring the gap between potential and actual rice yields in the Philippines, *Food Research Institute Studies*, 14: 163–81.

Hertford, R., Ardila, J., Rocha, A. and Trujillo, C. (1977) Productivity of agricultural research in Colombia. In Arndt, Dalrymple and Ruttan.

Hertford, R. and Schmitz, A. (1977) Measuring economic returns to agricultural research. In Arndt, Dalrymple and Ruttan.

Hewitt de Alcantara, Cynthia (1976) *Modernizing Mexican Agriculture*. UNRISD, Geneva.

Hines, J. (1972) The Utilization of research for development: two case studies in rural modernization and agriculture in Peru, Ph.D. dissertation, Princeton: Princeton University.

Ibach, D. B. (1966) *Fertilizer Use in the United States*. US Department of Agriculture, ERS, Ag. Econ. Report No. 92.

International Agricultural Development Service (1979a) *Agricultural Assistance Sources*, 2nd edn. New York.

International Agricultural Development Service (1979b) *Preparing Professional Staff for National Agricultural Research Programs*. Report of a

Workshop, Bellagio, Italy, Feb. 16–21.

International Food Policy Research Institute (1976) *Meeting Food Needs in the Developing World: The Location and Magnitude of the Task in the Next Decade*, IFPRI Research Report No. 1. Washington, DC.

International Food Policy Research Institute (1977) *Food Needs of Developing Countries: Projections of Production and Consumption to 1990*, IFPRI Research Report No. 3, Washington, DC.

International Food Policy Research Institute (1978) *Criteria and Approaches to the Analysis of Priorities for International Agricultural Research*. Working Paper No. 1, Washington, DC, February.

International Rice Research Institute (1975) *Changes in Rice Farming in Selected Areas of Asia*. Los Banos, Philippines.

International Rice Research Institute (1977) *Constraints to High Yields on Asian Rice Farms: An Interim Report*. Los Banos, Philippines.

International Rice Research Institute (1978a) *Economic Consequences of the New Rice Technology*. Los Banos, Philippines.

International Rice Research Institute (1978b) *Interpretative Analysis of Selected Papers from Changes in Rice Farming in Selected Areas of Asia*. Los Banos, Philippines.

International Rice Research Institute (1979) *Farm-level Constraints to High Rice Yields in Asia 1974–77*. Los Banos, Philippines.

Irvine, D. E. G. and Knights, B. (eds) (1974) *Pollution and the Use of Chemicals in Agriculture*. Butterworths, London.

Islam, Nural (ed) (1974) *Agricultural Policy in Developing Countries*, Halstead Press, New York.

Jarrett, F. G. and Linder, R. K. (1977) Research benefits revisited, *Review of Marketing and Agricultural Economics* 45, No. 4 (Dec.): 167–78.

Jennings, P. R. (1974) Rice breeding and world food production, *Science*. 186, No. 4169 (Dec. 20): 1085–89.

Jennings, Peter R. (1976) The amplification of agricultural production, *Scientific American* (Sept.): 181–94.

Jodha, N. S. (1979) *The Processes of Desertification and the Choice of Interventions*. ICRISAT, Progress Report 2, Hyderabad, India.

Jodha, N. S., Asokan, M. and Ryan, James G. (1977) *Village Study Methodology and Resource Endowments of the Selected Villages in ICRISAT's Village Level Studies*. ICRISAT, Occasional paper 16, Hyderabad, India.

Johnston, B. F. and Kilby, P. (1975) *Agriculture and Structure Transformation*. Oxford University Press, London.

Kahlon, A. S., Bal, H. K. Saxena, P. N. and Jha D. (1977) Productivity of agricultural research in India. In Arndt, Dalrymple and Ruttan.

Kassas, M. (1975) Arid and semi-arid lands: an overview. In *Overviews in the Priority Subject Area: Land, Water and Desertification*, UNEP. UN Environ. Programme, Nairobi, Kenya.

Khan, Mahmood H. (1975) *The Economics of the Green Revolution in Pakistan*, Praeger, New York.

Kislev, Y. (1977) The economics of agricultural research, some recent findings, *Food Policy* (May): 148–56.

Koppel, Bruce (1979) The changing functions of research management: technology assessment and the challenges to contemporary agricultural research organization, *Agricultural Administration* No. 6: 123–39.

Knutson, Marlys and Tweeten, Luther G. (1979) Toward an optimal rate of growth in agricultural production research and extension, *American Journal of Agricultural Economics* 61, No. 1: 70–6.

Kumar, P., Maji, C. C. and Patel, R. K. (1977) Returns on investment in research and extension: a study on Indo-Swiss cattle improvement project, Kerala, Indian Journal of Agricultural Economics 32 No. 3 (July–Sept.): 207–16.

Latimer, R. (1964) Some economic aspects of agricultural research and extension in the US. Ph.D dissertation. Lafayette: Purdue University.

Leach, Gerald (1979) *Energy*, Report prepared for the Conference Agricultural Production: Research and Development Strategies for the 1980's, Bonn, Oct. 8–12.

Lele, U. J. (1972) The Green Revolution: income distribution and nutrition. In *Proceedings of Western Hemisphere Nutrition Congress III*, 1971, P. L. White (ed) Futura, Mount Kisco, New York.

Lele, U. J. and Mellor, J. W. (1972) Jobs, poverty and the Green Revolution, *International Affairs*, 48, No. 1 (Jan.): 29–31.

Levine, Gilbert, Oram, Peter and Zapata, Juan A. (1979) *State of Knowledge Report for the Water Resources Task Groups*. International Conference on Agricultural Production: Research and Development Strategies for the 1980s. Bonn, Germany, (Oct. 8–12).

Levine, Gilbert, Oram, Peter and Zapata, Juan A. (1979) *Water*, Report prepared for the Conference Agricultural Production: Research and Development Strategies for the 1980's Bonn, Oct. 8–12.

Liao, S. H. and Barker, R. (1969) An analysis of the spread of new high yielding rice varieties on Philippine Farms, *Economic Research Journal* 16, No. 1 (June): 12–19.

Lindner, R. K. and Jarrett, F. G. (1978) Supply shifts and the size of research benefits, *American Journal of Agricultural Economics*, 60, No. 1 (Feb.): 48–58.

Lipton, Michael (1978) Inter-farm, inter-regional and farm-non-farm income distribution the impact of the new cereal varieties, *World Development* 6, No. 3, 319–37.

Lockeretz, William (ed.) (1977) *Agriculture and Energy*. Academic Press, New York.

Lohani, B. N. and Thanh, N. C. (1977) Rural development and its environmental impact assessment in Southeast Asia. Paper presented at the International Conference on Rural Development Technology – An Integrated Approach. Bangkok, June.

Lu, Yao-Chi, Cline, Phillip and Quance, Leroy (1979) Prospectives for productive growth in US agriculture. US Department of Agriculture,

AE-435, Washington, DC.

Lu, Yao-chi and Quance, Leroy (1979) *Agricultural Productivity: Expanding the Limits*. US Department of Agriculture, Agr. Inf. Bulletin No. 431, Washington, DC.

McClung, A. Colin (1974) *Strengthening National Agricultural Research Systems, Some Concerns of the International Community*. CIAT Workshop, Cali, Colombia, Nov.

McInerney, John P. (1978) *The Technology of Rural Development*. World Bank Staff Working Paper No. 295, Washington, DC, Oct.

Mangahas, M. (1970) An economic analysis of the diffusion of new rice varieties in Central Luzon, Ph.D. thesis, University of Chicago.

Mangahas, M. and Librero, A. R. (1973) *The High-Yield Varieties of Rice in the Philippines: A Perspective*, Discussion Paper No. 73–11. Institute of Economic Development and Research, University of the Philippines, June 15, 1973.

Mangundojo, Sutardi (1971) Agricultural research in Indonesia. In *National Agricultural Research System in Asia*, Albert H. Moseman (ed.). The Agricultural Development Council, New York, pp. 39–49.

Manshard, Walther (1974) *Tropical Agriculture*. Longman, London.

Masefield, G. B. (1972) *A History of the Colonial Agricultural Service*. Clarendon Press, Oxford.

Mathieu, M. and J. de la Vega (1978). *Constraints to Increasing Fertilizer Use in Developing Countries and Means to Overcome Them*. The Fertilizer Society, Proceedings No. 173, London.

Mayer, Jean (1976) The dimensions of human hunger. *Scientific American*, (Sept.): 40–50.

Meadows, Donella H. et al. (1972) *The Limits to Growth*. Universe Books, New York.

Mellor, J. W. (1966) *The Economics of Agricultural Development*. Cornell University Press, Ithaca.

Mellor, J. W. (1975) *The Impact of New Agricultural Technology on Employment and Income Distribution – Concepts and Policy*. US Agency for International Development, Occasional Paper No. 2, Washington, DC May.

Mellor, J. W. (1976) *The New Economics of Growth: A Strategy for India and the Developing World*, Cornell University Press, Ithaca.

Mellor J. W. (1977) Relating research resource allocation to multiple goals. In Arndt, Dalrymple and Ruttan.

Mellor, J. W. and Lele, U. J. (1973) Growth linkages of the new foodgrain technologies, *Indian Journal of Agricultural Economics* 28, No. 1 (Jan. – March): 35–55.

Menon, K. P. A. (1971) Building agricultural research organizations – the Indian experience. In *National Agricultural Research Systems in Asia*, Albert H. Moseman (ed.). The Agricultural Development Council, New York, 23–38.

Monteiro, Augusto (1975) *Analiacao economica da pesquisa e extensao agricola: o caso do cacau no Brasil*, M.S. thesis. Universidade Federal de

Vicosa, Brazil.

Mooney, P. H. R. (1979) *Seeds of the Earth, A Private or Public Resource?* The International Coalition for Development Action, London.

Moseman, Albert H. (1970) *Building Agricultural Research Systems in the Developing Nations.* The Agricultural Development Council, New York.

Moseman, Albert H. (ed.) (1971) *National Agricultural Research Systems in Asia.* The Agricultural Development Council, New York.

Mudahar, Mohinder S. and Pinstrup-Andersen, Per (1977) *Fertilizer Policy Issues and Implications in Developing Countries.* FAI/IFDC Conference. (Dec. 1–3) New Delhi, India.

Nagel, Uwe Jens (1979) Knowledge flows in agriculture: linking research, extension and the farmer. *Zeitschift fur Auslandische Landwirtschaft* 18, No. 2: 135–50.

Nagy, Joseph and Furtan, W. Hartley (1978) Economic costs and returns from crop development research: The case of rapeseed breeding in Canada, *Canadian Journal of Agricultural Economics*, 26, 1: 1–14.

National Academy of Sciences (1975) *Population and Food, Crucial Issues.* Washington, DC.

National Research Council (1975) *World Food and Nutrition Study, Interim Report.* National Academy of Sciences, Washington, DC.

National Research Council (1977a) *Supporting Paper: World Food and Nutrition Study*, Vol. V: National Academy of Sciences, Washington, DC.

National Research Council (1977b) *World Food and Nutrition Study: The Potential Contribution of Research*, National Academy of Sciences, Washington, DC.

Nightingdale, H. L. (1970) Statistical evaluation of salinity and nitrate content and trends beneath urban and agricultural areas – Fresno, California, *Ground Water* No. 8: 22–8.

Norman, Colin (1979) *Knowledge and Power: The Global Research and Development Budget.* Worldwatch Paper No. 31, Washington, DC.

Olembo, R. J. (1976) Environmental issues in current food production, marketing and processing practices, *Proceedings of the World Food Conference of 1976.* Iowa State University, Ames, Iowa: 145–62.

Oram, Peter (1978) *Current and Projected Agricultural Research Expenditures and Staff in Developing Countries*, IFPRI, Working Paper 30. Washington, DC.

Oram, Peter et al. (1979) *Investment and Input Requirements for Accelerating Food Production in Low-Income Countries by 1990.* Research Report No. 10, IFPRI, Washington, DC. Sept.

Organization for Economic Co-operation and Development (OECD) (1979). *Development Co-operation 1979 Review.* Paris.

Osborn, Howard A. (1979) Technology and the Small Farm: *A Conceptual Framework.* US Department of Agriculture, Washington, DC. Aug.

Ozaki, Chujiro (1975) *Fertilizer Consumption, Distribution and Prices in APO Member Countries.* In Asian Productivity Organization, Impact of Fertilizer Shortages, Focus on Asia.

Paarlberg, Don (1970) *Norman Borlaug – Hunger Fighter*. US Department of Agriculture, PA 969, Washington, DC.

Palacpac, Adelita C. (1977) *World Rice Statistics*, IRRI, Los Banos, Philippines.

Palmer, Ingrid (1972) *Science and Agricultural Production*. UNRISD, Geneva.

Palmer, Ingrid (1975) *The New Rice in the Philippines*, UNRISD, Geneva.

Paulino, L. A. (1977) Allocation of resources for agricultural research, *Agricultural Research Management*, Vol. II.

Pee, T. Y. (1977) *Social returns from rubber research in Peninsula Malaysia*, unpublished Ph.D dissertation. Michigan State University.

Perrin, R. K. and Winkelman, D. (1976) Impediments to technical progress on small versus large farms, *American Journal of Agricultural Economics* 58, No. 5: 888–94.

Peterson, W. L. (1967) Return to poultry research in the United States, Journal of Farm Economics, 49 (Aug.): 656–69.

Peterson, W. L. (1975) *The Social Cost of a Cheap Food Policy: The Case of Argentina Corn Production*. Staff paper p. 75–28. Department of Agricultural Economics, University of Minnesota. (Nov.).

Peterson W. L. and Fitzharris, J. C. (1977) Productivity of agricultural research in the United States. In Arndt, Dalrymple and Ruttan.

Pimentel, David and Pimentel, Marcia (1979) *Food, Energy and Society*. Edward Arnold, London.

Pimentel, David et al. (1973) Food production and the energy crisis, *Science*, 182, (Nov.): 443–9.

Pimentel, David (ed.) (1978) *World Food, Pest Losses, and the Environment*. American Association for the Advancement of Science, AAAS Selected Symposium 13, Washington, DC.

Pinstrup-Andersen, Per (1970) *Estimating the Distribution of Benefits from Expanded Agricultural Production with Examples from Latin America*. Seminar, Cali, Colombia, Nov.

Pinstrup-Andersen, Per (1976a) Preliminary estimates of the contribution of fertilizer to cereal production in developing market economies, *The Journal of Economics* 2.

Pinstrup-Andersen, Per (1976b) *The Role of Fertilizers in Meeting Developing Countries' Food Needs*. Missouri Valley Economics Association, Tulsa, Oklahoma.

Pinstrup-Andersen, Per (1977) Decision-making on food and agricultural research policy: The distribution of benefits from new agricultural technology among consumer income strata, *Agricultural Administration* No. 4: 13–28.

Pinstrup-Andersen, Per (1978) Market price effects of new rice technology on income distribution, comment. In *Economic Consequences of New Rice Technology*. IRRI, Los Banos, Philippines.

Pinstrup-Andersen, Per (1979a) Selected economic aspects of agricultural research. In *Plant Cell and Tissue Culture*, by W. R. Sharp et al. (eds). Ohio

State University Press, Columbus, Ohio.

Pinstrup-Andersen, Per (1979b) *The Impact of Technological Change in Agriculture on Production, Resource Use and the Environment: Towards an Approach for Ex Ante Assessment.* International Institute for Applied System Analysis, Working paper No. 79–108. Vienna, Austria.

Pinstrup-Andersen, Per (1979c) The market price effect and the distribution of economic benefits from new technology, *European Review of Agricultural Economics* 6 (1) 17–46.

Pinstrup-Andersen, Per (1980) *Kunstgodningens betydning for fodevareforsyningen.* DSR-Forlag, Copenhagen.

Pinstrup-Andersen, Per (1981) Energy Cropping and the Poor, *Mazingira* (Sept.)

Pinstrup-Andersen, Per and Byrnes, Francis C. (1975) *Methods of Allocating Resources in Applied Agricultural Research in Latin America.* CIAT, Series CE–11. Nov.

Pinstrup-Andersen, Per and Caicedo, Elizabeth (1978) The potential impact of changes in income distribution on food demand and human nutrition, *American Journal of Agricultural Economics* 60: 402–415.

Pinstrup-Andersen, Per, de Londono, Norha, and Hoover, Edward (1976) The impact of increasing food supply on human nutrition: Implications for commodity priorities in agricultural research and policy, *American Journal of Agricultural Economics* 58: (May): 131–42.

Pinstrup-Andersen, Per, de Londono, N. and Infante, M. (1976) A suggested procedure for estimating yield and production losses in crops. *PANS* 22, No. 3: 359–65.

Pinstrup-Andersen, Per and Diaz, Rafael O. (1975) A suggested method for improving the information base for establishing priorities in cassava research. In *Cassava Germ Plasm*, Berry Nestel and R. MacIntyre (eds). IDRC, Ottawa, Canada.

Pinstrup-Andersen, Per and Franklin, David (1977) A systems approach to agricultural research resource allocation in developing countries. In Arndt, Dalrymple and Ruttan.

Poleman, T. T. and Freebarin, D. K. (eds). (1973) *Food, Population, and Employment: The Impact of the Green Revolution*, Praeger, New York.

Proceedings of the World Food Conference of 1976 (1977) Iowa State University, Iowa State University Press, Ames.

Ramalho de Castro, J. P. and Schuh, G. E. (1977) An empirical test of an economic model for establishing research priorities: a Brazil case study. In Arndt, Dalrymple and Ruttan.

Ramalho de Castro, J. P. (1974) An economic model for establishing priorities for agricultural research and a test for the Brazilian economy, Ph.D dissertation. Department of Agricultural Economics, Purdue University.

Rao, C. H. H. (1975) *Technological Change and the Distribution of Gains in Indian Agriculture*, Macmillan of India, New Delhi.

Reynolds, L. G. (ed.) (1975) *Agriculture in Development Theory.* Yale University Press, New Haven.

Riquier, J. R. (1978) Land resources degradation, *The Courier* No. 47 (Jan.–Feb): 47–9.

Rosegrant, M. W. (1976) *The Impact of Irrigation on the Yield of Modern Varieties*, IRRI, Paper No. 76–28, Los Banos, Philippines., Dec.

Ruthenberg, H. (1976) *Farming Systems in the Tropics*. Clarendon Press, Oxford.

Ruthenberg, H. (1977) The development of crop research in the humid and semi-humid tropics, *Plant Research and Development* 6: 7–27 (edited and published by the Institute for Scientific Cooperation in conjunction with the Federal Research Centre for Forestry and Forest Products, Tubingen, West Germany).

Ruthenberg, H. (1979) Tendencies in the development of tropical farming systems. *Zeitschift für ausländische Landwirtschaft* 18, No. 3: 239–47.

Ruttan, Vernon (1975) Food production and the energy crises: a comment. *Science* 187 (Feb. 14): 560–1.

Ruttan, Vernon (1977) The Green Revolution: seven generalizations, *International Development Review* No. 4: 16–23.

Ryan, J. G. (1977) Human nutritional needs and crop breeding objectives in the Indian semi-arid tropics, *Indian Journal of Agricultural Economics* 32, No. 3 (July–Sept.): 78–87.

Ryan, J. G. and Asokan, M. (1977) *Effect of the Green Revolution in Wheat on Production of Pulses and Nutrients in India*. Occasional Paper No. 18, Economics Programme, International Crop Research Institute for the Semi-Arid Tropics, Hyderabad, India, Oct.

Ryan, J. G., Sheldrake, R. and Yadaw, S. P. (1974) *Human Nutritional Needs and Crop Breeding Objectives in the Semi-Arid Tropics*, Occasional Paper No. 4, Economics Programme, International Crop Research Institute for the Semi-Arid Tropics, Hyderabad, India. Oct.

Schmitz, A. and Seckler, G. (1970) Mechanical agriculture and social welfare: The case of the tomato harvester, *American Journal of Agricultural Economics*. 52, No. 4 (Nov.): 569–78.

Schuh, G. Edward and Tollini, Helio (1979) *Costs and Benefits of Agricultural Research: The State of the Art*. World Bank Staff Working Paper No. 360, Washington, DC.

Schultz, T. W. (1961) A policy to redistribute losses from economic progress, *Journal of Farm Economics* 43, No. 3 (Aug.): 554–64.

Schultz, T. W. (1974) *Transforming Traditional Agriculture*. Yale University Press, New Haven, Connecticut.

Schultz, T. W. (1977) Uneven prospects for gains from agricultural research related to economic policy, In Arndt, Dalrymple and Ruttan.

Schultz, T. W. (1979) The economics of research and agricultural productivity. Paper presented at the Seminar on Socio-Economic Aspects of Agricultural Research in Developing Countries. May 7–11. Santiago, Chile and IADS Occasional Paper.

Schutjer, Wayne A. and Van Der Veen, M. G. (1977) Economic Constraints on Agricultural Technology Adoption. US Agency for International

Development, Occasional paper No. 5, Washington, DC March.

Scobie, Grant M. (1976) Who benefits from agricultural research? *Review of Marketing and Agricultural Economics*, Vol. 44: 197–202.

Scobie, Grant M. (1979a) The demand for agricultural research: a Colombian illustration, *American Journal of Agricultural Economics*. 61, No. 3 (Aug.): 540–5.

Scobie, Grant M. (1979b) *Investment in International Agricultural Research: Some Economic Dimensions*. World Bank Staff Working Paper No. 361.

Scobie, G. M. and Posada, T. (1977) *The Impact of High-yielding Rice Varieties in Latin America, With Special Emphasis on Colombia*. Series JE-01, CIAT, Cali, Colombia.

Scobie, G. M. and Posada, R. (1978) The impact of technical change on income distribution: the case of rice in Colombia, *American Journal of Agricultural Economics* 60, No. 1 (Feb.): 85–92.

Shigemochi, Hirashima (1978) *The Structure of Disparity in Developing Agriculture: A Case Study of the Pakistan Punjab*. Institute of Development Economics, Tokyo.

Shin, Dong Wan and Young Kun Khim (1975) *The Effectiveness of the Tongil Rice Diffusion in Korea*. Office of Rural Development, Suweon, Republic of Korea.

Shumway, C. R. (1973) Allocation of scarce resources to agricultural research: review of methodology, *American Journal of Agricultural Economics* 55, No. 4 (Nov.): 557–66.

Shumway, C. R. (1977) Models and methods used to allocate resources in agricultural research: A critical review. In Arndt, Dalrymple and Ruttan.

Sidhu, S. (1974a) Economics of technical change in wheat production in the Indian Punjab *American Journal of Agricultural Economics* 56, No. 2 (May): 217–26.

Sidhu, S. (1974b) Relative efficiency in wheat production in the Indian Punjab, *American Economic Review* 64, No. 4 (Sept.): 742–51.

Singh, Inderjit (1979) *Small Farmers and the Landless in South Asia*. World Bank Staff Working Paper No. 320, Washington, DC.

Singh, I. and Day, R. H. (1975) Microeconomic chronicle of the green revolution, *Economic Development and Cultural Change*. 23, (July): 661–86.

Sisler, Daniel G. and Colman, David R. (1979) *Poor Rural Households, Technical Change, and Income Distribution in Developing Countries: Insights from Asia*. Cornell University, A.E. Res. 79–13, Ithaca, New York.

Sivard, Ruth L. (1980) *World Military and Social Expenditures, 1980*. World Priorities, Leesburg, Virginia.

Smith, G. E. (1967) *Fertilizer Nutrients as Contaminants in Water Supplies*. American Association for the Advancement of Science, Pub. No. 85, 173–86.

Steward, Frances (1977) *Technology and Underdevelopment*. Macmillan Press, London.

Stout, P. R. and Burau, R. G. (1967) The extent and significance of fertilizer buildup in soils as revealed by vertical distribution of nitrogenous matter between soils and underlying water reservoirs. In *Agriculture and the Quality of our Environment*, N. C. Brady (ed.) American Association for the Advancement of Science, Pub. No. 85 Washington, DC. 283–310.

Swanson, Burton E. (1975) *Organizing Agriculture Technology Transfer*. International Development Research Center, Indiana University, Bloomington, Indiana.

Tang, A. (1963) Research and education in Japanese agricultural development, *Economic Studies Quarterly* 13, 91–9 (Feb. and May): 27–41.

Thiesenhusen, W. C. (1971) *Technological Change and Income Distribution in Latin American Agriculture*, Land Tenure Center Paper No. 78, University of Wisconsin, Madison.

Timmer, Peter C. (1976) The demand for fertilizer in developing countries, *Food Research Institute Studies* 13, 3.

Timmer, Peter C. and Falcon, Walter P. (1975) The political economy of rice production and trade in Asia. In Reynolds, Lloyd G (ed.) *Agriculture in Development Theory*, Yale University Press, New Haven and London, 1975, 373–410.

Toquero, Z., Duff, J. B., Anden, T. L. and Hayami, Y. Marketable surplus functions for a subsistence crop: rice in the Philippines, *American Journal of Agricultural Economics* 57 No. 4: 705–9.

Tuckman, B. (1976) The Green Revolution and the distribution of agricultural income in Mexico, *World Development* 4, No. 1 17–24.

United Nations (1975) *Demographic Yearbook 1974*. New York.

United Nations (1977) *Desertification: An Overview*. UN Conference on Desertification, A/CONF. 74/1. (Aug.)

UNIDO/FAO/IBRD Working Group on Fertilizer (1978a). *Current Situation and Outlook, June 1978*.

UNIDO/FAO/IBRD Working Group on Fertilizers (1978b) *Current Situation and Outlook*, Nov. 1978.

United Nations Industrial Development Organization (1978) *Second World-Wide Study on the Fertilizer Industry: 1975–2000*. UNIDO/ICIS, Vienna.

US Department of Agriculture (1965) *Changes in Agriculture in 26 Developing Nations*. ERS FAE Report No. 27.

US Department of Agriculture (1977) *World Agricultural Situation*, Washington, DC, WAS–14, Oct.

Valdes, Alberto, Scobie, Grant M. and Dillon, John L. (ed). (1979) *Economics and the Design of Small Farmer Technology*. Iowa State University Press, Ames, Iowa.

Verghese, M. C. (1977) *Issues Facing the World Fertilizer Industry*. FAI/IFDC Conference, Dec. 1–3, New Delhi.

Viets, Frank G. (1971) Fertilizer use in relation to surface and ground water pollution. In *Fertilizer Technology and Use*, R. A. Olson et al. (eds). Soil Science Soc. of America, Madison, Wisconsin, 517–32.

Wade, Nicholas (1974) Green Revolution (I): a just technology, often unjust in use, *Science* 186, No. 4169 (Dec.20): 1093–96.

Wade, Nicholas (1975) International agricultural research, *Science* 188,

(May): 585–9.

Wellhausen, Edwin (1976) The agriculture of Mexico, *Scientific American* 235, No. 3, (Sept.) 128–53.

Welsch, Delane (1979) The place of accelerated production campaigns in efforts to expand agricultural output. Paper presented at the IAAE Conference. Sept., Banff, Canada.

Wennergren, E. B. and Whitaker, M. D. (1977) Social return to U.S. technical assistance in Bolivian agriculture: the case of sheep and wheat, *American Journal of Agricultural Economics* (Aug.): 565–9.

Wharton, Clifton, B. (1969) The Green Revolution: cornucopia or Pandora's Box, *Foreign Affairs* 47: 464–76.

White, Bill (1978) Energy, food and fertilizers, *Fertilizer Progress* (July–Aug.) 13–16.

Winkelmann, Donald L. (1977) Promoting the adoption of new plant technology, *Proceedings, The World Food Conference of 1976*. Iowa State University Press, Ames, Iowa: 567–79.

Winkelmann, Donald and Moscardi, Edgardo (1979) Aiming agricultural research at the needs of farmers. Paper presented at seminar on Socio-economic Aspects of Agricultural Research in Developing Countries. May 7–11, Santiago, Chile.

World Bank (1979) *The World Bank and Agricultural Research Systems in Developing Countries – A Policy Paper*. Agricultural and Rural Development Department, Washington, DC.

World Food Council (1980a) *Current World Food Situation*. WFS/1980/6, March.

World Food Council (1980b) *Report of the Consultative Group on International Agricultural Research*, WFS/1980/8, Feb.

Wortman, Sterling (1973) Extending the green revolution, *World Development* 1, No. 12: 45–51.

Wortman, Sterling (1977) *Accelerating Agricultural Development*. The seventh annual Coromandel lecture, New Delhi, India.

Wortman, Sterling and Cummings, Ralph W. (1978) *To Feed This World, the Challenge and the Strategy*. Johns Hopkins University Press, Baltimore, Maryland.

Yrarrazaval, Rafael, Navarrete, Rodrigo and Valdivia, Victor (1979) Costos y beneficios sociales de los programas de mejoramiento varietal de trigo y maiz en Chile, *Cuadernos de Economia* No. 49: 283–302.

Yudelman, M. Butler, G. and Banerji, R. (1971) *Technological Change in Agriculture and Employment in Development Countries*. OECD Development Centre, Paris.

Zandstra, Hubert et al. (1979) Caqueza: Living Rural Development: International Development Research Centre, IDRC–107e, Ottawa.

Index

White, Bill, 186
Wickham, T. H., 214
Winkelmann, Donald L., 131, 214
World Bank, 9, 22, 87–8, 89, 216
World Food Council, 8, 10, 219

Yield Gap, 198–9
Yield limiting factors, 82, 196–202
Yrarrazaval, Rajael, 102, 103

Zambia, 162, 166